Brilliant Internet

Dom Brookman

Harlow, England • London • New York • Boston • San Francisco • Toronto • Sydney • Singapore • Hong Kong
Tokyo • Seoul • Taipei • New Delhi • Cape Town • Madrid • Mexico City • Amsterdam • Munich • Paris • Milan

Pearson Education Limited
Edinburgh Gate
Harlow
Essex CM20 2JE
England

and Associated Companies throughout the world

Visit us on the World Wide Web at:
www.pearsoned.co.uk

First published 2006

© Pearson Education Limited 2006

ISBN-13: 978-0-13-173399-2
ISBN-10: 0-13-173399-0

British Library Cataloguing-in-Publication Data
A catalogue record for this book is available from the British Library

Library of Congress Cataloging-in-Publication Data
A CIP catalog record for this book can be obtained from the Library of Congress

10 9 8 7 6 5 4 3 2 1
10 09 08 07 06

Prepared for Pearson Education Ltd by Syllaba Ltd (http://www.syllaba.co.uk)

Editorial management by McNidder & Grace, Alnwick

Typeset in Arial Narrow 11pt by Shoemaker Dodds, Northumberland
Printed and bound in Great Britain by Ashford Colour Press Ltd., Gosport.

The publisher's policy is to use paper manufactured from sustainable forests.

Brilliant guides

What you need to know and how to do it

When you're working on your PC and come up against a problem that you're unsure how to solve, or want to accomplish something in an application that you aren't sure how to do, where do you look? Manuals and traditional training guides are usually too big and unwieldy and are intended to be used as end-to-end training resources, making it hard to get to the info you need right away without having to wade through pages of background information that you just don't need at that moment – and helplines are rarely that helpful!

Brilliant guides have been developed to allow you to find the info you need easily and without fuss and guide you through the task using a highly visual, step-by-step approach – providing exactly what you need to know when you need it!

Brilliant guides provide the quick easy-to-access information that you need, using a detailed index and troubleshooting guide to help you find exactly what you need to know, and then presenting each task in a visual manner. Numbered steps guide you through each task or problem, using numerous screenshots to illustrate each step. Added features include 'See also...' boxes that point you to related tasks and information in the book, while 'Did you know?...' sections alert you to relevant expert tips, tricks and advice to further expand your skills and knowledge.

In addition to covering all major office PC applications, and related computing subjects, the *Brilliant* series also contains titles that will help you in every aspect of your working life, such as writing the perfect CV, answering the toughest interview questions and moving on in your career.

Brilliant guides are the light at the end of the tunnel when you are faced with any minor or major task.

Publisher's acknowledgements

The author and publisher would like to thank the following for permission to reproduce the material in this book:

British Telecommunications plc, Wanadoo UK plc, AOL (UK) Ltd, Networking Links Ltd, BBC, Situation Publishing Ltd, www.ADSLguide.org.uk, Mark Jackson (ISP Review), ONSPEED - a subsidiary of Z GROUP plc., Ntl Group Ltd., Google UK, Yahoo, Guardian Newspapers Ltd 2005, CNET download.com, GRISOFT s.r.o., Firetrust Ltd, Symantec Corp., PCSecurityShield, www.stopzilla.com, J Mason (Spam Assassin), Steganos GmbH., Barclays Bank plc., Skype, Tesco, Amazon UK, LOVEFiLM.com, eBay UK, 1837online.com (Trace 2 Ltd), www.thetrainline.com, Multimap.com, Tele Atlas NV, NHS Direct, Expedia, Napster, Live365 Inc., Apple Computer Inc., Epitonic, Miniclip Ltd, www.moonfruit.com (Greek Attic Ltd), CuteFTP, www.TechGuy.org, www.PCPitstop.com, Tiscali.

Microsoft product screen shot(s) reprinted with permission from Microsoft Corporation.

Every effort has been made to obtain necessary permission with reference to copyright material. The publishers apologise if inadvertently any sources remain unacknowledged and will be glad to make the necessary arrangements at the earliest opportunity.

Author's acknowledgements

Thanks to: Steve Jenkins for his generosity in letting me use his Windows XP PC during many a long night and weekend. I'd also like to thank David and Susan Brookman, Rob Clymo, Tom Evans, Dan Ford, Rebecca Milford, Dawn & Rob Neatby, Angela Orchard, Craig Payne, Kate Phelps, Matt Powell, Robert Powell and Jenny, Steve and Ollie Sanders, for all their help, ideas and inspiration.

Dedication

Dedicated to Rozalind Neatby for her consistent support and immense patience during the production of this book.

About the author

Dom Brookman is editor of *eBuyer and Online Seller* magazine, the UK's only monthly guide to eBay and buying and selling online. He has worked on a series of titles for Paragon Publishing over the last seven years, including *Internet User*, *Web Pages Made Easy*, *Windows XP Made Easy* and *PC Home*, and has wide experience of the consumer Internet market. Away from work, he enjoys following Liverpool FC, travelling the world and going to music concerts.

Contents

Introduction

Welcome to *Brilliant Internet*, a visual quick reference book that shows you how to make the most of the rich resources available on the internet. Discover the very best websites, programs and services *and* the most efficient way of using them to their maximum potential.

Find what you need to know – when you need it

You don't have to read this book in any particular order. We've designed the book so that you can jump in, get the information you need, and jump out. To find the information that you need, just look up the task in the table of contents, index, or Troubleshooting guide, and turn to the page listed. Read the task introduction, follow the step-by-step instructions along with the illustration, and you're done.

How this book works

Each task is presented with step-by-step instructions in one column and screen illustrations in the other. This arrangement lets you focus on a single task without having to turn the pages too often.

Step-by-step instructions

This book provides concise step-by-step instructions that show you how to accomplish a task. Each set of instructions includes illustrations that directly correspond to the easy-to-read steps. Eye-catching text features provide additional helpful information in bite-sized chunks to help you work more efficiently or to teach you more in-depth information. The 'For your information' feature provides tips and techniques to help you work smarter, while the 'See also' cross-references lead you to other parts of the book containing related information about the task. Essential information is highlighted in 'Important' boxes that will ensure you don't miss any vital suggestions and advice.

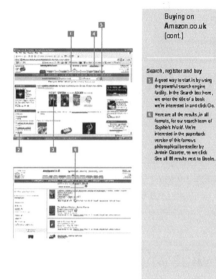

Troubleshooting guide

This book offers quick and easy ways to diagnose and solve common problems that you might encounter using the Troubleshooting guide. The problems are grouped into categories that are presented alphabetically.

Spelling

You will notice that we have used American spelling conventions throughout this book. We do regret having to do this in a book aimed at UK and Irish readers. However, nearly all the software that we illustrate (Microsoft's being the most prevalent) is written by American developers and in order to be consistent with the spelling you will actually encounter whilst using your PC, we have conformed. Please rest assured that our grammatical conscience struggles as much as yours does with disk, color and program!

Troubleshooting guide

Getting online: your first steps

Introduction

Hello and welcome to our indispensable guide to getting the most from the internet. Later on in the book, we're going to look at the very best websites out there to help you chat with other users, sort out your finances, search for a job, do your weekly shopping, rent a DVD, research your family tree, listen to the radio, download music, book a holiday, get the latest travel information… and much, much more. Before all that, though, we need to cover some of the basics about the internet and how to find your way around – after all, if you don't know how to use the basic tools in front of you, you're not going to get very far.

Surprising as it may seem, the internet has actually been around for over 30 years. A definition of what we've come to know as the 'internet' is hard, but essentially it's a network of networks, or a grid of computers carrying information across the world. You can't just access the internet at will – you need a computer, relevant equipment and the help of an ISP – Internet Service Provider. Hopefully by now you'll have a PC, preferably a newer model with Windows XP pre-installed. You've probably spent some time getting used to the XP Operating System, familiarising yourself with your desktop and the practicalities of moving around with your mouse. Click on the Start menu in the bottom-right of your screen and go up to My Computer to see the really important parts of your computer and its settings.

So what about setting up internet access, then? It's this task which has seen the battlelines been drawn by ISPs over the last few years, as they all battle to get your custom and, of course, your money. Only a few years ago, people were used to 'dial-up' internet access – a slow, laborious system where, in order to connect to the internet, your PC would dial a telephone number supplied by the

What you'll do

Find out broadband and ISP information

Set up and install broadband

Look at the different kinds of ISP

Analyse the latest ISP price deals

Explore the ONSPEED service

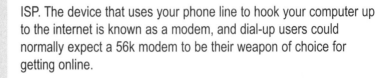
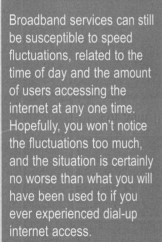
ISP. The device that uses your phone line to hook your computer up to the internet is known as a modem, and dial-up users could normally expect a 56k modem to be their weapon of choice for getting online.

Dial-up connections do, indeed, still exist, but the good news is that in the last couple of years, the outdated technology has been taken over by something known as broadband – high-speed internet access delivered into your home via your telephone line, cable or satellite. The most common form of broadband is ADSL – which stands for Asymmetric Digital Subscriber Line. We won't go into the technicalities here, but basically ADSL helps deliver internet access to your home at speeds which are up to 40 times faster than a normal dial-up connection. And the good news is that as the competition hots up, broadband deals are getting cheaper, faster and more comprehensive.

So, broadband helps you enjoy the rich wealth of content, audio and video that the internet delivers, at much faster speeds. But how do you get connected? Are there any barriers to you getting broadband? What kind of prices are out there, and which ISP should you choose? We'll aim to answer these questions over the next couple of pages.

The amount of technical mumbo-jumbo we could bombard you with to do with broadband connections is pretty high, but we're going to cut through the nonsense and try and give you as rounded a picture of the current broadband scene as possible. A good first step is to read some background literature about broadband and the internet – this book is a good start, and there are still monthly computer magazines out there which act as good beginners companions, although unfortunately less than there were at the turn of the century. Let's kick off with a look at some different ISPs, and general websites which will help you make a decision when it comes to choosing a broadband ISP.

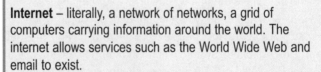

Jargon buster

Internet – literally, a network of networks, a grid of computers carrying information around the world. The internet allows services such as the World Wide Web and email to exist.

First things first – do some research. If you're going to the time, trouble and expense of getting online with a broadband ISP, you should make pretty sure that you know your facts and are confident of what you're getting yourself into.

The major problem is the fact that the broadband market is so volatile, with companies folding and deals changing at the drop of a hat. If you're a beginner, you may find it a good move to hook up with one of the major players in the business. In August 2005, ISP advice site ISP Review listed these ten companies as the top ISPs by users, in descending order: BT Retail (www.bt.com,), Wanadoo (www.wanadoo.co.uk), AOL UK (www.aol.co.uk), NTL (www.ntl.com), Tiscali (www.tiscali.co.uk, Telewest (www.telewest.co.uk), Breathe (www.breathe.co.uk), Clara.net (www.clara.net), Brightview (www.brightview.com) and Pipex (www.pipex.net). Sign up with one of these and you should be relatively sure that none of them are going to go bust the next day – a scenario which was all too depressingly common in ISP-land only a couple of years ago. Even now, though, your ISP may change its name or merge with another big player without warning, so you need to be on your guard.

Obviously all these ISPs have different offers, enticements and services to try and woo you in, which makes dedicated research even more important.

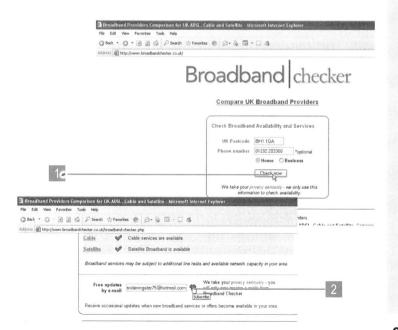

Finding out broadband and ISP information

Can I get it?

1. One of the first things that you can do is check whether you can get broadband. We'll presume that you're either on a dial-up computer, or using a friend's computer if you haven't got round to buying a PC yet! Go to www.broadbandchecker.co.uk and enter your postcode and your phone number (optional), say whether you're likely to be a home or business user, and click Check now.

2. Lucky us! In our area in Bournemouth, ADSL, cable and satellite broadband are all available. Hopefully, this will be the case for the vast majority of you now that broadband is so prevalent across the UK. If you want occasional updates on what's happening in the broadband world, enter your email address in the box provided and click on the green arrows.

Finding out broadband and ISP information (cont.)

Get the lowdown

3 BT's pretty proud of its broadband service, and proudly gives you the interesting figure from its home page at www.bt.com/broadband that 99% of all UK homes and businesses can already get broadband. Note that there's another chance here to find out if you can get ADSL – there's a Can I get Broadband? box on the right-hand side that allows you to enter your BT phone number to see.

4 You also get the chance to get some beginners' guides to broadband – in the bottom-left corner, for example, you can click on Find Out How Broadband Works.

5 The BBC's website at www.bbc.co.uk is so good that we're going to return to it time and time again in the course of this book. Its broadband information sub-site, at www.bbc.co.uk/broadband, is also well worth a visit, and allows you to understand just what broadband is and how you can get it.

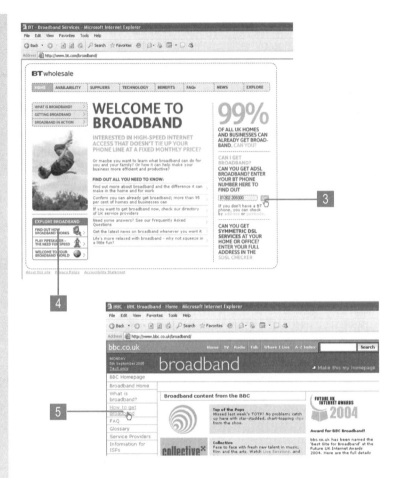

For your information

A good way to work out which broadband ISP is for you is to ask yourself before you take the plunge: what kind of user am I? Questions to ask include:

How often do I use the internet? Am I a light, average or heavy user?

How important are family controls and security settings to me?

Does it matter if my ISP has a limit on the amount of data that I can download or upload?

What hobbies do I have? Is music, film, online games or sport important to me? (Some ISPS have features relevant to one particular hobby.)

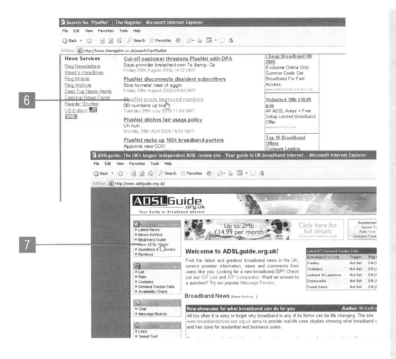

More info

6 If you're after well-written, authoritative and occasionally biting comments on the state of the broadband industry (and the IT industry in general), you could do a lot worse than The Register, at www.thregister.co.uk. This daily news site has a comprehensive broadband section that you can click on from the home page to access all the latest headlines – click on a headline to read the story below it.

7 The site at www.adslguide.org.uk is also brilliant for giving you a comprehensive guide to the world of broadband internet access. Whether it's the latest news, a beginner's guide, explanations of how ADSL works, reviews, chat or comparisons of different ISPs, this is one of the best general broadband info sites around, and we heartily recommend it.

Timesaver tip

ADSL Guide (www.adslguide.org.uk) has a speed test that you can access which you can access from the menu down the left-hand side. This will show you the speed of the internet access you're enjoying, and if you're not satisfied, could be a major contributing factor in your decision to swap broadband ISP, if you already have a broadband connection.

Did you know ?

You can now get 1 Mb broadband for less than a tenner, if you look hard enough – proof that broadband prices have absolutely plummeted during the last couple of years. Be aware the most broadband providers now have a series of packages, covering 1, 2, 3 Mb and higher connections, which muddies the waters still further. In August 2005, NTL announced that in 2006, its broadband packages would be set at 10 Mb as standard.

Finding out broadband and ISP information (cont.)

A typical ISP

8 You've done a lot of background research so far, so how about looking at some of the home pages of the major ISPs? Try any of the addresses of the Top 10 providers which we listed in our intro to this chapter – here, we're at the home page for Wanadoo (formerly known as Freeserve, and set to be known as Orange in 2006 – but that's another story), at www.wanadoo.co.uk. Obviously, when you go to the home page of an ISP, you'll get a very biased view of the broadband service on offer – they want your custom, after all. Nevertheless, taking a trip round the major players, maybe even armed with a pen and paper to note down the very latest deals, can't do any harm, and may even help swing your mind in one direction or another. Remember that all deals are subject to change at the drop of a hat, unfortunately.

Timesaver tip

Some broadband ISPs tie you to a 12-month contract; others let you disconnect and move on whenever you want. Make sure you read that small print and make sure that you're aware of the stipulations of your chosen ISP.

For your information

Comparison websites let you compare and contrast all the broadband deals that are out there. Although it's better known as a device to check the prices of consumer goods such as DVDs or computers, there's nothing stopping you going to a price comparison website such as Kelkoo (www.kelkoo.co.uk), typing in Broadband and then comparing the list of results that you get.

We're now going to look at a quick setup with the BT broadband service. Obviously we can't know the exact specifications of your computer setup, so there may be differences between our approach and the steps you have to take, but the general principles should remain the same.

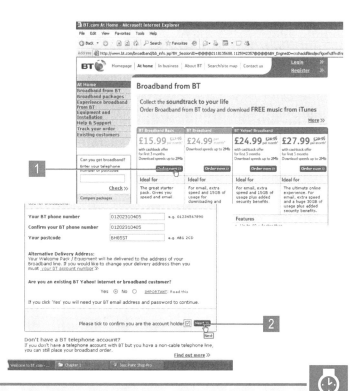

Timesaver tip

The ISP that you eventually plump for should make sure, either on its site or in the instructions it sends you (or preferably both), that you're not left to sink or swim when it comes to setting up broadband. Of course, if you have a technology-friendly chum nearby, you can always get them to set up broadband for you, but it's so much better when you can understand everything yourself, or at least follow instructions that help you through the whole process as painlessly as possible. Opt for Tiscali, for example, and at www.tiscali.co.uk/help/broadband you can access loads of broadband help and advice, from how to set up your connection to how to connect your broadband filters and what to do if you move to a new address. All ISPs should provide a similar service.

Setting up and installing broadband

1

We want BT

1 After a lot of consideration, we've plumped for BT Broadband Basic from www.bt.com, with download speeds of up to 2 Mb, a price of £15.99 per month, 5 email addresses and free online help. As the blurb says, this is an excellent package for beginners, although by no means the only beginner-friendly package out there. Click Order now under the package title.

2 BT then asks for the details of the telephone line that you'll be using for broadband. Enter the number, read and answer the other questions, then click Next.

For your information

Another excellent source of broadband news and views can be found at www.net4now.com/.

Setting up and installing broadband (cont.)

What do we need?

3 BT reckons that installing its broadband is simple – so simple, in fact, that you don't need an engineer. You may gulp at this, but installing broadband isn't that hard – you'll need a compatible computer (obviously), a broadband modem (which comes free if you order online) and microfilters, which split your phone line, enabling you to be online and on the phone at the same time. BT provides two microfilters with its broadband packages. Click Is my PC compatible if you're worried.

4 The options available to you can all be explored under Why Broadband from BT – click See for Yourself to explore aspects such as sharing your broadband PC or online gaming. It's then just a matter of sorting out your payment details and confirming everything, then waiting to get your kit and moving on to the all-important stage we'll mention over the page – setting it all up!

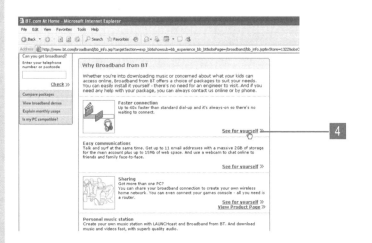

Important

Watch out for any restrictions on your broadband service which your ISP may have buried away in the small print somewhere. Some ISPs, for example, 'cap' your service, by restricting the amount of data you download per month – a far cry from the unlimited, 'always on' service that broadband promises to provide. Make sure that you know all about any potential capping on your service, and whether or not this is likely to interfere with your day-to-day computer activity.

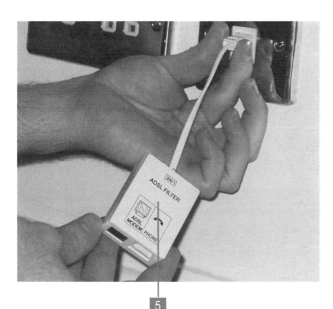

5

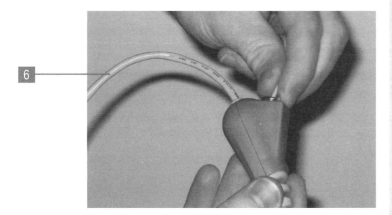

6

Set up your kit

5 Hopefully your broadband ISP will have provided you with the kit you need to get up and running quickly and easily; if not, you might need to go to a website such as DSL Warehouse, at www.dsl-warehouse.co.uk. When you've got your kit, and if you've plumped for a normal ADSL broadband service, the first thing you'll need to do is install your modem's drivers from the CD that should have been provided. Plug a microfilter into every phone socket that you need for ADSL.

6 Time to set up the modem. Grab the long cable that came with your modem and then plug it into the jack on the modem.

Timesaver tip

Once you've got broadband, make the most of it! Some of the things that we're going to mention in this book, including watching the BBC news online, making free phone calls via the internet, listening to internet radio and playing graphically-rich games work so, so much better with a broadband connection. Major online player such as the BBC will, on their broadband areas, provide exclusive broadband content which will be all the more enjoyable now that you've joined the high-speed internet revolution.

Setting up and installing broadband (cont.)

Set up your kit

7 The next step involves you simply plugging your phone line into one of the microfilter's jacks, and your modem cable into the other end. Take your time over these steps – you won't get anywhere rushing things, and would be more likely to make a mess of things by being unduly hasty.

8 Finally, it's time to invoke the power of the USB . Plug your external modem's USB lead into the USB socket of your PC. You're now ready to connect – good luck!

Jargon buster

USB – stands for Universal Serial Bus, and is fast becoming the technology used to connect devices such as joysticks and modems to your PC.

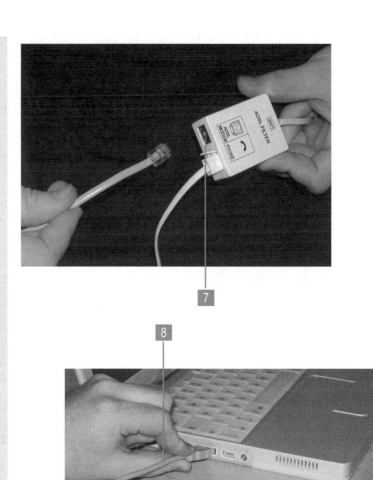

7

8

For your information

When it comes to broadband, of course, don't forget the different flavours that are available – the major three being cable, satellite and ADSL. Major cable broadband providers include NTL (www.ntl.com) and Telewest (www.telewest.co.uk). Satellite broadband is still in its infancy, but keep your eye out for this emerging technology over the next couple of years.

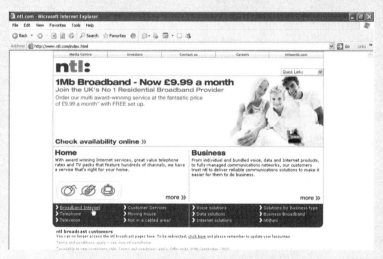

One internet service provider we haven't mentioned yet is the famous giant that is AOL. This family-friendly ISP, at www.aol.co.uk, offers a different internet experience than you get with conventional rivals such as BT or Tiscali. AOL has its very own browsing software which, when you load it up, plunges you into a friendly internet interface chock-full of content channels full of sport, news, entertainment, gossip and chat. AOL Search is powered by Google, its antivirus, pop-up blocking and parental control features have all been beefed up in recent versions of the software, and its Instant Messaging program is a big plus as well. Prices are relatively low and AOL has managed to muscle its way into the top 3 ISPs in the UK, mainly on the back of its cheapness, strong internet content and reputation for being excellent when it comes to online security tools. Unsubscribing from AOL can be a bit of a nightmare, and it takes a bit of time to get used to the AOL world when you subscribe, but this is one internet service that's well worth a look.

Analysing the
latest ISP price
deals

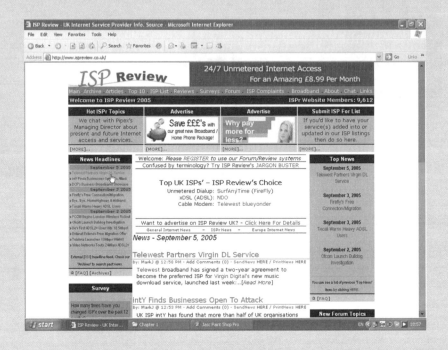

We've already mentioned a couple of cracking sites that will help give you the lowdown on what's out there in the world of ISPs. When it comes to checking prices, we could give you a price rundown of all the major deals right here – but there'd be no point. Prices are changing so rapidly, as it's such a competitive market, that information you receive today is totally out of date by tomorrow. It really is that cut-throat and competitive. So computer magazines and books such as the one in your hands right now can't give you the up-to-date pricing info you need – you'll need to log on to the internet in real-time and see what the very latest deals are. One excellent site that has reviews, charts, pricing details, forums, surveys, chat, news and info about what to do if you have a complaint is ISP Review – www.ispreview.co.uk. You can tell a lot of time, effort and care goes into keeping this site regularly updated with all the hottest news – the comprehensiveness is staggering. Basically, if you want the latest pricing details, you should either check the home page of your ISP, ring its customer service line, or check out in-depth consumer guides such as ISP Review.

You may find that, for whatever reason, you'd like an alternative to dial-up which isn't broadband – but is still a technology that lets you get on the internet at high speeds. In that case, you're going to need to try ONSPEED, at www.onspeed.com. This 2 minute software download, easy to install and pretty simple to use, utilises compression technology to give you speeds that it describes as 'up to 5 times faster' than regular dialup. You can expect to be charged around

£24.99 a year for the service, which is pretty good value, and there's no need to sign contracts or change your existing ISP. ONSPEED has been enthusiastically received by the computer press, and although you may find problems using the technology in conjunction with certain web pages, if you're looking for a low-cost, yet still relatively speedy, alternative to broadband, then you could do much worse.

Finding your way around the web

2

Introduction

Internet Explorer is the single most important piece of software on your PC. This mighty piece of browsing software, an integral part of Windows XP, is a crucial part of your day-to-day surfing activities and has a massive domination of the market (although we'll look at alternatives to Internet Explorer in due course). We're going to get to grips with some of its main features in this chapter.

Internet Explorer 6, which is the version we're going to be studying here, can help you browse the web smoothly, and has a host of customisable settings for you to play about with and control. Whether you want to search the web quickly, block pop-ups, access favourite websites with one click, print out a web page, use security features, save websites and much, much more, Internet Explorer can help you do it, with the minimum of fuss.

Internet Explorer isn't perfect, of course – some people resent the fact that they seem almost 'ordered' to use Internet Explorer, and go off to use flexible alternatives such as Opera and Mozilla Firefox, which we'll feature later. Nevertheless, it's pretty much perfect for beginners, which is why we're going to devote a lot of time into peering into its innermost workings.

Once we've got you up and running with Internet Explorer, we'll go on to perhaps the first website you'll ever visit, and certainly one of the most useful – Google (www.google.co.uk). This search engine is used by millions of people the world over, admired for its simplicity and staggering comprehensiveness – if it's not on Google, basically, it's not worth being on the internet. And Google does so, so much more than just carry out a basic web search for you – a point we'll be making very strongly in due course. In the meantime, let's crack on with getting on top of Internet Explorer.

Setting your Favorites in Internet Explorer

Set your Favorites

 Yep, you've guessed it – Google is one of our favourite websites, and we want it to be added to the hall of fame. The first thing to do is to go up to Favorites in the menu bar that runs across the top of your browser.

 Our Favorites as they stand need a bit of organisation, so we click on Organise Favorites.

Whether you're in your first week as an internet surfer or your five hundreth, you'll have a set of websites that are your Favorites (shame about the American spelling, but never mind) – the ones you return to time and time again. Sites such as Google, the BBC, Amazon and the home page of your ISP are likely to feature here, but chances are that you'll have plenty of sites unique to yourself or your family that you frequent several times a week.

If this is the case, you're unlikely to want to go through the rigmarole of typing in the URL (web address) of those popular websites each and every time you want to pay a visit. Internet Explorer may 'auto-complete' web addresses you type into the Address Bar at the top of your browser interface, which can save time, but a much better way of grouping together all your favourite destinations is to make full use of the Favorites function. Let's see just how it works over the next few pages.

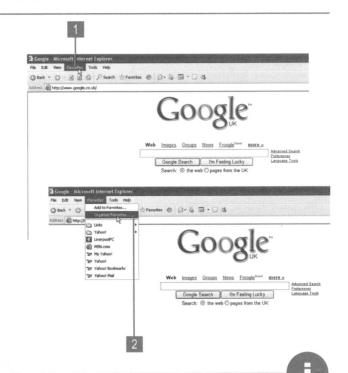

Setting your Favorites in Internet Explorer (cont.)

Organise

3 This is a key part of your Favorites life – organisation. Even with Internet Explorer's help, it's still perfectly possible to have your Favorites all over the shop and unorganised, which kind of defeats the object of having them in the first place. In this dialog box, you can create new folders, move sites into folders, rename sites or delete them. We choose to delete Radio Station Guide, so highlight it in the right-hand window, and then click Delete.

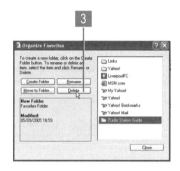

4 All these separate Yahoo! sites you can see in the drop-down window could now, for example, be moved to the Yahoo folder for ease of future reference. It's up to you how you want to go about things – you may like sites grouped separately, so you can see at a glance exactly what link will take you where. To illustrate another feature of the Favorites menu, we go to the Liverpool football club website and click Add to Favorites again.

Finding your way around the web 17

Setting your Favorites in Internet Explorer (cont.)

Add it

5 A new window will appear, confirming that Internet Explorer will add this page to your Favorites list. You'll see its title in the Name window. Click OK if you're happy to let Internet Explorer do its business.

6 A key part of organising your sites is to have clear site names, or names that mean something to you when you see them. We're keen on giving the Liverpool website a slightly catchier name, so we click on Rename.

! Important

There is another way to sort your Favorites, rather than using Organise Favorites. After loading Internet Explorer and clicking the Favorites menu, you can right-click on any item in the list to bring up a new dialog menu. From here you can, for example, click on Sort by Name, which will then list all your Favorites in alphabetical order. Smart!

Setting your Favorites in Internet Explorer (cont.)

Final touches

7 Type in your new name (ours doesn't differ significantly, but is shorter), and then click Close when you're done.

8 Now, when you're on a site such as Google and want to go to a favourite website quickly and easily, just click on Favourites and then the name of the site from the drop-down menu. You'll then be whisked off to your chosen destination in a matter of milliseconds, without the need to type any troublesome web addresses in!

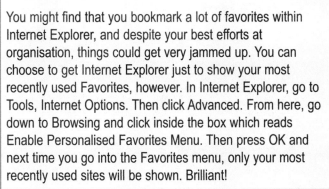

Timesaver tip

You might find that you bookmark a lot of favorites within Internet Explorer, and despite your best efforts at organisation, things could get very jammed up. You can choose to get Internet Explorer just to show your most recently used Favorites, however. In Internet Explorer, go to Tools, Internet Options. Then click Advanced. From here, go down to Browsing and click inside the box which reads Enable Personalised Favorites Menu. Then press OK and next time you go into the Favorites menu, only your most recently used sites will be shown. Brilliant!

Using the Search function

There are a number of ways of searching for information on the web, of course, and we're going to look at Google in a short while, but for the moment let's see what happens when you click on the Search button in Internet Explorer. Internet Explorer has a search engine built into it, and we'll see how it works below.

Search in Internet Explorer

1 Here we are browsing the internet, and the fantastic BBC site at www.bbc.co.uk. To get started on the road to searching heaven, click on the big Search button near the top of the screen.

2 Your normal browsing window will now split in two. On the right-hand side is your normal browsing window, whilst on the left a search window has opened – MSN Search. What do you want to search for? We're planning a mini-break in Liverpool soon, so we enter 'liverpool hotels' in the box provided and click Go.

? Did you know ?

To get rid of the search engine frame in the left of your screen, you can simply click the little 'x' next to 'Search'. The frame will now close.

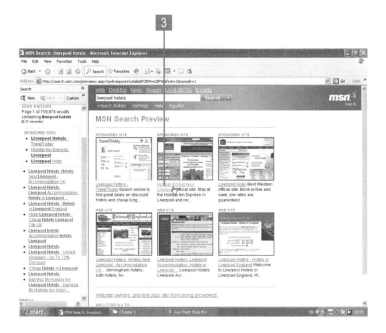

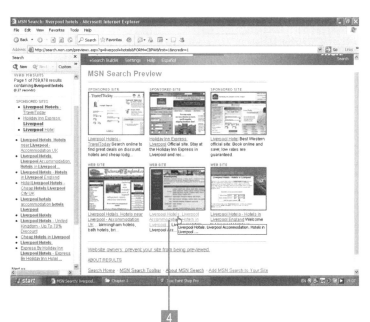

Using the Search function (cont.)

2

Results time

3 In the search window, after a couple of seconds (at most), you'll see a list of websites matching the criteria you suggested. Just look at all the alternatives for Liverpool hotels! The main browsing window has also changed to a preview screen where you can see screenshots of some of the top results, with a brief description. Note that for some results, you'll get Sponsored Sites – these are websites which have paid the search engine money, for the privilege of appearing at the top of the results list. We click on the Holiday Inn Liverpool link, to be taken to its website.

4 You can, of course, try as many different sites as you like to get to the result that you want. Here, we click on the Liverpool Hotels link in the main window, after taking a look at the screenshot and seeing that it could offer us just what we want.

Finding your way around the web 21

Using the Search function (cont.)

Where do you want to go?

5 You'll be taken to the website in question – we're at www.liverpoolhotels.com, which has some excellent suggestions for hotels in the city. What you'll find with search engines is that one simple search can lead off into dozens of corners of the web – here, we click on Crowne Plaza Liverpool to taken to info about this particular hotel.

6 If you're not getting the results you expect, and you're confident that your own searching techniques are up to scratch, you can click on Help us improve under Didn't get the results you expected? to offer some feedback.

Timesaver tip

Get rid of the search preview window on the right by unticking the Show Search Preview box at the bottom of the Search frame.

5

6

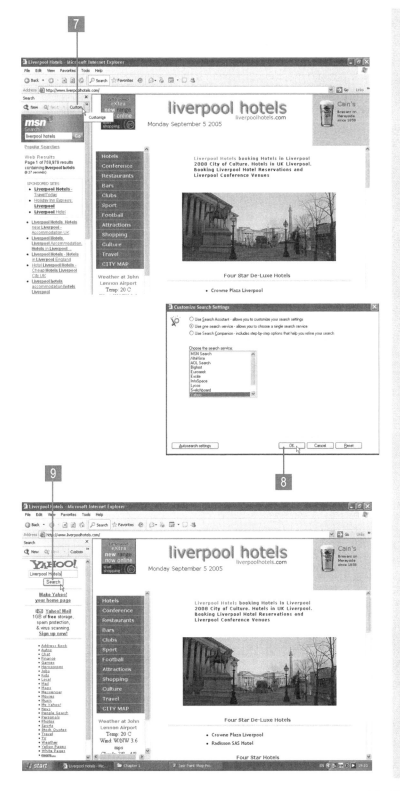

Using the Search function (cont.)

Final steps

7 You can also customize the search engine to look how you want. Click the Customize button just above the search window.

8 You can now customize a couple of options, including getting Internet Explorer to just use a single search service when it comes back with your results. We choose Yahoo! and click OK.

9 When you search now, you'll get Yahoo!'s results, which you may or may not find as significantly different to what you were getting with MSN. Play around to your heart's content and see which search engine suits your needs best.

Using the History function

Start off

1. How your History button is shown depends on whether or not you've configured the icons in Internet Explorer or not, but you should see an icon marked History in the top toolbar, or a visual representation of a clock and a backwards-pointing arrow, as here. Click on the icon to access your History.

2. On the left-hand side, a pane will open with a series of folders, documenting where you've been in the last 3 weeks. We click on Today to see where we've been – to go to any of the destinations listed, just click on the link.

3. Each website address can be split even further into sub-categories, too – if, like here, you visited a few different destinations whilst on the main Liverpool FC site. Again, click on the sub-category to go to that exact page.

As you surf the web, visiting different sites as you please, Internet Explorer is working away in the background, recording what is known as your 'History' in its History folder.Why is this useful? Well, if you get into the habit of visiting a lot of websites, you might visit a really good site one day, and then completely forget its address the next day. It's not hard, when you consider the staggering amount of websites out there.Your browser's History, however, has a full record of all the websites which you've visited over the last 20 days, so you can pick the relevant day and see just what the forgotten address was. A couple of mouse clicks and you can be right back in the action.The History function is pretty useful, and isn't very hard to understand at all – let's clear up how to use it in the next 4 pages.

Timesaver tip

Want to alter how long Internet Explorer stores your History records? Click Tools in the Internet Explorer menu bar, then select Internet Options from the drop-down menu. A new dialog box will appear. In the General tab you'll see an area at the bottom called History, and from there you can enter a value in the Days to keep pages in History box.

Using the History function (cont.)

Further back

4   You can go further back in time than just today or yesterday, of course. Here, we click on Last Week.

5   A massive list of the website destinations from last week opens, in alphabetical order. Click on a link to access the website.

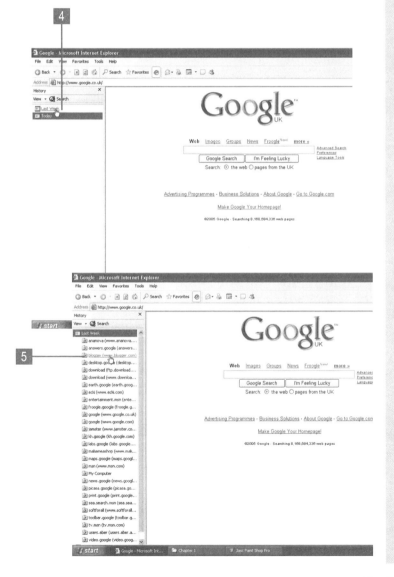

Timesaver tip

To clear your History, go to Tools, Internet Options and then click on Clear History.

Using the History function (cont.)

Different options

6 The great thing about the internet is that clicking on one simple link can take you off to all sorts of destinations. Just as happened when we tried a simple internet search, accessing our History takes us off all over the web. Here, at the Bookcrossing website (www.bookcrossing.com is a fantastic little site which encourages you to set your books 'free' by leaving them in public places, for other people to pick up and read – you can then track your book's progress across the world and read other people's comments. It's great fun, and we highly recommend it), we're instantly given links to loads more sites such as Amazon and eBay – we decide to go off to eBay.

7 You also have a choice of ways that you can view your History – it's all about configuring things to how you want. Under History in the top-left corner, click on View.

Using the History function (cont.)

How do you want it?

8. You can now decide how you want your History to be viewed – by date, by site, by most visited, or by order visited today. A black dot appears next to the option which you've currently chosen. We go for By Most Visited.

9. The new order then shows up, so you can see which sites really are your most popular. Unsurprisingly, Google is at the top, with MSN and fun cricket game Stick Cricket narrowly behind. Click on the site name to access your favourite.

Timesaver tip

To get rid of the History panel, click on the little 'x' in the top-right corner of the History window.

Finding your way around the web 27

Using the View menu

A different View

1 First things first – click on View from the top menu bar.

2 Click on Toolbars to choose which toolbars you want to be shown in Internet Explorer.

3 Those currently being shown will have a tick next to them – click on the tick to untick an option. You'll see that Lock the Toolbars is ticked – you may want to untick that if you want to start moving things around. We click Links.

4 The Links toolbar is here, on the far-right of your Internet Explorer window. You can place Favorite websites in the Links toolbar. The Favorites you created earlier in this chapter will have a Links folder, and you can drag and drop sites from there into your Links toolbar to start building up a fine collection of links.

You'll already have noticed that we're een on stressing that you should endeavour to get Internet Explorer to work for you, by customising its many options and settings. Remember, it's highly unlikely that you'll 'break' Internet Explorer by experimenting with things – sure, you might want to think a little before clicking wildly, but otherwise you should feel free to play around and see which settings suit your method of working. Pretty much anything you set can be reversed with just a few clicks of the mouse, so there really shouldn't be anything much to worry about.

The View menu is at the very top of your Internet Explorer browser, sitting next to File, Edit, Favorites, Tools and Help. The View menu, as its name suggests, has useful commands for you to alter the way Internet Explorer looks, giving you the ability to hide or show certain toolbars, change the size of text, refresh the browser, put it in full-screen mode, and much more. Let's put it through its paces.

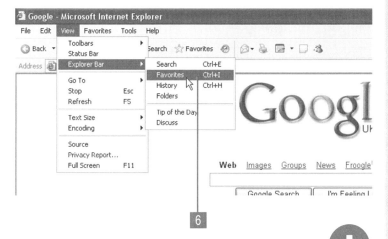

2

Explorer Bar

5 The Explorer Bar, accessible from the View menu, shows useful functions of Internet Explorer such as Search, History and Favorites. Note the shortcuts next to each of these options – to get quickly to your History folders, for example, you need to press 'Ctrl' + 'H'. Clicking any of these options opens a new panel in the left-hand side of the main browsing window.

6 Just as a further example, clicking on Favorites brings up the Favorites panel on the left. The shortcut for bringing up this panel is 'Ctrl' + 'I'.

For your information

Internet Explorer has three built-in toolbars for you to play with; the Standard Buttons toolbar which includes button such as Home, Back and Refresh; the Address Toolbar below that, where you type in the web address of a site and press Enter or Go, and the Links toolbar, which allows quick access to your favourite sites. To move these toolbars around, click on the little dotted line that appears at the left of each toolbar, and drag the double-headed arrow that appears to your desired location. If you find that you can't do this, your toolbars could be 'locked' – to unlock them, go to View, Toolbars and unclick Lock The Toolbars. We'll look at this option again when we come to customising Internet Explorer later in the chapter.

Timesaver tip

To change the name of a link, right-click on it with your mouse and choose the Rename option from the menu that appears.

Using the View menu (cont.)

More options

7 Go To from the Internet Explorer View menu lets you quickly access a selection of your most recently visited sites, without having to go into the History folder or typing in the URL.

8 We go to the BBC home page here by clicking on its link.

9 You may want to play around with the text size of words in your Internet Explorer browser, especially if you have eyesight problems, or someone likely to use the computer has. Click on View, Text Size.

10 You can then choose between a variety of sizes, ranging from 'smallest' to 'largest'. We go for 'larger'.

11 You can instantly see the difference in the Google main window, with the text appearing larger than before.

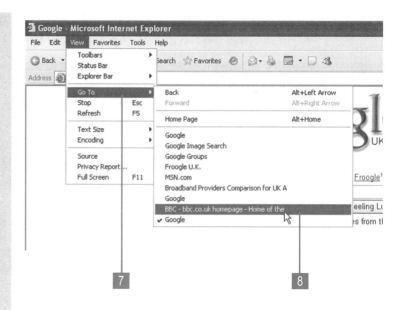

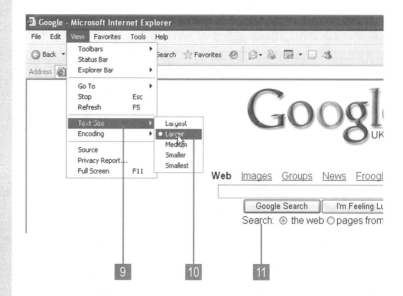

Timesaver tip

Refreshing a web page, which can be done by going to View, Refresh, can also be done quickly by just pressing F5.

Privacy Report

Based on your privacy settings, no cookies were restricted or blocked.

Show: All Web sites

Web sites with content on the current page:

Site	Cookies
http://www.google.co.uk/	
http://www.google.co.uk/intl/en_uk/images/logo.gif	

To view a site's privacy summary, select an item in the list, and then click Summary.

Summary

Learn more about privacy...

Settings... Close

`12` `13`

Web   Images   Groups   News   Froogle^{Ne}

Google Search   I'm Feeling Lucky
Search: ⊙ the web ○ pages from the

Advertising Programmes - Business Solutions - About Go

Final steps

`12` Click on View, Privacy Report to see this window. Here, you can set various privacy options, as well as opting to see a privacy summary for a certain website. To do this, select an item in the site list and then click Summary. If you want to know more about privacy settings, click on Learn more about privacy.

`13` Going to View, Full Screen – or pressing 'F11' on your keyboard gives you a full-screen arrangement for your browser. It looks nice and dramatic, but is perhaps not a too wise idea for beginners, as it can be a tad disorienting when you can't see your usual array of helpful toolbars and icons.

See also

You'll notice we haven't mentioned the View, Customize option. That's because we're going to mention it later in the chapter, when we concentrate on customising Internet Explorer. Turn to the 'customising your browser task on page 40 to learn all about this option.

Timesaver tip

Stop a website from loading by going to View, Stop. Or alternatively, just press Escape.

Finding your way around the web 31

Printing out a web page

There are plenty of times where you might want to print out the information contained in a web page. You may want a permanent record of an internet transaction, for example, which could be important in the unlikely event of anything going wrong. Or you could just want to print out a selection of cinema times from a particular day, or train times. Whatever your requirements, Internet Explorer can make printing a doddle, and we'll see just how everything works.

Set your options

1 Here we are at the excellent Multimap.com website. When you get used to this site, featured in Chapter 7 of this book, you'll see that it does actually have a print option contained in its interface (map sites, of course, should be well aware of the likelihood that you'll be printing the directions or maps that you're given out, ready to use in the car), but we're more concerned with how Internet Explorer itself approaches printing here. You can either click the icon of a printer on the Standard Buttons toolbar, or go to the File menu in the top-left as we do. First off, we opt for a Print Preview.

2 A preview of how your printout will look appears. To change how closely you're zoomed in, change the percentage value in the box next to the plus and minus magnifying glasses. We opt to go up from 75 to 100%.

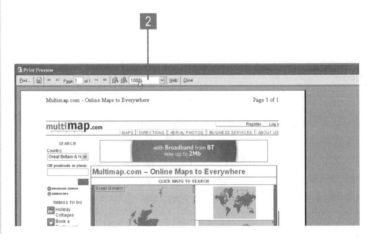

Timesaver tip

Many websites are clued up to the fact that you want to print out web pages, and offer a 'printer-friendly' icon on their page. Click on the icon and you'll be able to get a version of the website's information which will fit nice and snugly, with the correct formatting, on your printout.

Printing out a web page (cont.)

Set your options

3 Here's the map of the little Warwickshire town of Kenilworth, 100%. You can see that you're currently on page 1 of 2 – to move to the second page, click on the right-facing arrow.

4 To dive further into print configuration options, we click on the little Page Setup icon in the top-left of the screen.

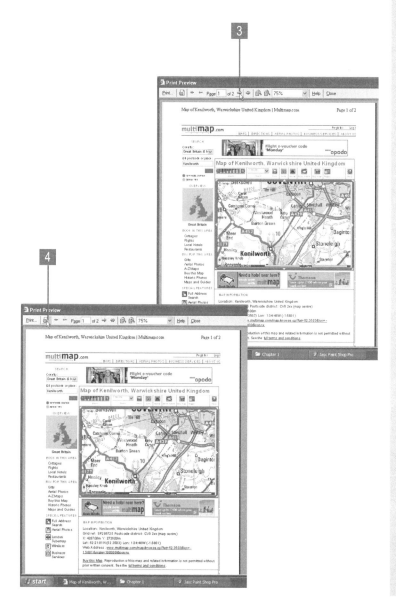

Timesaver tip

To print a frame or item in a web page, simply right-click on the frame or item, and then just select Print or Print Frame.

Printing out a
web page (cont.)

Page Setup

 In the Page Setup window, set
the size of the paper that you
want. Obviously check the
setup of your own printer to see
what is necessary!

 Once you're happy with the
print options you've set here,
you can go back to the website
and get going. Obviously, you
don't have to set all these
options each and every time
you print – we're just showing
you all the possibilities on offer.
Go to File and Print.

Timesaver tip

On the lookout for a new
printer? You can buy one
online at a number of stores –
try Amazon
(www.amazon.co.uk), eBuyer
(www.ebuyer.com), PC World
(www.pcworld.co.uk) or HP
Store (www.hpstore.hp.co.uk).

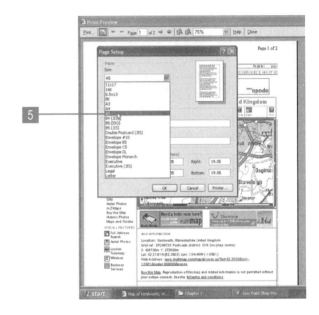

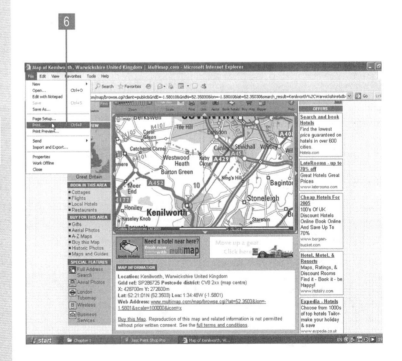

Printing out a web page (cont.)

Printing

7 The final options are here, including selecting your printer, choosing the page range (you may want to just print a single page, for example) setting any further preferences and selecting any copies you want – note we've gone for '2' here.

8 When you're absolutely happy with everything, click Print. And that's it!

2

Finding your way around the web 35

Saving websites

Saving a web page or a website for future reference is yet another useful feature of Internet Explorer. In some ways you've already been doing this by creating a series of Favorites and web links, but we're going to show you how to save pages to your hard drive. The advantage of this is that it lets you read, say, text-heavy and information-heavy pages at your leisure at a later time which is more convenient to you – rather than having to skim over vital information.

Let's take a look at the various saving options available to you, over the next four pages.

Start off

1. Here we are at cricket365.com, a content-rich area of cricketing news and views. We'd like to save this for future reference, so we go to File, Save As.

2. A web page is made up of a text file called an HTML file, which contains all the text on the page, along with references to any graphics and pictures, which tell your web browser how to lay everything out. You now have a choice of where you want to save the page to – desktop, hard drive or disc. We opt for disk.

3. You can rename the page if you like; make sure the Save as Type box reads 'Web page, complete' so that everything on the page is saved.

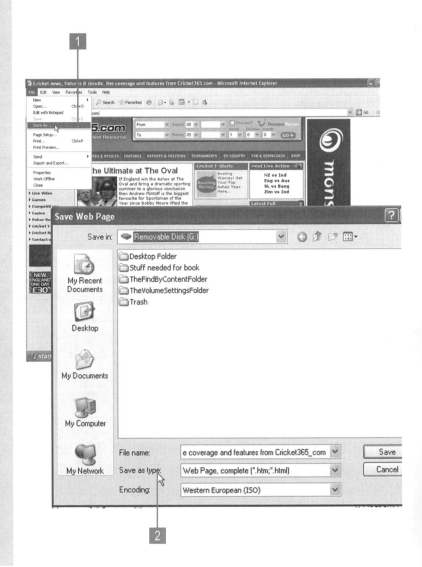

Saving websites (cont.)

New folder

4 Clicking this icon lets you open a new folder to place your web page in. Keeping your pages in good order, with them clearly named, is vital if you're going to be saving lots of websites in the future.

5 Now name your folder. We reckon we're going to save a few web pages in here in the future, so we name our folder 'Dom's websites'.

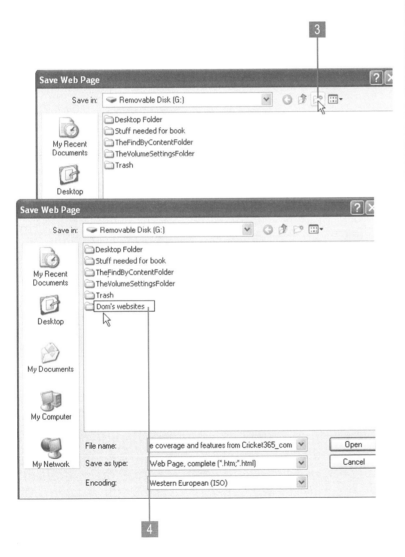

Saving websites (cont.)

Save it

6 Then just click Save to save your web page.

7 Internet Explorer will now save all the relevant files from your page. Wait a few seconds for it to do its job – it shouldn't take very long.

Timesaver tip

If you visit one website time and time again, why not make it your 'home page'? A home page is the first page that your web browser opens when it is started up. Initially, you'll find it set to a default Microsoft site, but say you wanted to change it to, for example, the BBC (www.bbc.co.uk). Go to Tools, Internet Options. Under the General tab, you'll see Home page at the top of the screen. Simply type in the web address of the site you want to become the home page (www.bbc.co.uk, in this case) and then click OK. Next time you open up Internet Explorer from scratch, it will automatically go to the BBC's site.

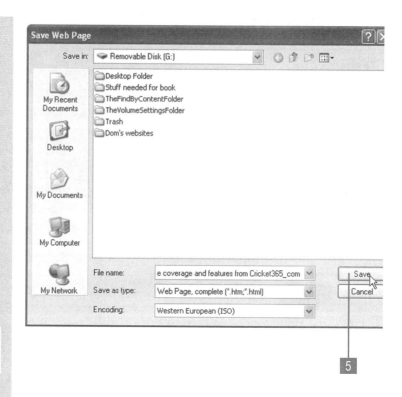

5

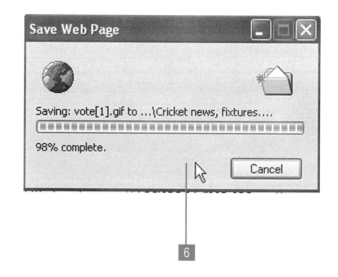

6

Job done

8 Now you can switch your computer off and return later. On our return, we go into our disc and click on 'Dom's websites', where we can already see a preview of what we've saved.

9 And here is our HTML file. We can now double-click on it to open it up and start reading it again.

8

Did you know ?

Again, you can check www.download.com for programs that make the process of saving websites even easier – try a few different searches in the Search box at the top of the screen and see what you get.

Customizing your browser

Customizing the ways Internet Explorer looks and works is vital to enjoying your internet experience. Without experimenting with the customizable options, you may find yourself getting, well, a tad bored with the rather grey and formulaic look of Internet Explorer – where's the fun in having a browser that looks the same every day of your life, and does exactly the same things?

We've already looked at a few options to do with moving toolbars, changing the size of text on a page and so on, but there's much, much more you can do. Far more than we can cover in just these 4 pages, in fact, but we'll give it a go...

You'll see later on in the book just how importantly we take the area of staying safe and secure online – we've got a whole chapter devoted to the topic in Chapter 4. For the basic truth is that no matter how exciting and thrilling using the internet is, there are always things to watch out for, or unscrupulous individuals trying to spoil your fun.

Get customizing

1 As we mentioned earlier, the View menu offers excellent opportunities for you to change things around, especially when it comes to the Standard Buttons bar, the Address bar and the Links bar. Do you want all three of these bars? And do you want them in the same place as Internet Explorer suggests? To get rid of a bar, simply click on its tick icon to 'untick' it. And if you want to move things around, click on the tick next to Lock The Toolbars, which will unlock them (bear with us – it does make sense, honest!), allowing them to be moved.

2 You'll need to look very carefully to see what we're doing here. Having unlocked the toolbars, we've clicked on the dotted lines at the far, far left of the Internet Explorer window, to change the cursor to this double-headed arrow appearance. We can now stretch and manipulate the bars to our heart's content. This may seem like a minor adjustment, (cont.)

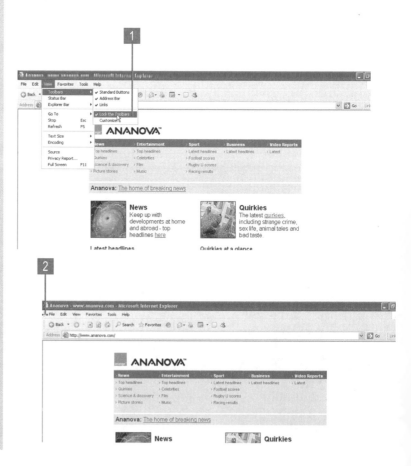

Customizing your browser (cont.)

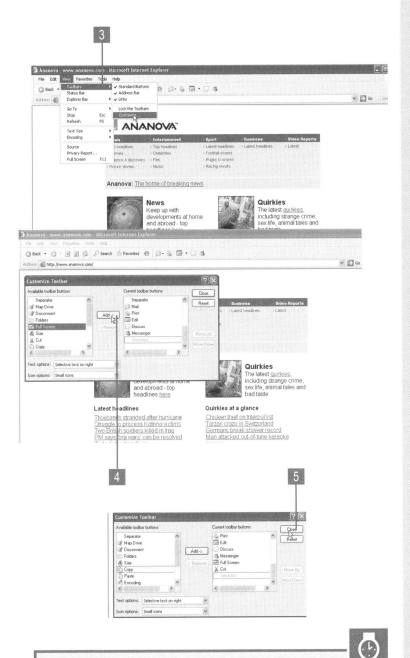

2 (cont.)
but if you're going to be using Internet Explorer every day, which is more than likely, why not take that extra bit of time to make sure everything's right?

Serious customizing

3 Now let's get into some serious customising and button shifting. From the View menu, go to Toolbars and then Customize.

4 Here we get an excellent chance to change some serious settings. On the left are the available toolbar buttons; on the right is what you already have. If you want to add something, as we do here with the Full Screen button, highlight the chosen button, and then click on Add.

5 In the same way that you can add, so can you remove. Just highlight a button on the right and click Remove. When you're happy, or if you just want to see how everything looks, click on Close.

Timesaver tip

Made a few mistakes with your adding and removing of buttons? Then simply click on the Reset button in the Customize Toolbar window to set everything back to its original state.

Customizing your browser (cont.)

See them lined up

6 Back online, you can see our new icons all lined up in the Standard Buttons toolbar – icons such as the Full Screen button are now present and correct. Click on any of them to check that they're working as they should be.

7 Back in the Customize Toolbar dialog box, you may be happy with what icons are now showing, but are you happy with their order? If not, highlight one of your current toolbar buttons, and click Move Up or Move Down to change where it sits in the order of things.

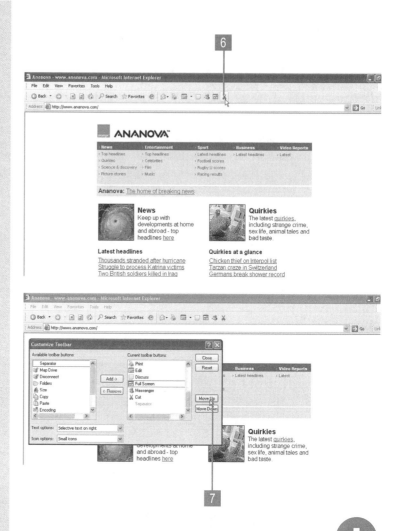

For your information

There are a number of different toolbars which you can download from the web to customize and alter your day-to-day activities in Internet Explorer. Try: the eBay Toolbar (http://pages.ebay.co.uk/ebay_toolbar), the Yahoo! Toolbar (http://uk.toolbar.yahoo.com), Google's Toolbar (http://toolbar.google.com) and the Ask Jeeves Toolbar (http://dl.ask.co.uk/toolbars/ajtoolbar31/download.html), just for starters. Obviously, they all do different things, but you should find in one way or another that they enhance your surfing experience.

2

Text options

8 You also have some text options to play with, as well. The icons in the Standard Button toolbar can have a word underneath them to show what they represent, if you're unsure – like History or Home. Click on the downwards pointing arrow next to the Text options box to set whether you want to show labels or not.

9 You can also set how large you want the icons to be, with the Icon options settings.

10 You can now go back and admire your handiwork and see what's changed – we've now got words underneath our Standard Buttons, for example. It's best to stick with that if you're a beginner. And if you don't like what you've done, change it – you're the one who's going to have to live with it all every day in your internet surfing!

Timesaver tip

To potentially make your Internet Explorer surfing smoother and faster, you can try clearing out your Temporary Internet Files folder, or your 'cache'. The Temporary Internet Files folder is what Microsoft refers to as a 'kind of travel record of the items you have seen, heard or downloaded from the web'. After a while these files take up some significant space on your computer, slowing you down online. To clear them, go to Tools, Internet Options and in the General tab, in the Temporary Internet Files section, click Delete Files and OK twice.

Using Security features

The good news is that Internet Explorer 6 can help make your web experience as safe and trouble-free as possible, with the help of a few options. There's no need to panic and think that if you don't know about all these options, nasty things are going to happen to you online – but it's as well to be prepared and knowledgeable about what's on offer to you. Let's see just what security provisions Internet Explorer has.

Pop-up blocker

1 Once a year or so, Microsoft releases updates to Windows XP. These updates are known as Service Packs, and contain all the most up-to-date versions of drivers, tools and utilities. If and when you install Service Pack 2, you'll see a pop-up blocker turned on. Pop-ups are little ads that display a message when you browse the internet; some are legitimate and useful, whilst others are very annoying. Go to the Tools menu in Internet Explorer and scroll down to Pop-up Blocker, then Turn On Pop-up Blocker. If you want to set further pop-up options, or demand that you see pop-ups from a certain site, click on Pop-up Blocker Settings.

2 Once you've sorted out the Pop-up Blocker satisfactorily, you can access a wealth of further security options. Go to Tools, Internet Options.

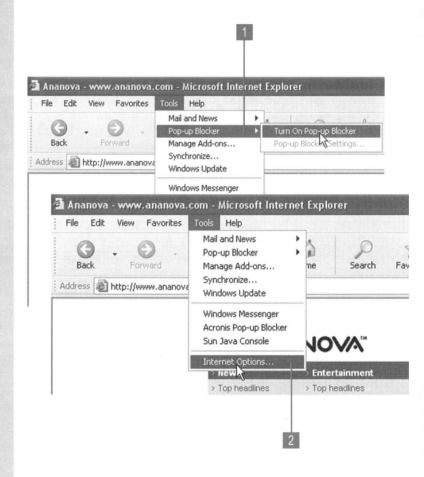

For your information

The latest update for Windows XP is Service Pack 2, which has a host of goodies and can be downloaded via http://update.microsoft.com/windowsupdate/v6/thanks.aspx?ln=en&thankspage=2&, or ordered from CD.

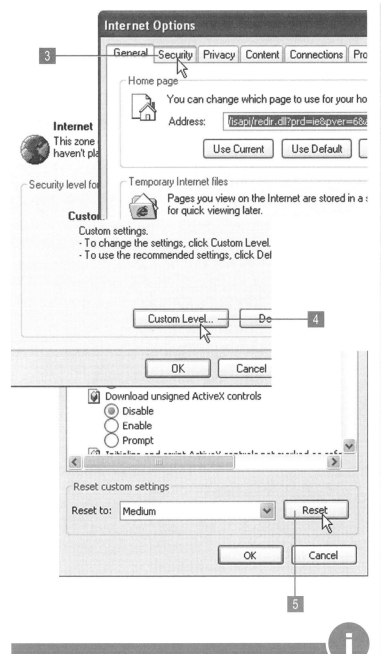

Security levels

3 You'll be on the General tab, but we want the Security tab, so click Security.

4 You can now set a few basic security options. Click Custom Level to change the settings of your security zone.

5 These buttons give you control over your browser's security settings. If you wonder what ActiveX is, it's a programming language, which may occasionally cause you problems in Internet Explorer, so you can choose to alter some settings to do with it if you please. You can also reset the custom settings if you wish by clicking on Reset.

See also

For more on pop-up blockers and essential security programs, see Chapter 4 of this book, 'Staying safe online'.

For your information

Find out more about the Internet Explorer pop-up blocker, and learn how to troubleshoot potential problems, at www.microsoft.com/windowsxp/using/web/sp2_popupblocker. mspx.

Using Security features (cont.)

Further settings

6 You can now choose to set either 'trusted sites', which you trust not to damage your PC, or 'Restricted sites' – troublesome sites that you'd like to bar from your Internet Explorer experiences. We highlight Trusted sites and then Sites.

7 You can then add websites to the trusted zone, by typing in a websites' address and clicking on Add.

8 Click Restricted sites to start setting sites that you'd like to be barred.

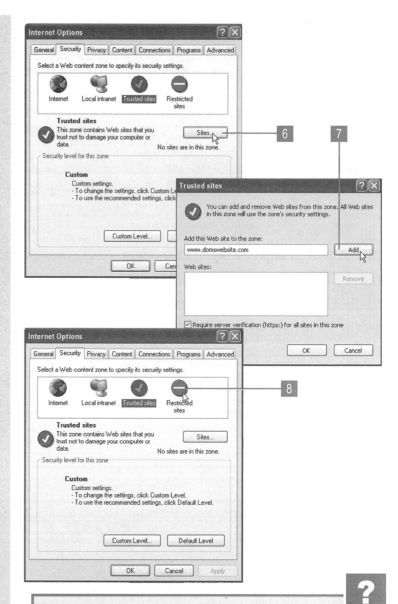

Timesaver tip

To turn off the Content Advisor, go to Tools, Internet Options, Content and Disable. You'll then be prompted to enter your password again, followed by OK.

Did you know ?

If, when you try to add a trusted site to the Trusted site zone, you're asked for confirmation by Internet Explorer, it could be the case that you're adding a site which isn't totally safe and secure. If a site has 'https://' in its web address then you can know that it's secure. If you're determined to add an unsecured site to the list, untick the box at the bottom of the Trusted sites window which reads 'Require server verification (https:) for all sites in this zone'.

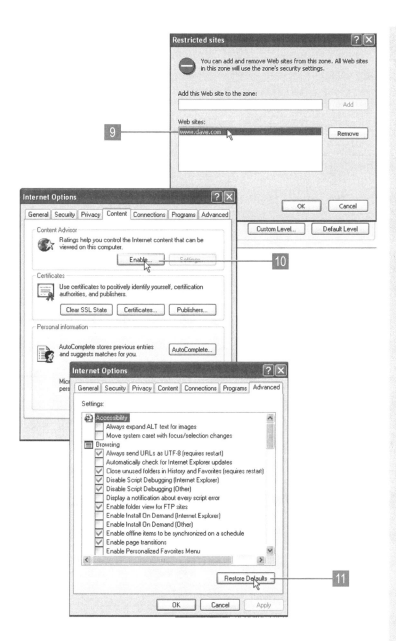

Ban or allow?

9 You can add a website to the restricted zone like before, or if you change your mind about a site, highlight it and then click Remove.

10 Play around with these options until you're happy; you can always return to them later. Back in the Internet Options window, click on the Content tab to see a few more options, including the Content Advisor, which Internet Explorer describes as 'Ratings [which] help you control the Internet content that can be viewed'. Click Enable to create a list of approved sites that the whole family can access. You'll be asked to create a supervisor password which only you or a fellow adult should know, which will allow you to bypass any child restrictions that you set.

11 Happy? Then click on the Advanced tab for a selection of further options. If you change a few settings and then have a change of heart, click on Restore Defaults to get everything back to how it was.

Important

These options are very useful when you need to control the websites that your children have access to on the web. Remember that your kids are vulnerable when they're surfing inquisitively, to the worst of the internet.

Finding alternatives
to Internet Explorer

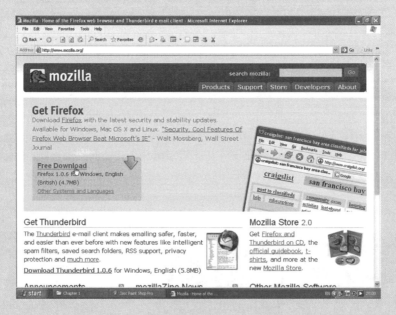

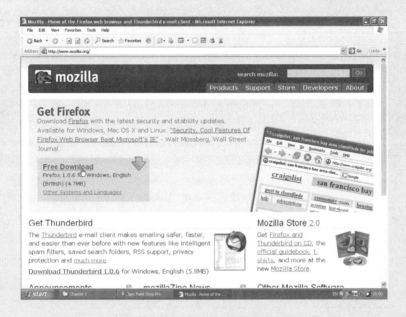

Internet Explorer has lost quite a bit of market share over the last couple of years, to a generation of new upstarts in the world of browsing – different browsers which claim to offer increased flexibility, power and security.

You might want to take a peek at Opera (www.opera.com) and try this powerful, security-conscious browser out with a free download. With pop-up blocking, tabbed browsing, and an impressive email program, Internet Explorer has a worthy competitor here. Opera is also highly customisable, so you can play around with its settings to your heart's content.

Meanwhile, more and more people swear by Mozilla Firefox (www.mozilla.org) – 80 million or so,

according to the site! Again, tabbed browsing, pop-up blocking and smart searching pay a large role here, and with so many converts, is it about time you popped along to the site to see what all the fuss is about? The latest version of Netscape (http://browser.netscape.com) shouldn't be forgotten, either.

Finally, of course, sign up with AOL (www.aol.co.uk) and you get a totally new browsing experience, thanks to AOL's wealth of content channels and family-friendly settings.

So the browser war certainly isn't over – and there's enough strength in depth for Internet Explorer to be looking over its shoulder nervously for a good while to come!

Using a basic search engine

Basic searching

1 Here we are at Google.co.uk. Look how everything is laid out, and how clear and uncluttered this home page is. Carry out a basic search in Google by entering your search term. We type in 'Cricket'.

2 Then click Google Search.

3 Watch out, here come the results! It was quite a general enquiry, obviously, and we get hundreds of thousands of results. Each result is given an underlined title, site description and website link in green. Click on the underlined title to be whizzed straight to the site in question.

Once you've found your way around the web with Internet Explorer, how do you get to the content you want as quickly as possible? After all, with so many millions of sites out there, it could turn into an absolute nightmare if you just hit and hope whenever you go online.

That's why search engines are such big business on the web – and why Google (www.google.co.uk) is so famous.
Google is pretty much without question the leading search engine on the web. Competition has thankfully increased significantly over the last couple of years, mainly because more and more sites are cottoning on to the undeniable fact that there's some serious money to be made in the business of searching, but Google still stands top of the tree. It's clean and uncluttered, and tremendously comprehensive and useful – especially when you look at its ever-increasing add-ons, such as Google News, Google email (Gmail) and Google Local, which we'll look at presently. For the moment, however, we'll concentrate on some basic searches in Google, before moving on to a few advanced tricks.

Basic searching

4 Here's the site in question, which you can now navigate around as usual.

5 You can ask Google to search the whole of the web or, if you're hankering after a bit more of a 'local' set of results, just the UK. Here, we've clicked in the little circle next to 'pages from the UK' to do just that.

Timesaver tip

Many search engines have language tools which allow you to translate web pages into another language, and Google is no different. Click on Language Tools from the home page, or go to www.google.co.uk/language_ tools, to translate text into a variety of different languages.

Did you know ?

Every so often, on days of cultural and historical significance such as Independence Day or Shakespeare's birthday, the Google home page will change its logo to a drawing reflecting the special event. This doesn't mean much necessarily, but is a nice touch for Google fans and a sign that there's a human team behind the massive search engine giant.

Using a basic search engine (cont.)

Basic searching

6. Add an element of surprise to your search results by entering your search term and then clicking I'm Feeling Lucky. This will take you immediately to one relevant site of Google's choice. Obviously, unless it's a bit of an obscure query, this method is fairly unlikely to get you where you want immediately.

7. At the bottom of the screen you can click on more pages of results, if you haven't got what you wanted from the first page of results.

8. You can also click on Download now to download Google's exciting new Desktop Search program, which searches your own computer files for relevant info. This kind of thing shows how Google is refusing to stand still as it aims to cement its reputation as the world's leading search engine.

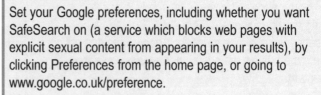

Timesaver tip

Set your Google preferences, including whether you want SafeSearch on (a service which blocks web pages with explicit sexual content from appearing in your results), by clicking Preferences from the home page, or going to www.google.co.uk/preference.

9

Basic searching

9 Click Make Google your homepage to quickly and easily set www.google.co.uk as the site that Internet Explorer instantly goes to when you open it up. If you do a lot of searches, as most of us do, this could be a great time-saving move.

2

10 Click on the underlined 'more' link from www.google.co.uk to access this amazing array of Google extras – just look what's on offer! We'll cover some of Google's add-ons at the end if this chapter, but for the moment, take a look at what's on offer, including Google Scholar for students, Google Labs for sneaky glimpses at new services, Google Alerts to get news alerts via email, Google Groups to start chatting with like-minded users... and much, much more!

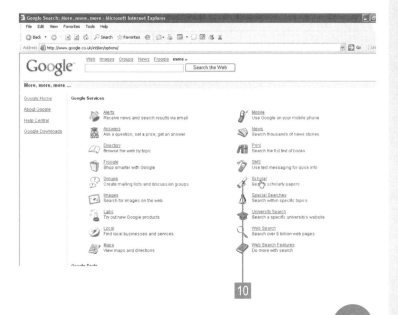

10

For your information

Google has a number of business solutions, such as Google AdSense, which may be able to help you earn more money from your website. To find out more about these possibilities, click on Business Solutions from the Google home page, or go to www.google.co.uk/services.

Doing basic image searching

Search for an image

 The first thing to do, at www.google.co.uk, is to click on Images.

 You can now specify your image search query. We're after pictures of cult pop star Beth Orton, so we enter her name into the search box, and then click Search Images.

Timesaver tip

As we'll see, you can do an advanced Google web search, and you can also do an advanced image search. After you've clicked Images from www.google.co.uk for an image search, click on Advanced Image Search from the right-hand side. You can then set stipulations about the size of images you want to see, the file type and other options.

Google can do far more than just basic text searching, as we're sure you've become aware of by now. Another major factor of Google is its Image Search, which lets you search for pictures of, well, anything really, at the speed of light. We'll investigate how it works. We've looked at basic word and image searches in Google – now it's time to check out Advanced Searches on the site. These fall into two camps – useful tips and tricks that you can do from the main Google interface to give you more precise results, or literal 'Advanced Searches', which is an option available from Google's home page. An Advanced Search lets you specify strict criteria for your searches – to only look for exact words or phrases, in a certain language, or from a certain date, for example.

We'll now get to grips with advanced searching tips.

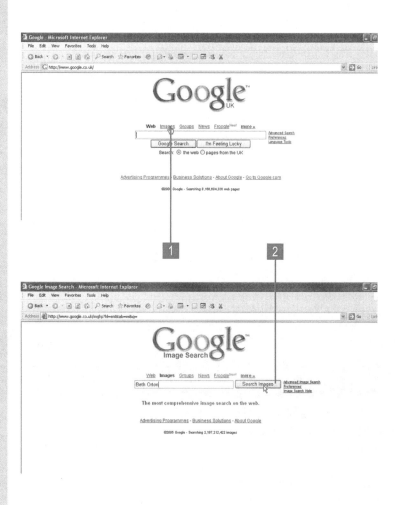

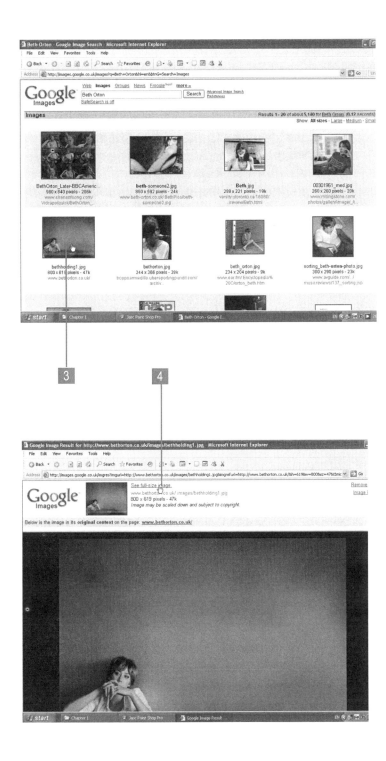

Find an image

3 Google will search its massive database and come back with lots and lots, hopefully, of photographs of the singer in question. We do indeed get plenty of images, presented in thumbnail style on this results page, with their file details and the address of the website where the image came from. Click on a photo to see it on its own, and bigger if possible – we click on the first photograph on the left in the second row.

4 The photo is now isolated, and you can choose to see the full-size image, and, in the window below, the image in its original context on the web page in question. We click on See full-size image.

Timesaver tip

Feeling a bit in the dark about image searches? Get some Google help at www.google.co.uk/help/faq_images.html.

Doing basic image searching (cont.)

More possibilities

5 Here's the image in full-size (not that much bigger than the thumbnail really, in this case). If the image is copyrighted, you'll need to contact the rights holder if you want to use the image on your website or for commercial use. We just want to print it, so we go to File, Print and set our print options before clicking Print.

6 Seeing the pic may have just stirred your interest in an actual website, so to see the site where the picture came from, click on the underlined link next to 'Below is the image in its original context'. Obviously if the site opens in the window below the pic you won't need to do this, but sometimes it is quicker to just click on the link.

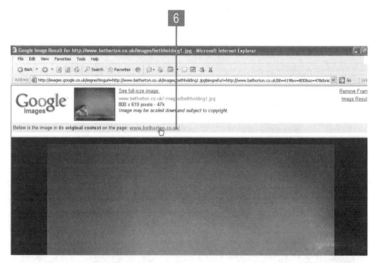

For your information

If you need to find personal photos on your computer, try Google's free downloadable digital photo organizing software Picasa, available at http://picasa.google.com/index.html.

Doing basic image searching (cont.)

Last steps

7 Here is the photo placed in context in its website. As we thought, it's stimulated us to check on some further links – there's a story about Minnie Driver on the right which we decide to click on.

8 It's best to stay safe when you're doing image searches, as without the safe search filter on, you could get some results of a sexually explicit nature. Underneath the search window on a results page you'll see the underlined words Moderate SafeSearch is On, or SafeSearch is Off. If you get the latter, click on the link to change your preferences to turn the filter on and guard yourself from dodgy results.

For your information

Other search engines have powerful image searches as well. On uk.yahoo.com, change the pull-down menu in the search window to 'in Images' to do an image search. At www.ask.co.uk, simply click Pictures from the home page. And at www.lycos.com, click on Images & Audio.

Carrying out advanced searches

Get advanced

1 Typing a search command with speech marks around it asks Google to search just for that exact phrase. So here, only results with the exact phrase 'Internet Made Easy' will come back to me, rather than results with combinations of any or all of these words.

2 Click Google Search as usual to carry out the modified search.

3 What a difference to the results – at the top is the very magazine that we're searching for. Click the underlined link to access the website as usual.

4 Type in the AND command and Google will be forced to look for results with both terms in them. So here we're looking for results that not only mention the internet, but also 'Dom Brookman'. Click Google Search.

Timesaver tip

Go to www.google.co.uk/help/refinesearch.html to get some Google-endorsed advanced search tips.

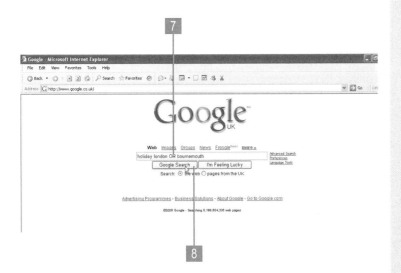

Different results

5 Again, very good results come back, and we can click on an underlined link to go the website we want to view.

6 Just to prove the validity of Google's results, here's the site in question, which details a previous internet book written by this very author.

7 You can also use the OR command to good effect. Here we ask Google to come back with holiday results that mention either London OR Bournemouth.

8 Click Google Search as usual.

Timesaver tip

Google has even provided a handy print-out-and-keep 'cheat sheet' of all the different symbols you can use in search strings and what they do – you won't use many of them, but some of them could prove invaluable from time to time. See www.google.co.uk/help/cheatsheet.html.

Carrying out advanced searches (cont.)

Different results

9 The results which come back are full of London and Bournemouth holiday details; click on a link that interests.

10 Entering 'DVD player £50..£100' – those 2 dots are crucial – will get Google to come back with results for DVD players that cost between 50 and 100 pounds.

11 Entering 'Star Wars Episode +1' – again, it's the '+' symbol which makes the difference here – gets Google just to look for the exact movie title Star Wars Episode 1.

12 Click Google Search again.

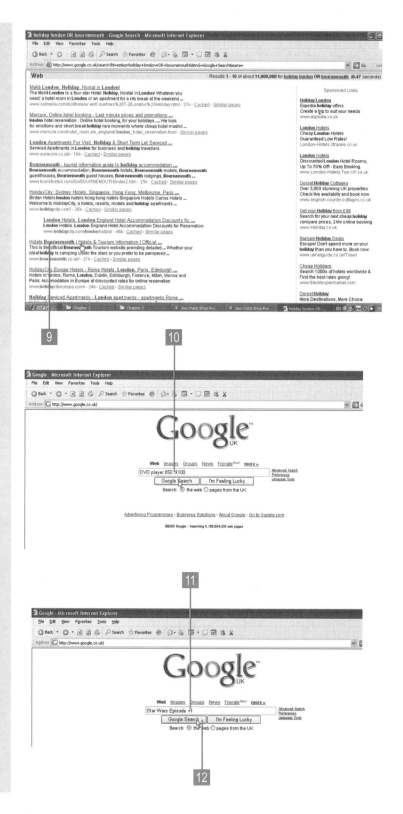

Different results

13 Star Wars Episode 1 results only return (at least at the top of the results – some of the others are a bit iffy). Click on a link to go the website.

14 Just so you know, here's what the Google Advanced Search screen looks like – there are oodles of criteria which you can set. Remember, the more precise you are, the less results you'll get – which you may regard as a good or a bad thing!

Timesaver tip

There are plenty of general websites out there offering search engine advice and tips – after all, everyone pretty much uses search engines these days, as the internet is so big, so there's a large market for decent pointers. One of our favourite help sites is Search Engine Watch (www.searchenginewatch.com), which has some excellent pointers, and even helps you out if you're thinking of submitting your website for the perusal of the leading search engine players.

Finding alternatives to Google

As we've said, Google is pretty much the world's number one search engine – but the competition is fierce, with search engines offering more and more features, and more personalisation options, to try and get your custom. There are plenty of people out there who dislike Google and prefer one of the many alternatives – so don't be afraid to experiment and see which one suits you best.

You should take a look at the friendly and ever-improving Ask Jeeves (www.ask.co.uk), the massive internet portal Yahoo! (uk.yahoo.com), the entertainment-driven Lycos (www.lycos.co.uk or www.lycos.com), and the Google-alike AltaVista (www.altavista.com).

62

New players on the block such as Blinkx (www.blinkx.com) also take a different approach to the subject – Blinkx is able to search relevant information not only on the web, but on your desktop and in your files. Blinkx actually tailors searches based on what content you're viewing online, and it's this personalisation which could be the next big thing in search technology. Google has fought back with its own Desktop Search feature – expect this battle to run and run!

Take a look at all the search engines and make up your mind as to which you think is the best one for your own highly unique needs.

2

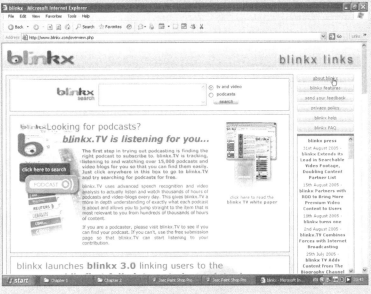

Exploring Google add-ons

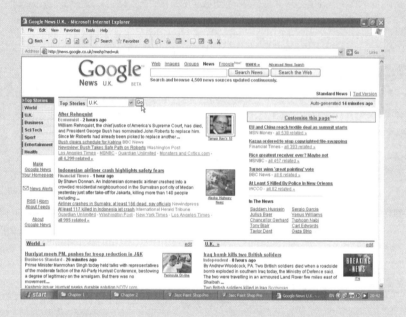

We've mentioned the fact that Google regards itself as much, much more than a search engine already – and it has so many different features these days that it's hard to catch up. Google seems to be trying to become your number one choice in a number of fields, with a first example being that of news-gathering. Google News (http://news.google.co.uk) searches and browses 4,500 news sources continuously to give you the most up-to-date links to the most up-to-date stories from across the world. This really is a tremendous news-gathering site, and you even sign up to news alerts to your Inbox, so you never miss the very latest happenings in a certain topic area.

The punningly named Froogle, meanwhile (http://froogle.google.co.uk) acts as an invaluable shopping resource, helping you find thousands of consumer items from across the web.

Google Local (http://local.google.co.uk) uses the power of Google to search your own 'manor' for local businesses and services – brilliant. And Google Earth (http://earth.google.com) goes the opposite way, offering you stunning maps and satellite images and putting the world's geographical detail at your fingertips. Broadband is definitely recommended for this stunning service.

And we haven't even mentioned so many other services, including Google's attempt to take on the major email providers, with Gmail (mail.google.com), which boasts over 2 Gb of storage.

One of the best places to catch up on Google developments is Google Labs (http://labs.google.com) – just be prepared to check back there every day, as this is one web giant definitely not prepared to stand still!

Communicating with others

Introduction

It's no exaggeration to say that the internet has revolutionised the way we communicate with each other, and continues to blaze a trail when it comes to helping us talk to people across the world. In the early days, it was email that was the real 'killer app' of the internet – here was a fantastic way of keeping in touch with people no matter where they were in the world, just by typing a few lines in a program and pressing Send. Email not only fundamentally changed inter-personal relationships and communication, but also the way we conduct business. All of a sudden, you could conduct your business with someone thousands of miles away in a matter of minutes, without having to fork out on expensive travel fares or phone calls.

Some people, of course, reckon that email has actually affected the way we speak to people in a negative way. Speaking to someone face-to-face seems not the 'done thing' any more, when you can just fire off an email in a matter of seconds. The informality of email also encourages mistakes, inappropriate language, gossip and poor standards of English – according to some. We, however, prefer to regard email as a brilliant, powerfully effective communication tool; it's hard to imagine, indeed, a world before email existed.
We'll be looking at setting up an account with the default mail client Outlook Express in this chapter, as well as pointing out some of its rivals, such as Hotmail, Eudora and Yahoo!

There's more than one way to chat and get yourself heard than email, of course, and the rest of the chapter will be dedicated to a raft of ways where you can get in touch with people. Newsgroups, chat rooms, online dating and the new craze of 'blogging' will all be featured, as we explain how to get involved quickly and simply in some fantastic methods of communication. Chat rooms, of course, have come in for some bad press over the last couple of years with

What you'll do

Set up an account in Outlook Express

Use some Outlook Express features

Send and receive emails

Send and save attachments

Find alternatives to Outlook Express: separate programs

Find alternatives to Outlook Express: webmail

Access a newsgroup

Send messages in a newsgroup

Look at the subjects covered by newsgroups

Access a chat room

Chat online and learn about good 'Netiquette'

Use an Instant Messaging program

Learn about chat room dangers

Find different Instant Messaging programs

Sign up for Guardian Soulmates dating

Learn about different forms of online dating

Start your own blog with Blogger.com

Find some alternatives to Blogger

various unsavoury incidents of paedophiles 'grooming' young children in chat rooms before striking – scary stuff. Microsoft acted quickly to radically change the setup of its free-to-all MSN chat rooms, and others followed suit, leaving the chat room landscape looking rather barren. Internet giants Yahoo, through partnership with Lycos, still offer chat, however, and it's their service that we'll be highlighting.

There are various aspects of safety that you must remember when you're chatting online, and we'll be pointing these out as we go along. Simple, basic facts like not giving your contact details out on national chat rooms really need to be heeded, so you can concentrate on the business of chatting and having fun.
A word about 'blogging' – this is the new craze that's swept through the internet over the last couple of years. The word sounds technical, but it basically just refers to writing an online diary, sharing your thoughts with the rest of the world. It's great fun, and incredibly addictive, and we'll show you how to start your own blog as the chapter draws to a close. So without further ado, let's see how the standard email account Outlook Express works.

Outlook Express is the default email client that you get when you buy a new PC, so will thus be familiar to millions of people across the world. It's not perfect, but does the job required without fuss or frills – whether you like it or not pretty much depends on whether you want an email account with lots of bells and whistles, or just want a simple way of sending and receiving your messages. We'll take a look at setting up an account in Outlook Express, before going on to a few more simple features of the program.

Setting up an account in Outlook Express

Account setup

1 There are a few ways of accessing Outlook Express quickly. You may want to go click the Start button in the bottom-left of your desktop, go to All Programs and click Outlook Express. In our case, Outlook Express has already been added to the list of main programs down the left-hand side, so we simply click on its icon.

2 It loads up, and the first thing we want to do is configure a new mail account, so we click on Set up a Mail account. You'll need to have some information for the next few steps – the type of email server you use, the name of the incoming email server, and the name of the outgoing email server. If you're unsure about this info, check with your ISP.

3

Setting up an account in Outlook Express (cont.)

Account setup

3 The Internet Connection Wizard is now here to help you out. Click the check box next to Create a new internet mail account if this screen pops up.

4 Then click Next.

5 Enter your Display name here – what other people will see when they get mail from you. We recommend using your full name for the moment.

6 Click Next again.

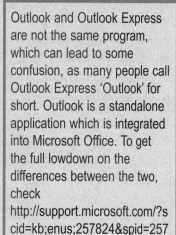

For your information

Outlook and Outlook Express are not the same program, which can lead to some confusion, as many people call Outlook Express 'Outlook' for short. Outlook is a standalone application which is integrated into Microsoft Office. To get the full lowdown on the differences between the two, check http://support.microsoft.com/?scid=kb;enus;257824&spid=2578&sid=global.

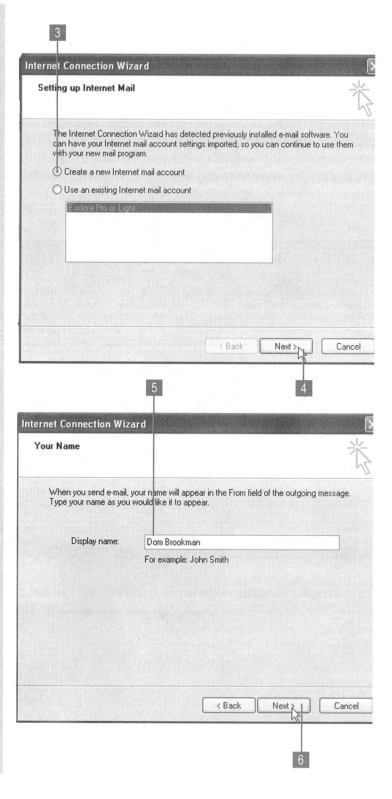

3

Internet Connection Wizard

Setting up Internet Mail

The Internet Connection Wizard has detected previously installed e-mail software. You can have your Internet mail account settings imported, so you can continue to use them with your new mail program.

⦿ Create a new Internet mail account

◯ Use an existing Internet mail account

Eudora Pro or Light

< Back   Next >   Cancel

5   **4**

Internet Connection Wizard

Your Name

When you send e-mail, your name will appear in the From field of the outgoing message. Type your name as you would like it to appear.

Display name: Dom Brookman

For example: John Smith

< Back   Next >   Cancel

6

Account setup

7 Carry on through the next couple of steps, entering your email address, and then type in the information which you may have gathered from your ISP about the names of your incoming and outgoing mail servers. Now, type in your account name and password, ticking the check box next to Remember Password if you want Outlook Express to remember you next time you pop in.

8 Click Next, and then Finish. The setting up procedure should now be complete.

Important

Choose your password for Outlook Express carefully, especially if you're going to be using it often. There's actually a series of 'best practices' to use when it comes to password selection, and you can see what they are at www.microsoft.com/windows/IE/community/columns/passwords.mspx.

Internet Connection Wizard

Internet Mail Logon

Type the account name and password your Internet service provider has given you.

Account name: dom_brookman

Password: ••••••••

☑ Remember password

If your Internet service provider requires you to use Secure Password Authentication (SPA) to access your mail account, select the 'Log On Using Secure Password Authentication (SPA)' check box.

☐ Log on using Secure Password Authentication (SPA)

[< Back] [Next >] [Cancel]

Using some Outlook Express features

We'll now take a look at playing with a couple of the basic options in Outlook Express – there's plenty to investigate, so don't feel afraid to experiment!

Carry out some tasks

1. You may have Address Book settings that you want to import into Outlook Express, for speed and convenience. If you do, click on File, Import and then Address Book.

2. Printing any emails you get is easy, as you'll probably guess from the large printer icon in the main Outlook Express window. Click on it to bring this window up, select your different options and then click Print. Easy!

Timesaver tip

Backing up your copy of Outlook Express is a good idea, to prevent any catastrophes in the future. The process is a bit too long-winded to go into here, but you can find a step-by-step guide to what do from Microsoft at www.microsoft.com/windows/IE/community/columns/OEtopten.mspx. You can also find the Outlook Express Backup Wizard at http://www.outlook-express-backup.com.

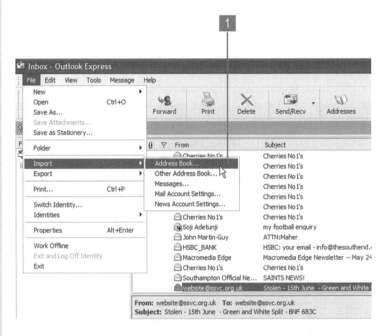

Change the order

3 Any messages you do get, you may want to sort into some kind of order – maybe grouped together by sender or subject, for example? To sort messages by alphabetical subject title, click on View, Sort By and Subject.

4 Your messages are now sorted out, in this example, by subject title. Where there's only a few emails like this, imposing this kind of order on proceedings is hardly vital, but the more mail you get, the more you may want to get things shipshape – especially if you're likely to be trawling through mail looking, for example, for a particular person's mail.

Timesaver tip

Outlook Express does have a Help menu which may be able to sort you out if you run into problems. If you're unsure whether everything is as it should be once you've set your account up, simply find a mate who's online at the same time as you. Send them an email, and if they get it and can read it OK, you're in business.

Timesaver tip

Close Outlook Express quickly by pressing 'ALT' + 'F4'.

Using some Outlook Express features (cont.)

Options, options...

5 Go to Tools, then Options to see a selection of different tabs.

6 The General tab has a number of basic options, such as whether or not to play sound when you receive messages.

7 The Read tab controls how you read messages.

8 The Receipts tab lets you request a 'read receipt' for all messages you send.

9 The Send tab controls your sending mail settings.

10 The Compose tab lets you configure how your messages will look.

11 The Signatures tab lets you add a signature to all your messages.

12 The Spelling tab lets you set whether you want to spellcheck your mail.

13 The Security tab, which we're on here, has a whole host of important security settings for you to configure.

14 The Connection tab allows you to hang up your connection.

15 The Maintenance tab lets you conduct essential Outlook Express housework.

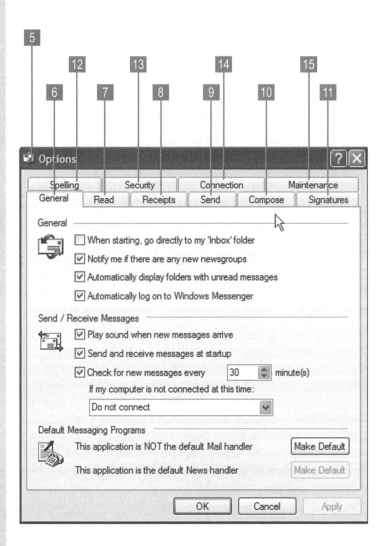

Timesaver tip

Don't forget, of course, that you can send emails to multiple recipients at the same time. In the 'To' field, simply separate each different email address by a comma. The message will then go to all the different people.

Sending and receiving emails in Outlook Express is an absolute doddle, even if you've barely used a computer. Everything is clearly signposted to avoid confusion, and you'll be sending messages with the best of them after just a few minutes. Let's take a very quick tour through sending your mail.

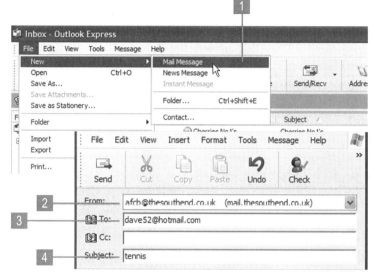

Send a message

1 Right, we want to send a new message to someone. Again, there are a couple of ways of doing this, and you'll probably find one that's most convenient to you after a bit of experimentation. Go to File, New, then Mail Message.

2 A new window opens. Type in the address of the person that you're sending the message to in the To box, making sure you don't make any mistakes. If they're in your Address Book you can just copy and paste them in from there.

3 Decide if you want to 'cc' anyone in on the message (see our tips for more on this option).

4 Type in a relevant subject title.

3

Timesaver tip

Got more than one person in the house who uses email, and who wants their own personal address book, message store and settings? Then you need to use the Outlook Express Identities feature, and give a separate Identity to each user, enabling different people to get to their messages without having to shut down your PC. Each identity should be configured with its own separate email account address as well, to avoid different people getting the same messages. Add the appropriate email account once you've entered Outlook Express with the new Identity.

The first person to use Outlook Express and set it up will have the main Identity. To create an additional Identity, you need to go to File, Identities, then Add New Identity. Then type a name for the new identity and select whether or not to set a password.
For further help on this potentially crucial area of Outlook Express, the Help menu can also come to your aid.

Sending and receiving emails (cont.)

Send a message

5 Type your message in the window. Don't shout, check for punctuation, and check for spelling if you like by going to Tools, then Spelling.

6 When you're happy, click Send. And that's it! The message will be added to your Outbox, and hopefully you'll get a reply soon.

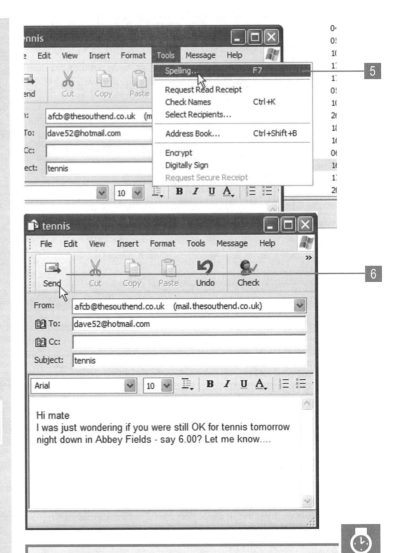

Once you've got the hang of sending basic messages, you may want to branch out with sending what are known as 'attachments'. These could be pictures, music files, Word documents... anything that you need to go as an accompaniment to your basic main message. Let's see just how easy it is to send an attachment with Outlook Express.

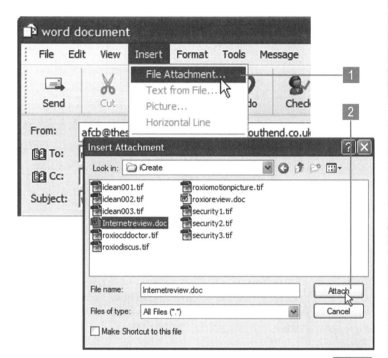

Sending and saving attachments

Send an attachment

1. Here, we're sending an attachment screenshot to a work colleague. We go to Insert, File Attachment. Alternatively, you can click on the Attach icon, which should be lurking on the right of your email window as well.

2. We then browse through our hard drive for the relevant picture. Once we've found it, we click Attach.

3

Timesaver tip

Email's very convenience and speed can be both a blessing and a curse. Imagine you're in a bad mood, for example, and send off a furious email to a friend, work colleague, or even your boss. You may be furiously angry as you type away, but think very carefully before you press that Send button. Once an email has been sent, it's extremely difficult to retrieve it, so a good rule of thumb is – have you said anything in the email that you'd be unwilling to say face-to-face? If so, you may need to have second thoughts. Email seems informal, and it's that informality which can lead to misunderstandings, people taking offence, or sending a rant to the wrong people, as you haven't checked the address fields carefully enough in your haste.

For your information

Check your spelling, try not to talk in CAPITALS as it looks like you're SHOUTING, and if you're in the workplace, keep personal emails to lunch hours, if at all – some firms have really stiffened up their rules and regulations on what is and isn't acceptable during business hours.

Sending and saving attachments (cont.)

Send an attachment

3. You'll see the filename, size and a little icon appear in the Attach field of the email. Then click Send.

4. If you want, any attachments that you receive can be saved. Simply go to File, Save attachments, and then click Save.

Timesaver tip

To create a signature in Outlook Express – your name and workplace details, which will go on the bottom of every message you send – click on the Tools menu, then Options, and the Signatures tab. Click New, enter your new signature, and then check the Add signatures to all outgoing messages box.

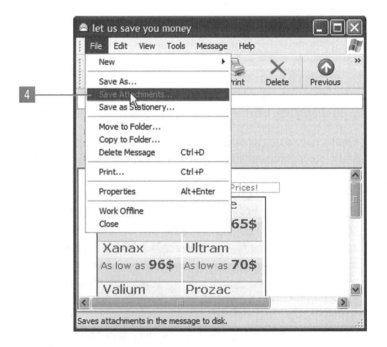

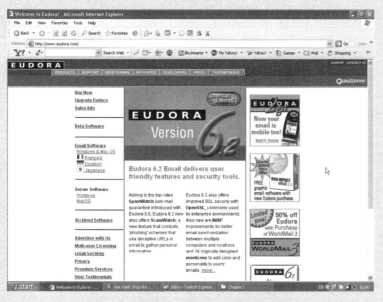

3

There are many people who claim that Outlook Express is a tad long in the tooth these days, and to cater for this market, you can go online and choose a different email service to fit in with the way you live. We'll look at 'webmail' accounts, but as far as downloadable email programs go, one of our favourites is the plucky underdog Eudora, at www.eudora.com. This program first came to our attention as the one used in our workplace – its large, friendly design and accessible interface were a great hit. Features such as 'MoodWatch', which marks up offensive emails with chillies depending on their nastiness, work pretty well, and recent versions of the program have introduced features such as 'ScamWatch', which tries to combat those dodgy 'phishing' fraudulent messages that seem such a depressingly constant inevitability of modern day emailing. You can choose a paid-for form, sponsored or light version of the program, so take a look and see if it's for you.

Other alternatives include the bright and garish IncrediMail (www.incredimail) and Pegasus Mail (www.pmail.com). Don't be afraid to experiment with your email service, and find one that suits how you work and the frequency with which you send mail.

Finding alternatives to Outlook Express: webmail

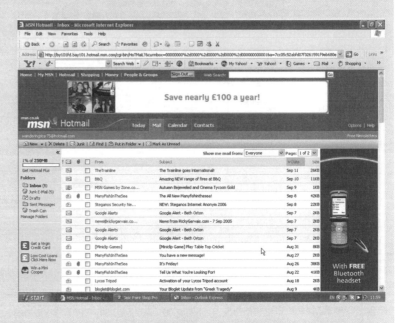

Webmail accounts are, as the name suggests, based online. You simply use your browser to go to the home page of the webmail provider, enter your username and password, and then access your messages, before composing new ones, should you so wish. Wherever you are in the world, therefore, as long as there's a computer and internet connection, you can access your mail. Being based online has its advantages and disadvantages, but one of the major plus points is the ease with which you can set up a new account and start using mail away from home or the workplace. One of the most famous and popular webmail providers is hotmail (www.hotmail.com), which Microsoft has made significant strides with over the last couple of years. Hotmail used to be plagued by annoying junk mail, but the situation is much, much better now; you may even choose to upgrade to Hotmail Plus, which offers a whopping 2 GB Inbox for you to play with.

Yahoo!'s email is another webmail giant – take a look at mail.yahoo.co.uk to see what this computer giant has to offer. Again, you'll see the increased emphasis on security and spam protection, which can only be good in today's world, where we're bombarded by email seemingly all day long. Most major ISPs provide you with your own email accounts, too, so check with them about what's on offer. You might also want to try FastMail (www.fastmail.fm), which has won lots of fans for its fast, professional and reliable service.

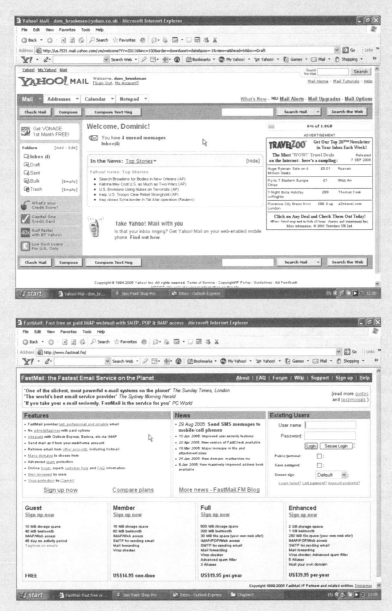

Accessing a newsgroup

Find a relevant newsgroup

1. Go the famous home page of Google at www.google.co.uk and click on Groups.

2. We're interested in accessing newsgroups about the famous '80s and '90s computer the Commodore Amiga, so we type in 'Amiga' into the search box and then click Search Groups.

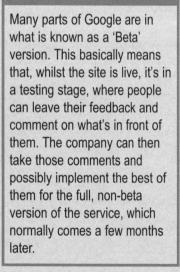

Newsgroups are another way of chatting to people and getting your voice heard online. They are basically just forums for sharing information – a place where like-minded people can gather and talk about, for example, Big Brother, or model airplanes, or The Premiership – you name it, they'll be a newsgroup dedicated to it somewhere online. You can both post messages and reply to other users, so many newsgroups get a 'healthy' debate which, unfortunately, can occasionally topple over into verbal abuse – so tread carefully and try and use a newsgroup which looks professional and where the tone is adult and sensible. In the past, people used a worldwide bulletin system known as Usenet to access newsgroups; Usenet grew and grew and became incredibly popular. Special newsreaders were needed to access such groups. Usenet.com still exists, as a gateway to some 100,000 newsgroups, but isn't the only way to access some top-quality discussion these days.

The mighty Google, as part of its new 'Groups' service at http://groups-beta.google.com, acquired the archive of Usenet postings and now offers an archive of more than a billion messages, offering a fantastic and amazingly comprehensive way of discussing those burning topics.

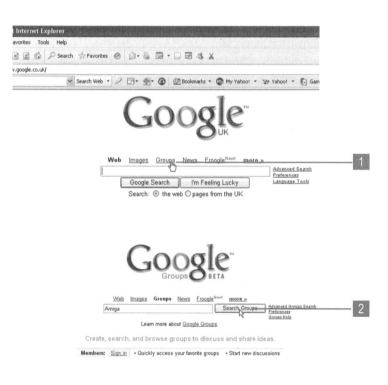

Google Groups BETA

Web   Images   **Groups**   News   Froogle^New!   **more »**

Amiga   [Search]   Advanced Groups Search
Preferences

Members: Sign in
New users: Join

Google Groups

☑ Groups Alerts

Create a new group

About Google Groups

Searched all groups

Related groups: comp.sys.amiga.hardware
comp.sys.amiga.marketplace
comp.sys.amiga.games
182 more »

Ottawa **Amiga** Show 2003
Ottawa **Amiga** Show 2003 **Amiga**.info http://www.technomages.net/amigashov
Ontario, Canada On Saturday November 22, 2003, the **Amiga**.info user group v
comp.sys.amiga.misc - Oct 21 2003, 7:10 pm by Thomas Leroux - 1 messag

Accepted **amiga**-fdisk 0.04-10 (source i386 m68k)
-----BEGIN PGP SIGNED MESSAGE----- Hash: SHA1 Format: 1.7 Date: Sat, 3
21:36:04 +0200 Source: **amiga**-fdisk Binary: **amiga**-fdisk-cross **amiga**-fdisk-b
linux.debian.changes.devel - Sep 4, 10:40 am by Christian T. Steigies - 1 m

[link] Drive into a wildly imaginative psychic adventure. Psychonauts! The screenshot
luring me quite. -- ive
read more »   **9 new** of 9 messages - 4 authors

☆ **How about some new games - finally**
i_b_ - Jul 10, 5:20 pm
Congratulations guys, again, you've written it all. As boring, and as boring as it was, t
you have put it all in here. Thank you, and God bless each and every single one of yo
comp.sys.amiga.advocacy preferably, at least in my case. Ehm? -- ive
read more »   **1 new** of 1 message - 1 author

☆ **which Amiga games are you currently playing ?**
Sodan - Jul 10, 2:05 am
Hello ! Ok, to post something more appropriate to this group (instead of talking about
workbench legality ;)), let's talk about games you currently play or have played not lo
am currently playing: Wonderdog: Have again started to play this game. I started aga
5 where I had been given the password years ago when I last played, but could never
read more »   **34 new** of 34 messages - 14 authors

☆ **looking for a game**
solons...@gmail.com - Jul 9, 4:23 pm
I know this isn't quite good place for this but the best i've found I'm looking for a game
amiga it was named CHAR (or at least that's what I think it was named) it was up to 8
turn based tank game, you shot and enemies using all sorts of ammo (lots of lava for
and also had a shield (like repel one) I can't find it
read more »   **10 new** of 11 messages - 5 authors

☆ **Workbench Reality Check**
The Hornet - Jul 9, 2:45 pm

Find a relevant newsgroup

3 You'll be presented with a list of relevant newsgroups that deal with the Amiga and Amiga-related issues. The addresses of the newsgroups are in green. We click on one near the top.

4 You'll see a list of topics that have been started in the newsgroup you chose. If a particular topic interests you, simply click on read more.

3

Timesaver tip

Treat people on newsgroups like you'd like to be treated – so don't be rude, abusive or inflammatory. It's a lot safer and nicer in the long run!

Sending messages to a newsgroup

So we've seen how to access a newsgroup – how do we send messages? It's incredibly simple with Google Groups, although you do need to go through a registration process, which we'll guide you through here.

Send a message

1 If you want to reply to a topic, first of all, simply click on the Reply link.

2 To be able to reply properly, you need to be registered with Google. You may be so already, but if you're not, simply click on Sign up now.

3 To open a Google account, enter your email address, choose a password and a nickname (this latter choice is optional), go through the security word verification step, read the terms and conditions and click I have read and agree… .

4 You're all set up to reply now, so enter your comment in the dialog box, remembering to be polite and courteous, and then click Post message. And that's it!

Timesaver tip

Don't forget that Google has stacks of other options on offer for you to play with, including email, local search and news. All the services are detailed at www.google.co.uk/intl/en/options.

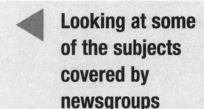

The good news is that we've only just scraped the surface when it comes to newsgroups – there literally are hundreds of thousands of them out there, covering a massive range of topics. Any quick search on Google (ironically enough) will prove that. Just looking at Google Groups here, you can see science and technology, music, language and history all well represented – and there are countless more topics to get to grips with.

Newsgroups tend to be more serious-minded than chat rooms, so access them if frivolous chat isn't really your thing, and you're after some decent information-gathering or debate. Obviously you'll still see silly things in newsgroups as well, but generally to a lesser degree than when you are in chat rooms. Have fun and start broadening your knowledge!

3

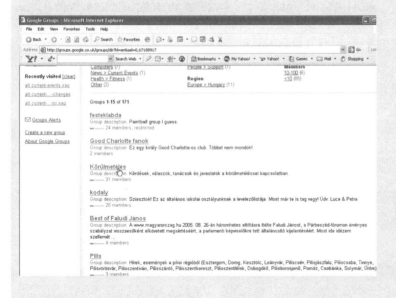

Accessing a chat room ▶

First steps with Yahoo! Chat

 There are plenty of ways to get to Yahoo!'s chat facility quickly and easily, but we'll take the route via the UK home page, at uk.yahoo.com. On the left of the home page, you'll see loads of options, one of which is Chat. Click on it.

 You'll see plenty of information now about the Yahoo! chat service, operated by Yahoo! Parental supervision for children under 18 is recommended – the UK and Ireland chat rooms, whilst not moderated as such, do have 'Navigators' available in some rooms, who can sort out problems with other chatters and answer any queries you might have. When you've had a bit of a look around, click on Enter the new chat on the right.

ⓘ For your information

Each deck has a series of rooms for you to choose from – you'll probably want to go to one with lots of people in at the beginning, and maybe just watch a conversation for a while and see what happens.

As we've already mentioned, chat rooms have been going through a bit of a rough time over the last couple of years, to say the least. Although chat rooms were there pretty much at the start of the internet boom – people always want to talk, after all – they only really came to the public consciousness when a series of alarming security breaches were reported in the national press – security breaches which, in some cases, led to innocent children being attacked by paedophiles in real life after being 'groomed' in the supposedly safe and comforting area of the internet. Public outcry was such that chat room giants MSN shut down its chat rooms, a move which whilst praised by some, was attacked by others – would it just drive chat 'underground' and move the problem elsewhere? MSN chat is now available on subscription only, but the basic fact remains that online chat can be safe, fun and enjoyable – with the right precautions. Parental controls and decent education about online safety should both be considered by any company wishing to set up a chat service, to help protect its users.

Anyway, the upshot of it all is that finding a large, well-controlled chat forum on the internet is surprisingly difficult – type in 'chat' into Google and you're more likely to get dating sites and dubious organisations than anything else. Nevertheless, Yahoo!, in conjunction with Lycos, still runs 'the biggest and most advanced chat community in Europe' at uk.yahoo.com/chat, and we're going to look at how it's all set up here. Hopefully we'll convince you that whilst you're unlikely to get any deep, meaningful chat in chat rooms, you can still have safe fun and enjoy yourself. Let's see first of all just how to access a chat room.

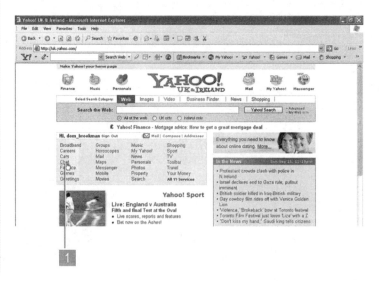

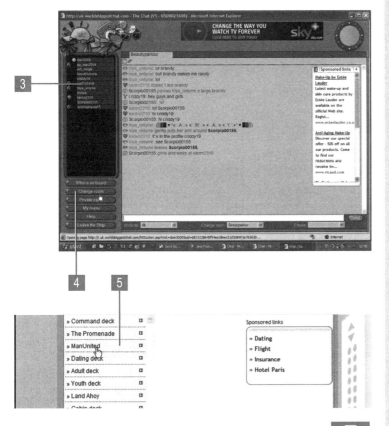

Choose a room

3 If you're already a member of Yahoo!, you'll need to confirm your password now. Otherwise, you'll have to start at the beginning and register with Yahoo! Once you've chosen a suitable username (keep it clean), you can choose a chat room that you'd like to go into. Note the list of people in the chat room down the left-hand side, including ourselves – dom5000.

4 Here's the main chat window. Note that in this room, the conversation isn't exactly stimulating or sensible ('brandy makes me randy' – hmmm), so we make a quick decision to try another room – there's plenty on Yahoo! Chat. So we click on Change room.

5 The chat system works here on a system of 'decks', such as the Adult deck and the Dating deck. Anyway, make your choice and proceed forwards. We'll look at some dos and don'ts of how to behave next.

Timesaver tip

If you're a parent responsible enough to educate yourself about the pros and cons of online chat, and the advantages and disadvantages, put your mind at rest and suck up information at http://uk.docs.yahoo.com/parents_guide. This series of articles lets you know all about safe online surfing and how to have fun.

Communicating with others 87

Chatting online and learning about good 'Netiquette'

Dos and Don'ts of chatting

1 We've found a chat room where there is some vaguely intelligent conversation going on, in the Philosophy Lounge (not much philosophy, though). Follow the chat, and then to type in your own comment, simply write your words in the box at the bottom of the screen and click Send.

2 What we've written, of course, manages to break at least three separate Netiquette rules, all in one go. So this kind of thing is what you should never write in a chat room (don't worry, we didn't press Send!). For a start, it's got spelling errors. Secondly, it's insulting and likely to cause offence. Thirdly, it's written all in CAPITALS, which makes it look like you're SHOUTING and won't do you any favours whatsoever. So don't ever write something like this!

3 What might help is to just look at what everyone else is writing, and how they're writing it – that way, hopefully, you might learn some basic do's and don'ts.

Now that we're in, what are the rules of chat rooms? These informal but widely-used rules and conventions form part of something known as 'Netiquette' – if you don't show good Netiquette, you're likely to be 'flamed' (an internet term for 'insulted', basically) and have a pretty miserable time of things. The techniques to remember are pretty simple to understand, however, so let's look at the basics of how to behave.

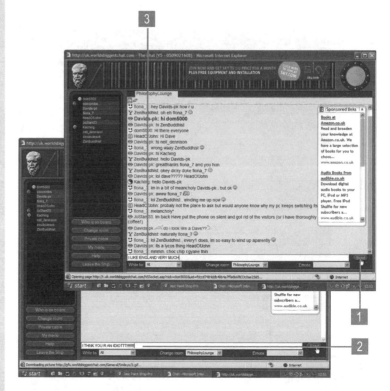

Timesaver tip

Yahoo's laws for safer and fun chatting are printed at http://uk.docs.yahoo.com/chat/laws.html. They comprise seven 'laws', which are: Never agree to meet anyone in real life. Never give out your real identity over the internet. Never give out your telephone number. Never give out your mobile number. Never give out your pager number. Never give out your home address. And never give out your work/school/college address. Pretty simple stuff, really, but you'd be surprised just how many people disregard this kind of advice, and suffer the consequences later.

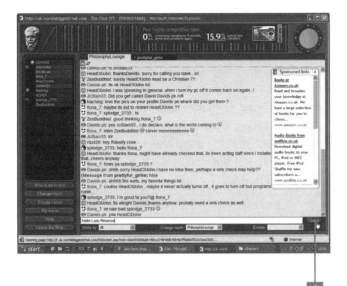

There are several possible reasons why you have arrived at my Netiquette site...

- You are new online and are on a quest for **Netiquette** or as some refer to it, **E-mail Etiquette** knowledge. Well, pat yourself on the back - I am thrilled to have you visit and wish there were more like you! Information is power but only if you use it! ;-) **Shall we start Netiquette 101?**
- A fellow Netizen has pointed you this way for your own good. See, they know how you are perceived without **Netiquette knowledge and E-mail skills** and felt that you should become aware of what has eluded you thus far. **Start Your Netiquette 101**
- Are you seeking a site to send Newbies to who do not yet practice Netiquette or E-Mail Etiquette? Each day seasoned Netizens land here at NetManners.com looking for such a resource on **Netiquette and E-mail Etiquette** and they then take advantage of my **Send a Dose of Netiquette** feature. Use my **Send a Dose of Netiquette** to let those you communicate with learn about the importance of communicating with knowledge, understanding and most importantly courtesy.
- You are smart and want to keep up with **e-mail etiquette issues** and technology trends that are constantly evolving which pertain to online communications and doing business online. Subscribe to my **Netiquette Matters! quarterly newsletter** sent out the first Wednesday of each quarter.

Timesaver tip

The advice website Internet Guide (www.internet-guide.co.uk) gives these examples of netiquette:

Not using someone else's name and pretending to be them.

Not posting or distributing material that is deemed illegal.

Not using abusive or threatening language.

Not posting racist remarks regarding peoples' sex, race or gender.

Not spamming message boards or chat rooms with useless or repeated messages.

Not trying to obtain or use someone else's password.

Not trying to obtain personal information about someone.

Chatting online and learning about good 'Netiquette' (cont.)

Further info

4 Whilst you're chatting away, you'll see people both exit and enter the room – many people only stay for a few minutes, while others remain for an age. When people enter, it's good Netiquette to welcome them to the room – it might not sound like much, but it's a nice thing to do, and puts fellow users at ease. Chat rooms are meant to be a pleasant, non-intimidating place, after all. Here, we welcome a new user to make her feel at home.

5 So, online chat can be fun, if you remember these rules and accept that in the nationally popular sites, you're unlikely to get anything that taxes the brain too much. But then, if you've had a hard day working, a bit of banter can be the ideal way to unwind. If you're still unsure about how to behave, try the Yahoo! helpsites that we've mentioned, or sites such as NetM@nners.com, at www.onlinenetiquette.com. They're full of advice about how to use resources properly.

Communicating with others 89

Using an Instant Messaging program

Instant Messaging takes the principles of email, newsgroups and chat rooms one step further. With email, there are plenty of barriers to actually having what we would term as a 'conversation' – your contact may be away from their desk or not there at all, their servers may be slow... basically you could be waiting ages for a reply. As the title Instant Messaging suggests, however, you can chat in 'real time' using this technology, allowing for extremely swift swapping of messages and banter. Often in Instant Messaging, you'll have a 'Buddy List' which tells you when someone in your Address Book is online – when they are, you can instantly hook up with them and type messages back and forth, at an immediacy which just isn't possible with email.

Instant Messaging is pretty addictive – many an employee has probably been caught Instant Messaging a mate when they should be concentrating at work! Major players in the Instant Messaging market include AOL, MSN and Yahoo!, who are all trying to outdo the other with more and more added cool features on their Instant Messaging software. We're going to see what the Yahoo! approach to Instant Messaging is here.

Get to grips with Yahoo! Messenger

1. A quick way of accessing Yahoo! Messenger is to go to http://messenger.yahoo.com. That will take you to this home page. Click on Features to see what you can expect from the program.

2. When you've done that, click on Get it now, to start the download process.

3. You can now choose between the UK and US version, but being based in England we go for the former. This screen lets you know that there's been some decent improvements to Yahoo! Messenger since its rather humble beginnings. Click on Get the UK version.

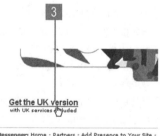

Important

Safety when you're Instant Messaging people is still very important, which is why it's worth going to http://uk.messenger.yahoo.com/msgr_safety.html and picking up tips on how to control who contacts you by this fun method of communication. Follow the advice carefully to make sure you don't trip up.

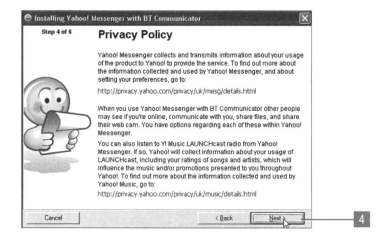

Get to grips with Yahoo! Messenger

4 The download process should be fairly quick and painless. You'll be taken to an installation process – click Next to cycle through the options.

5 Once it has downloaded, you'll be prompted to log in. Hopefully by now, if you've been following the book closely, you'll be a member of Yahoo! already, in which case all you need to do is use the login ID and password which you use when, for example, you're using Yahoo! Mail. If you are a new user, you need to click Get a Yahoo ID and follow the on-screen prompts.

6 Otherwise, enter your existing details and click Sign In.

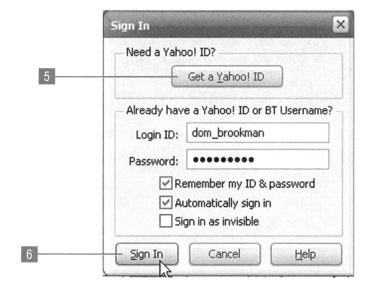

3

For your information

Yahoo! Messenger is now an impressively versatile program which has a whole feast of features on offer for you to take advantage of. Sign up and you get BT Communicator, which helps you make free phone calls online (see Chapter 5), Yahoo! Games, LAUNCHcast Radio, and fun sets of emoticons and avatars for you to play with. An avatar is an image which you can easily use to represent yourself online, taking the place of the more conventional photo.

Using an Instant Messaging program (cont.)

Get to grips with Yahoo! Messenger

7 Note the Yahoo! Games window underneath, which gives you access to such delights as Chess, Pearl Hunter and Word Racer. Click on the dice to access Yahoo! Games.

8 Yahoo! Messenger itself is in this window, with plenty of text prompts and icons for you to experiment with.

9 Underneath Yahoo! Messenger is yet more fun – LAUNCHcast Radio, which lets you listen to some cracking tunes as you work (or play). We click on the top icon in the radio window, to listen to 90s Flashback. Obviously check that your speakers and sound setup for your PC are present and correct.

10 One of the best things about Yahoo! Messenger is how it integrates itself with your other Yahoo! programs. So if you do use Yahoo! Mail, and millions of people do, your Address Book that you keep in that program can be accessed in your Instant Messaging window. Click on Address Book to prove it.

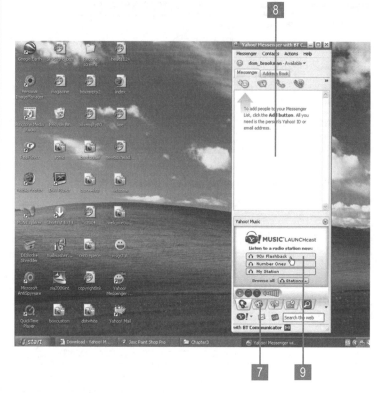

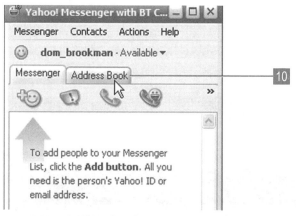

For your information

On Windows, Yahoo! Messenger has been localised for a whole series of countries – not just the UK and Ireland. Germany, Italy, Spain and the US all have their own versions; for the full list take a look at http://messenger.yahoo.com/messenger/intl.html.

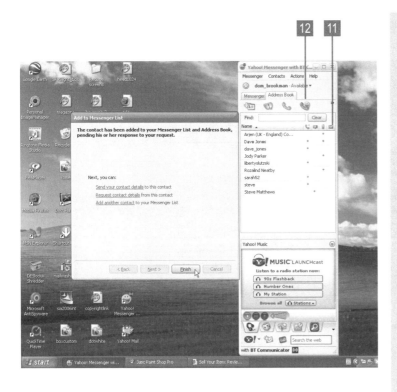

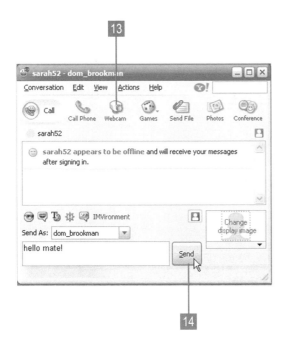

Get to grips with Yahoo! Messenger

11 You can now add one of your contacts to your Messenger List of buddies, by sending them an invitation. Choose a name from your Address Book, and when you're ready to send the invitation, simply click on the envelope.

12 Then simply click on the '!' button in the main Instant Messaging window...

13 ... to start chatting to one of your friends who you know is online as well. A new conversation window opens, with a series of icons at the top which let you cycle between options such as Games, Photos and Webcam usage.

14 Type your comment in the little window at the bottom, and then click Send. The conversation which hopefully follows will appear in the large window above, and you can look forward to having a quick-fire chat without some of the hassle and bother that even email can bring. Brilliant!

3

Communicating with others 93

Learning about chat room dangers

We've talked about the importance of observing the rules of Netiquette, and not giving away your personal details online. It would be false to say that there aren't people out there seeking to use chat rooms to prey on vulnerable individuals, so if you are a parent with a computer-literate or curious child, you need to combine a knowledge of the risks with a sensible attitude to trust and responsibility. There are plenty of websites out there which seek to educate and inform about potential chat dangers; www.chatdanger.com uses real life stories to drive home points, combining them with sensible answers to avoid getting into difficulties yourself. You should also find that any big firm responsible for internet chat, such as Lycos, has its own list of tips and dangers to avoid as well – see www.lycos.co.uk/content/flirtchat/safety2.html for their take on the situation. Ultimately, education is the key, and if you're wised up and sensible, online chat can be a perfectly enjoyable affair.

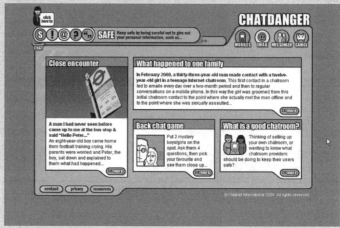

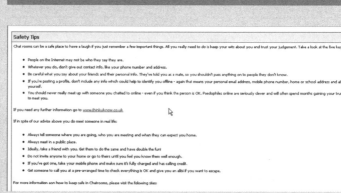

Jargon buster

Chat room – a special place on the web where you can go and talk to like-minded users about virtually every topic under the sun.

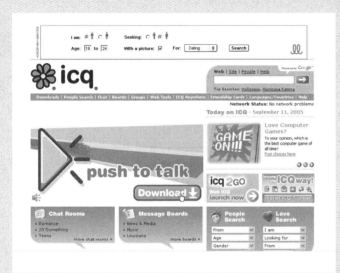

Instant Messaging is very popular, as we've seen, so unsurprisingly Yahoo! has a bit of competition when it comes to providing the software you need to chat. One of the biggest competitors is ICQ, at www.icq.com. As the software's home page says, you can do a lot more than just Instant Messaging people with ICQ – you can video/audio chat, send email, transfer files... and engage in PC-to-PC and PC-to-phone calls with ICQphone. The software is fun, friendly and very accessible. Computer giant AOL has its own Instant Messenger at www.aim.com, and you're also bound to have heard about MSN Messenger (http://messenger.msn.com). Microsoft seems to be growing ever more aware of the importance of Instant Messaging in people's everyday lives, so keep clicking back to the service to see what new features and functionality is on offer.

3

Signing up for Guardian Soulmates dating

Register with Guardian Soulmates

1 From the Guardian home page at www.guardian.co.uk, click on the Soulmates box which you should see in the menu bar running down the left-hand side. One of the first things you can do on the dating home page is a quick search to see what kind of matches exist out there for you. Choose your gender and what you're looking for as regards the sex, age range and location, then click Go.

2 You should see a list of compatible matches, which will hopefully convince you that the service is worth a go. You can take things in any order you like, but to get anywhere really you need to register, so press Back on your web browser to go back to the home page, and then click the line that says 'Complete our quick sign-up process' under Getting started.

Popular services such as DatingDirect, Match, uDate, Pocado and Guardian Soulmates are tapping into a massive market of people looking to be hooked up with like-minded souls and searching for love. These services normally work by asking you to register, type in a bewildering array of information about your likes and dislikes, say what kind of person you're looking for, supply a photo, and then let the computer search engine 'match' you up with people who fall into the criteria groups that you've suggested. Some of these services are free, but most are paid-for, typically at about £15 or £20 a month. Many people are willing to pay this kind of charge – after all, you can't put a price on love, and there is the chance that you could find your perfect partner online, and even someone who in real life lives just around the corner.

Go into internet dating with an open mind and you should be fine. The same dangers about revealing too much about yourself are also key here – don't hand out your personal details to strangers, and don't arrange to meet someone on a first date unless you're in a public place and your friends know where you are.
We're going to look at the Guardian Soulmates service, at http://www.guardiansoulmates.co.uk. It's the new online companion to the popular newspaper small ads that have been running for years, and offers a good chance of having a safe, fun and potentially successful online dating experience.

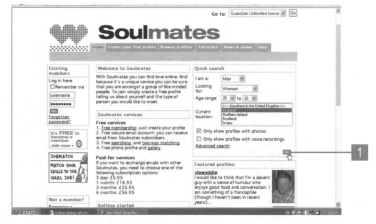

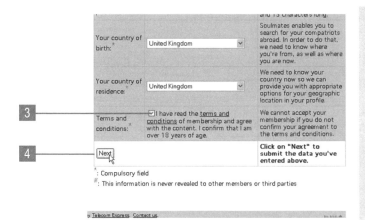

*: Compulsory field
#: This information is never revealed to other members or third parties

Register with Guardian Soulmates

3 It's now time to provide some information about yourself, including a username, email address and password. Make sure that you read and agree to the terms and conditions – click in the little box at the bottom of the screen.

4 Then click on Next to submit your data.

5 Now it's time for some personal characteristics. What languages can you speak? How often do you drink and smoke? What kind of relationship are you looking for? Do you have any children? Answer the questions as honestly as you can before progressing to the 'In your own words' section.

For your information

You'll see a guide to prices for the site when you click on the Subscribe button at the top of the screen, but keep your eye out for special bargains and deals online. 10% off deals are common on the site, so don't miss out.

Important

Be as honest as possible in your profile, for if you lie to try and make yourself sound good, you'll only get found out when someone meets up with you. Obviously you need to sell yourself, so a modicum of dramatic licence is OK, but don't let your imagination run away with you.

Signing up for Guardian Soulmates dating (cont.)

Register with Guardian Soulmates

6 More questions here – where would you like your matches to be based? How important is their location? What physical characteristics should they have, and how often should they visit the site? It's best to have these answers clear in your mind before you start registration, really, otherwise you'll waste time and end up confused.

7 You should get a message saying that your email address has been successfully confirmed.

Timesaver tip

If there's a profile you really like and want to return to, click on the Favourite link to add it to your list of Favourites.

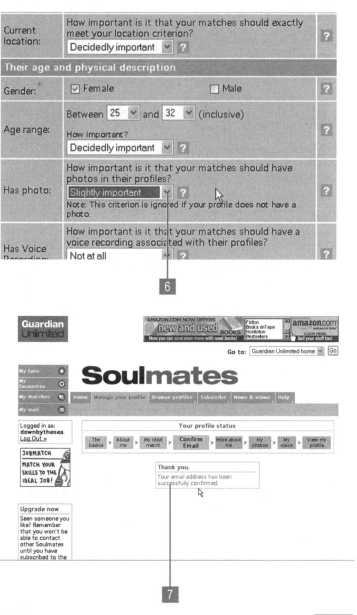

Timesaver tip

Profiles with photos get far, far more responses than those without – that's just the way it is on online dating. So get a decent photo of yourself, on your own and with your head and shoulders showing clearly, to give yourself as much chance as possible of success.

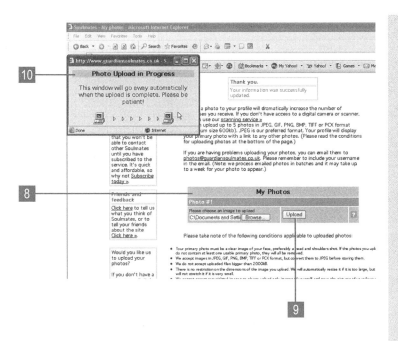

Timesaver tip

Don't try and do too much, too soon, and dive in feet first. Take the time to browse the site, and get to know people for a while if you get contacted. Be patient – you're highly unlikely to find everlasting love in your first week on the site!

Signing up for Guardian Soulmates dating (cont.)

Register with Guardian Soulmates

8 Time now to go to the My Photos section of the site.

9 Browse your hard drive for a suitable photo of yourself to upload, and then click Upload.

10 The progress of your upload will be shown in this box – be patient whilst the site processes it.

11 Click View my profile to see your profile in all its glory. Our photo could be tidied up a bit to get rid of all the background detail – it's only when you see photos fully uploaded that you can judge their effectiveness. Play around until you're totally happy – the more time you spend at this stage, the more likely you are to get some matches getting in contact. Note that you can't contact anyone until you've signed up for a subscription package, so that's your next step – to see the current rates, click on Subscribe today from the left-hand side.

3

Communicating with others 99

Alternatives to Guardian Soulmates

Dating sites are everywhere on the internet. As is the case with so many popular genres on the internet, some are more reliable and trustworthy than others – and some, to put it bluntly, just exist as crude pick-up joints for people on the look out for quick, no-strings sex. Dating Direct (www.datingdirect.com), Match (www.match.com), and uDate (www.udate.co.uk) are all very, very popular, which means that there'll be more potential matches on there. Pocado (www.pocado.com) is a free to register dating site, ManyFishInTheSea (www.manyfishinthesea.com) is a bit more risqué, and the offshoot of massively popular site Friends Reunited, Friends Reunited Dating (www.friendsreuniteddating.co.uk) has over 190,000 people looking for a date.

Basically, the choice is yours – be aware that the more you trawl, the more likely you are to see some risqué sites that are a bit 'out there', so be careful if you're easily offended. Generally, the more you're expected to pay, the better the service, although there are some decent free sites out there. Just have fun, don't expect too much all at once, and who knows, the internet could change the face of your love life for ever.

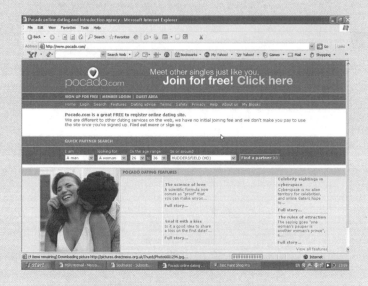

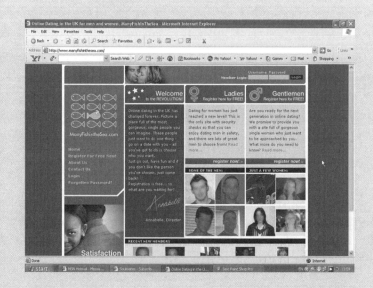

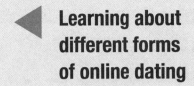

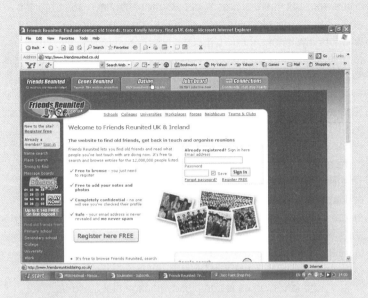

3

Don't forget that there are plenty of different kinds of dating sites out there, ready to cater for pretty much every taste and need. All age and lifestyle groups are catered for online, so if you've exhausted the conventional options, why not branch out a little? A good example of this is speed dating, which has become rapidly popular over the last few months. These work on the principle that if you're thrown in a room of between ten and thirty members of the opposite sex, and forced to talk to them for 5 minutes or so each, you're bound to come up with a match or two. After all, most people make up their mind about someone within the first few minutes of meeting them – sad but true. Obviously, speed dating online is a bit difficult to carry out, but speed dating sites do exist, primarily to act as a signing-up portal so people can then meet up in a pub or bar in real life. Try out www.speeddater.co.uk, www.speed-dating-guide.co.uk or www.slow-dating.com, and don't forget sites that take an interesting angle on the whole 'meeting up' thing, such as www.dinnerpoint.com, where you meet '4 to 8 interesting new people for dinner'.

Starting your own blog with Blogger.com

Register with Blogger

1. Here we are at www.blogger.com. Setting up a blog really is just a matter of minutes. If you'd still like to have a quick scoot around first, click on Take A Quick Tour.

2. Once you've done that, click on Create Your Blog Now to get cracking.

3. It's the first steps to creating your account. You'll need to create a username, password and display name, enter your email address and accept the terms and conditions. Don't be surprised if you get the message 'Sorry, this username is not available' – it can take a while to come up with a unique username, as there are so many people on Blogger.

4. Once you've got a unique username, click on Continue.

If you read the national press, you will probably have seen articles about the rise of 'bloggers' across the world, and been puzzled as to who this mysterious group of people are. Well, blogging is simply a term that refers to writing basically an online journal – and letting the world see your thoughts and reply to them.

Bloggers write about everything, from the trivial to the intense and serious, and the phenomenon basically taps into everyone's desire either to be 'famous' or at least to be heard, to get their voice out there and bring some meaning to the hurly-burly of everyday life. The first time your blog entry gets a response is a memorable occurrence – you get a real feeling of 'connecting' to someone, no matter how naff that sounds. You can share photos, music and all sorts of related multimedia in your blog, encourage friends to read it, or keep it secret and locked away – your own personal corner of the web. Although remember that the internet is a massive place, and what you fondly imagine is completely confidential could be being read by the person sitting opposite you!

Blogger.com is one of the major players in the blogging market, and was recently snapped up by – you guessed it – the ubiquitous Google. Let's see just how easy it is to start your own blog and write an entry.

Register with Blogger

5 Now the important bits – naming your blog and giving it the web address that people will need to type in to access it. Try and link up the blog name with the address, for convenience. Again, don't be surprised if something is already taken!

6 Click Continue again when you're happy.

7 You can now choose a preset template, for how your blog will look on the screen. There's a choice of four designs here. Click preview template to get a closer look.

3

Timesaver tip

You can decide for yourself whether you want people to reply to your blog or not, by clicking on the Yes or No button at the bottom of the blog window, underneath Allow New Comments on this Post. Feedback on your blog can be really exhilarating, although bear in mind people may exercise their right to free speech and give you less than flattering comments if they don't agree with something that you've said!

Timesaver tip

You can host your blog elsewhere other than Blogspot – if you wish to do so, click on Advanced Blog Setup from the screen that we're on here.

Starting your own blog with Blogger.com (cont.)

Register with Blogger

8 When you're happy with a particular template, click in the little circle next to its title. We click next to Minima.

9 Then carry on forwards by clicking Continue.

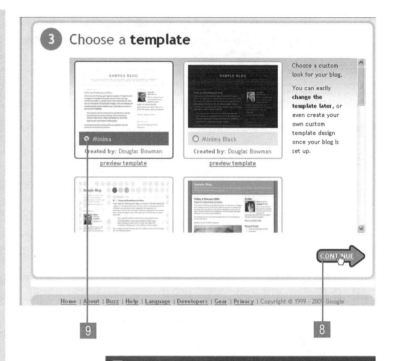

3 Choose a **template**

Choose a custom look for your blog.

You can easily **change the template later**, or even create your own custom template design once your blog is set up.

Minima
Created by: Douglas Bowman
preview template

Minima Black
Created by: Douglas Bowman
preview template

CONTINUE

Home | About | Buzz | Help | Language | Developers | Gear | Privacy | Copyright © 1999 - 2009 Google

9

8

Timesaver tip

Giving your blog some photos can really help liven things up – who wants to read page after page of text online, no matter how interesting it is? It might be wise to get the permission of the people whose photo you're putting up online, mind you, so they don't get a nasty shock next time they're surfing the web!

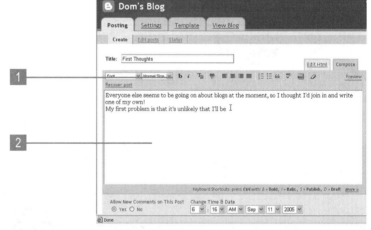

Timesaver tip

What's your blog going to be about? Is it going to be serious, and deal with weighty factual issues, or more personal, dealing with your own emotional thoughts and opinions? Ask yourself these questions well, well before you commit your blog to the screen, otherwise it will be all over the place and impress no one.

We've successfully registered, so let's now start writing in our blog, adding a photo and generally getting it in a decent state for the public at large to view it!

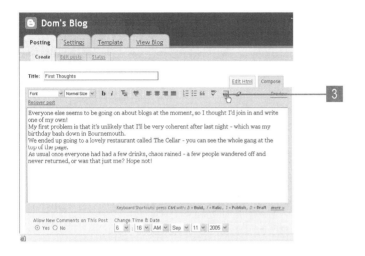

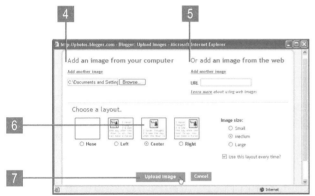

Starting your own blog with Blogger.com (cont.)

Edit your blog

1. You should get a message saying 'Your blog has been created!'. Click on Start Posting to be taken to this screen, which is the basic blogging interface. A lot of the icons, such as those along this top bar underneath the title of the blog entry, will be familiar to you from Microsoft Word.

2. Start writing your text in this main window.

3. Carry on writing as much as you need. In our description of a recent birthday, we've realised a photo would be really nice, so we click on the little icon of a photograph, in the top-right corner.

4. Search your hard drive for the image that you want.

5. You can also choose to add an image from the web, if you know its URL.

6. Choose a layout for your photo – i.e. how it's going to look in relation to your text. We choose Center.

7. Click Upload Image when you're happy.

Starting your own blog with Blogger.com (cont.)

Edit your blog

8 Our photo has been successfully placed inside the blog editing window! We can now carry on writing.

9 Carry on with as many different editing techniques as you like – remember, you can change the font, the size of the text, whether certain words are in bold or underlined... the works. Eventually, you'll finish your entry, and when you do, it's a good idea to preview it to see how it will look to your blog visitors. Click on Preview.

Timesaver tip

There's a Help button on any screen of the Blogger setup, so click it if you're experiencing difficulties. You can even speak to the dedicated support staff if you're having real problems.

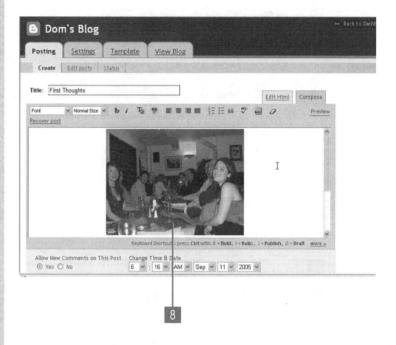

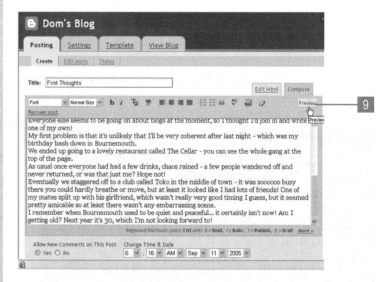

It's my party....

Everyone else seems to be going on about blogs at the moment, so I thought I'd join in and write one of my own!
My first problem is that it's unlikely that I'll be very coherent after last night - which was my birthday bash down in Bournemouth.
We ended up going to a lovely restaurant called The Cellar - you can see the whole gang at the top of the page.
As usual once everyone had had a few drinks, chaos rained - a few people wandered off and never returned, or was that just me? Hope not!

Starting your own blog with Blogger.com (cont.)

Edit your blog

10 Here's how it will look! Not bad, though we say it ourselves. Carry out any cosmetic changes if you like, then click on Publish Post when you're happy.

11 Brilliant – our first entry is live. You can now carry on with deciding whether you want people to comment on the blog, writing more entries, editing the links on the right-hand side, which take the visitor to your favourite websites and other blogs… the world is your oyster. Who knows, it may be you making the headlines soon!

3

Finding some alternatives to Blogger.com

It's fair to say that Blogger.com has a good hold on the market when it comes to blogging, but that's not to say there aren't other options – far from it. Indeed, in common with the fact that anyone can go online and start to blog, so does it seem that any company can set up its own blogging software – leading to a bewildering array of differently styled blogs out there.

Perhaps one of the biggest players in the blogging market is MSN's MSN Spaces (http://spaces.msn.com), a fun and friendly tool from the creators of MSN Messenger and Hotmail that lets you create a decent-looking blog and upload photos to it in a matter of minutes. Hundreds of thousands of people have signed up with MSN Spaces, and some of the blogs look pretty shocking, but there's still some interesting efforts out there if you're prepared to look. And your blog will be a cut above the average anyway, right?
Meanwhile, you could try Blogster (www.blogster.com), the 30-day free trial of TypePad (www.typepad.com) or Squarespace (www.squarespace.com), which describes itself as 'blogging evolved'.

The ultimate decision is down to personal choice, and how serious you are about blogging, or whether you just regard it as a hobby. Whatever the case, once you've joined the millions of fellow bloggers across the world, you'll begin to see just what a curiously addictive pastime it really is.

Staying safe online

Introduction

The proportion of good news to bad news in the national press about the internet does, in our view, seem somewhat out of kilter. Although you'll occasionally get an article about renting DVDs online, or finding love on the internet, the majority of press interest seems to be in the negative side of the internet. Consequently, barely a week goes by without some scare story about viruses taking over the internet and rendering millions of PCs unusable, spam (junk) email causing Inbox meltdown, shady spyware programs spying on your every move online, pop-up windows interrupting what should be a pleasurable afternoon online and causing you to tear your hair out in frustration.

The reality is, thankfully, somewhat different. First the bad news – viruses, spyware programs, time-wasting spam and annoying pop-up windows do exist online. You'd be a lucky internet user indeed if you never came across any of these problems in the course of a typical year online. However, the good news is that there exist countless comprehensive, reliable solutions to these problems, often in the form of software programs from major industry players such as Symantec (www.symantec.com) or McAfee (http://uk.mcafee.com). Sometimes you'll have to pay for these programs, other times you can nab free downloads – whatever the case is, it'll be worth the time and effort for a bit of peace of mind online.

So whilst it certainly pays to be prudent and careful when you're online, and start to adopt a couple of common 'best practices' as you surf, there's no need for the nastier side of the internet to ruin your fun and enjoyment. We're going to take a look at the best antivirus, spam-busting and pop-up crushing programs out there, giving you some ideas to be getting on with, and leaving you to concentrate on the countless useful and fun sites that make up the cheerier side of the internet. We'll also show you how to protect your privacy online, set parental controls to block kids access, and get a good overview of the security market in general.

Download and use an antivirus program

Protect yourself against spam

Banish pop-ups and spyware

Cover your tracks online

Set up parental controls

Explore the different security packages online

Downloading and using an antivirus program

Ask any computer user – especially one who owns a PC – what their biggest technological fear is, and it's a fair bet that being hit by a virus will come very high on their list. The online dictionary site NetLingo (www.netlingo.com) describes a virus as 'a computer program that replicates on computer systems by incorporating itself into shared programs'. Some viruses can be harmless, and just show an annoying message on screen; others can destroy files, or disable a computer or a network of computers in a matter of minutes. Viruses spread rapidly, and are often created by tech-heads with a grudge against a particular firm or corporation, or someone who just simply fancies their 15 minutes of fame, regardless of any pain or financial ruin they cause along the way. Once a virus has affected a computer and it crashes, it can worm its way into the heart of your PC and cause all sorts of damage. Scary stuff.

Apple Macs come off far better when it comes to viruses, but as far as PCs are concerned, you'll need to enter the world of antivirus software to begin to set up some effective protection for yourself. How you go about sourcing relevant software is up to you; you can either plight your troth with a big, reliable antivirus player such as McAfee (http://uk.mcafee.com), or pay a visit to popular download site Download.com (www.download.com) and see what's on offer. We're going to go with the latter option, and show you how to pick a piece of antivirus software, download it and set it to work.

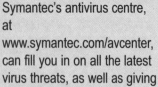

1

Go to Download.com

1. Download.com has recently had a good lick of paint, helping it cement its place as the place to go for downloading free software programs from the internet. Different categories include internet programs, audio and video, a spyware centre and desktop tools; for the moment, we click on Utilities.

2. Utilities splits into various sub-categories, including printers, firewalls, system utilities and, as luck would have it, antivirus programs. You can explore further by clicking on the sub-category. We decide to go for the popular AVG Anti-Virus Professional Edition.

3. You'll then be given more substantial information about the program and its publishers, including the editor's rating and an average user rating. It's pretty popular and well-reviewed, this product, so we decide to press on and click Download AVG Ant-Virus Free Edition.

Downloading and using an antivirus program (cont.)

Download the program

4 You may see this window, asking what you want to do with the download file. Simply click Run, as you can trust the source of this program and where it comes from.

5 Then it's just a case of waiting for the software to download. It really shouldn't take very long.

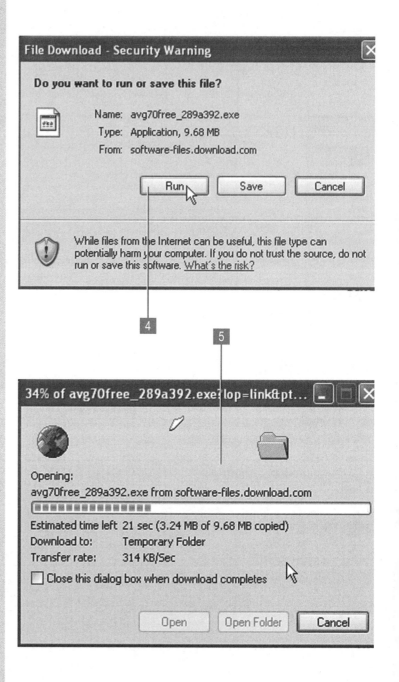

File Download - Security Warning

Do you want to run or save this file?

Name: avg70free_289a392.exe
Type: Application, 9.68 MB
From: software-files.download.com

Run   Save   Cancel

While files from the Internet can be useful, this file type can potentially harm your computer. If you do not trust the source, do not run or save this software. What's the risk?

4

5

34% of avg70free_289a392.exe?lop=link&pt...

Opening:
avg70free_289a392.exe from software-files.download.com

Estimated time left 21 sec (3.24 MB of 9.68 MB copied)
Download to: Temporary Folder
Transfer rate: 314 KB/Sec

☐ Close this dialog box when download completes

Open   Open Folder   Cancel

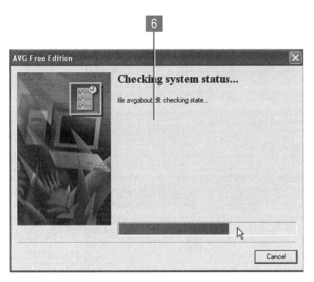

CONGRATULATIONS!

AVG Free has been successfully installed. A few simple steps remain to ensure your maximum protection. This First Run Wizard will guide you through the following recommended steps:

- Perform AVG Free update
- Create Rescue Disk
- Scan your computer for viruses

Clicking "Next" at any of the following steps will allow you to skip it. Of course, you can perform any step at later time.

Downloading and using an antivirus program (cont.)

Start the program

6 Once it's downloaded, the program will go through a brief initialising process. Again, this shouldn't take very long, so just let it do its stuff.

7 The program has successfully downloaded. As you'll see, you're recommended to go through the First Run Wizard, which will guide you through a couple of extra steps, and start the scan of your computer for viruses. Click Next to make your way through the steps and decide whether you want to skip any of them.

4

Jargon buster

Virus – a malicious computer program which spreads across computer systems, doing damage such as destroying files and crashing computers.

Important

Although the free version of AVG antivirus is a good start to your security life, you may want to consider upgrading to one of its paid-for options. The free version, for example, limits your technical support to just the FAQs page which we've mentioned at www.avguk.com/faq.html. Registered users of AVG Professional, however, can get full email support on any niggles or nasty problems that they may be experiencing.

Downloading and using an antivirus program (cont.)

Scan computer

8. You'll be asked whether you want to run the computer scan or not. The scan will check all the system areas and the hard drive of your PC, and if the worst-case scenario happens and a virus is found, AVG Free will either try and heal the infected file, or move it to a safe quarantined area where it can be dealt with later. We click Scan computer!

9. Here we see the program going through its scan. It may take some time, so you'll have to be patient – it's scanning every file, after all. We've had no viruses found so far.

10. If you do want to pause or halt proceedings for any reason, there are Pause and Stop buttons on the right-hand side.

Computer Scan

Would you like to scan your computer, now?

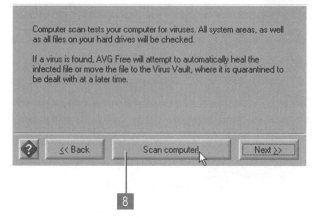

Computer scan tests your computer for viruses. All system areas, as well as all files on your hard drives will be checked.

If a virus is found, AVG Free will attempt to automatically heal the infected file or move the file to the Virus Vault, where it is quarantined to be dealt with at a later time.

| ? | << Back | Scan computer! | Next >> |

8

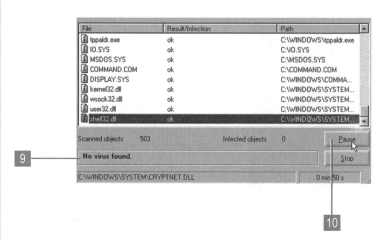

9

10

For your information

As we've said, there are plenty of antivirus programs out there to help your PC life, as a search on Google will prove. McAfee is one of the big players in the market, and its FreeScan product, available for downloading free from http://uk.mcafee.com, helps you detect thousands of viruses on your PC. After its scan, if viruses are found, you'll be given links as to how to clean your system and find out more about the viruses themselves.

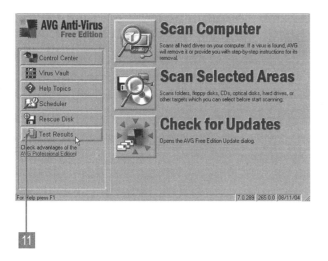

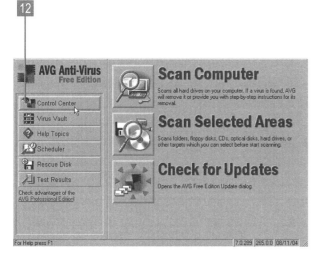

Explore the interface

11 This is the main interface of the program, with the features down the left-hand side; the Control Center, Virus Vault, Help topics and more. We've clicked on Test Results to find the results of the scan we've just performed, where luckily no viruses were found.

12 Next, we opt to take a look at the Control Center.

Timesaver tip

Remember that plenty of help sites exist on the internet to try and give you advice when you're in a fix. We'll discuss the Tech Support Guy forums at www.helponthenet.com in Chapter 10 of this book, but this is just one example where you can get free technical help on a PC problem. There's stacks of virus help and info online here, so you may want to give the site a go when the chips are down.

4

Downloading and using an antivirus program (cont.)

What's on offer?

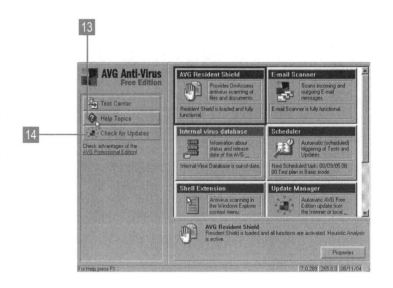

13 You'll see plenty of details about the various little utilities that can help you out, including the E-mail Scanner and the AVG Resident Shield. Note that the internal virus database is out of date; it's wise to keep everything updated as much as possible, so we click on Check for Updates on the left.

14 Remember that there are plenty of Help Topics for you to explore as well for further info – just click on the question mark icon to access them.

15 You'll be given update information, and a note reminding you that updating is essential if you want to ensure maximum antivirus protection. Choose where you want the update file to be located – we go for Folder.

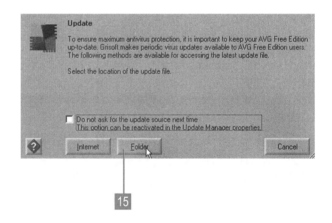

Jargon buster

Folder – useful devices for holding your PC files, documents and programs in some sort of order.

Important

These virus-tackling measures are not foolproof, but are an excellent start in the never-ending battle to ensure your computer is as safe as possible. Remember to update your virus protection software as often as possible, scan your PC frequently, and basically stay on your guard and be vigilant!

Timesaver tip

Another way of guarding against viruses is to use firewall software. There are plenty of firewall software options out there in the market; an excellent example is McAfee Personal Firewall Plus, which you can find at www.mcafeestore.com.

Important

When looking at security programs in general, ask yourself one question: do you want loads of different little programs, all of which might be effective in their own little field, or do you want one monster piece of software, which you might have to pay for, which does everything for you? Lots of programs have more than one capability; as shown here, MailWasher can stop viruses as well as deal with spam. Normally, we'd heartily recommend free trials, and indeed these are invaluable for getting to know a program, but in the long run, you may be better off buying an all-in-one product such as McAfee Internet Security Suite, available from all good online stores, such as www.amazon.co.uk.

Jargon buster

Firewall – is essentially a security barrier used by both organisations and individuals. It protects users from unauthorised access and hacks, monitors your internet connections and warns you if, for example, a spyware program is trying to watch you.

4

Protecting yourself against spam

The MailWasher approach

1 One of the best, most popular spam-busting programs out there is MailWasher, which has had over 5,000,000 downloads. You can try the program for free by downloading it from www.mailwasher.net.

2 The latest version of the program should be online for you to download and try out – note that the program also has antivirus capabilities as well. Click Download.

3 Choose your operating system and click Download Free Trial. Note that in your 30-day trial, you'll be sent three emails about using the program from the company (so don't think that they're spam, which would be rather ironic!), giving you handy hints and tips about ways to avoid spam and how to use filters.

4 The program will now, once you've clicked Install, work in conjunction with your email program in trying to block spam. The Friends List will allow any emails from designated email addresses to be automatically

It's probably easiest to think of spam as the electronic equivalent of the junk mail that you get through your letterbox. Spam is email sent to you without consent, often promoting a service which, unfortunately, is often sexual in nature. Viagra products, for example, seem to crop up in spam emails all the time, along with get-rich quick scams, pornographic links, 'miracle-cure' health solutions and chain letters.

The problem of spam is a huge one, and according to some doomsayers, could even spell the end of email and the internet as a viable form during the next decades. There's little doubt that it's intensely annoying to have to plough through rubbish in your Inbox before getting to the real, genuine messages; you may even miss a real email because you're so concerned with deleting the acres of nonsense. It's even more annoying if you actually answer a spam email and then either lose money due to an internet scam, or get put on even more mailing lists which bombard you with even greater amounts of garbage than you were receiving in the first place.

Thankfully, many ISPs, computer security firms and users themselves are battling back against the tide of spam, determined that it shouldn't spoil the enjoyment of all the positive things that the internet has to offer. Spam filters are becoming ever more advanced; these programs try and prevent spam mail from even reaching your Inbox in the first place, by setting various criteria for a genuine message, and deleting anything that doesn't match the criteria. Unfortunately, human correspondence isn't rigid enough for this to be by any means a foolproof method, but nevertheless there are plenty of different solutions out there, and we'll get a brief overview of them over the next few pages.

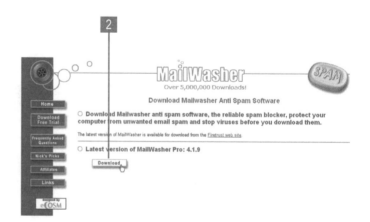

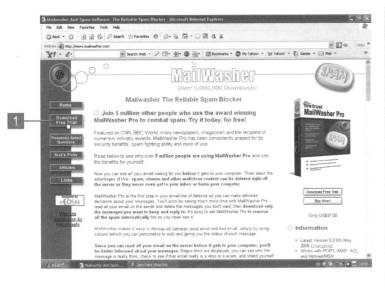

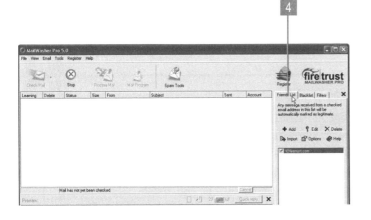

4 (cont.)

marked as legitimate; the blacklist will allow you to blacklist certain senders, and filters will let you set various criteria for what you want and don't want. Read the help emails from the firm carefully, and try experimenting with different levels of security until you're satisfied that you're blocking as much spam as necessary.

4

Important

You may get a spam email that asks you to click on a link to unsubscribe from the mailing list. Unfortunately this isn't someone being nice – the likelihood is that if you click on the link, it will just tell the spammers that your account is active, thus making them even more likely to bombard you with junk. Delete the email and don't be tempted into replying, no matter how annoyed you are.

Protecting yourself against spam (cont.)

Other programs

5 Symantec's NortonAntiSpam software is also an excellent product – here, at www.symantec.com/antispam, we're looking at the 2005 version of the software, which promises excellent automatic identification of spam, allowing you to block messages that you don't want, and still read the messages you do. As usual, there's a free trial on offer to help you out as well.

6 Try www.pcsecurityshield.com/weba pp/90024.asp for this anti-spam product that helps you clean Outlook and Outlook Express. The program promises to eliminate 99% of unwanted email – it's as well to take these claims with a pinch of salt until you've seen the program in action for yourself. Click Download Now if you're interested.

Timesaver tip

Top tips to avoid spam in the first place include: never posting your email address on forums or messageboards, setting up multiple email addresses (one email address, for example, could be used for all your correspondence with websites, while another could be kept secret, just for chums and family) and making effective use of email filters that should be contained within your email program.

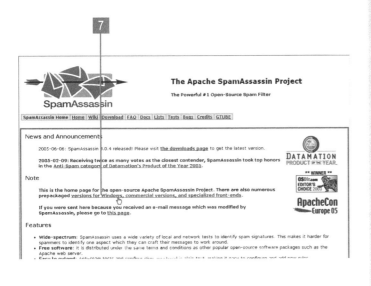

More resources

7 Spam Assassin, at http://spamassassin.apache.org, is an open-source spam filter – open source means that the code is available for modification by users and developers. Go to http://wiki.apache.org/spamassassin/StartUsing to get the full lowdown on the product. Note that there are also commercial, packaged versions of the product – click on the link for 'prepackaged versions for Windows' if you like.

8 Yahoo! has an anti-spam resource center, at http://antispam.yahoo.com/home, full of good ideas about dealing with spam, plus featured spam tools. You can even get a legal slant on the world of spam by clicking on Spam and the Law.

4

Jargon buster

Spam – unwanted junk e-mail which clutters up your Inbox.

Protecting yourself against spam (cont.)

Final thoughts

9 Anti-spam programs should be able to incorporate seamlessly into your program, with you barely knowing that they're there – here, for instance, we've downloaded SpamCatcher from www.download.com, its icon appears below the main toolbar that runs across the top of the Outlook Express interface, and you can set it to work quickly and effectively.

10 Finally, find out all about the Symantec Brightmail AntiSpam product at http://enterprisesecurity.symantec.com/products/products.cfm?ProductID=642%20. This piece of software is another effective weapon in the battle against spam. Click any of the tabs at the top of the screen to find out more about it.

Timesaver tip

A similar form of Net nasty is spyware, which are little pieces of software that gather information about you based on your surfing habits – often using that information for marketing or advertising purposes, and disturbing your internet experience. Some free downloads from the internet have spyware capabilities built into them, so it's as well to read the small print if you're worried. Anti-spyware products do exist, of course – you could try Microsoft Windows Anti-Spyware at www.microsoft.com/athome/security/spyware/software/default.mspx, SpySweeper at www.webroot.com/consumer/products, or Spyware Eliminator at www.aluriasoftware.com.

We'll be looking at more issues to deal with privacy, and covering your tracks online, in a short while.

Continuing our rather depressing tale of internet woe, we'll now look at pop-ups – which, simply, are online ads that 'pop up' in a new browser window, and can become rather annoying when you're just trying to have a peaceful browse through a particular website. Pop-ups basically interfere with what you're doing, which can't be good, and are similar to spyware programs, which spy on your activities online.

We'll take a look at a popular pop-up and spyware blocker over the next few pages.

1

2

Banishing pop-ups

Back to Download.com

1 Going back to Download.com is one option when you're on the hunt for pop-up blockers. This time, we click on the Internet section on the left-hand side, then Pop-Up Blockers.

2 Highly rated by the site is STOPzilla, which helps increase your surfing speed by blocking pop-up ads and protecting your PC from spyware. Click on the program name.

Timesaver tip

There's lots of anti-spam help and advice at
www.spamhelp.co.uk.

4

Jargon buster

Pop-up – a pop-up advert is a small window that appears on top of your current web page, often advertising an internet service.

Banishing pop-ups (cont.)

Download it

3 Read more about what the program does, then click on Download STOPzilla.

4 After a short time the program will download, and promise you the twin benefits of spyware protection and pop-up prevention. You can get STOPzilla to access real-time protection, where it checks your computer while you work, ensuring you remain protected at all times. If you want this, click in the circle next to YES.

5 Then click Next to work your way through the Setup Wizard.

Did you know

As if pop-ups weren't annoying enough, you may also get hit by pop-under ads, which appear surreptitiously in a new browser window behind your current window. No wonder pop-up blockers are becoming so popular...

Banishing pop-ups (cont.)

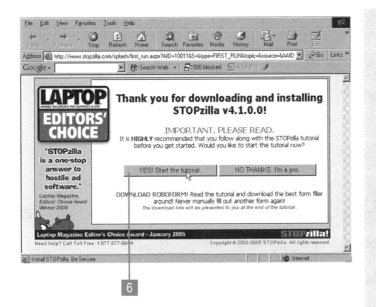

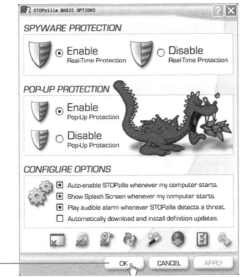

Let's use it

6 Beginners can opt to use the tutorial guide to help them get going – the program recommends this as a course of action, so click Yes! Start The Tutorial.

7 That done, you can access this basic options window, where you can set your preferences. As you can see, we've opted to enable real-time protection and pop-up protection, playing around with the Configure Options at the bottom as well. We then click OK.

4

For your information

STOPzilla's home page is at www.stopzilla.com. Here, you can find out more about the program, get technical help, access the FAQs and buy the full version of the product.

Timesaver tip

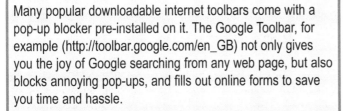

Many popular downloadable internet toolbars come with a pop-up blocker pre-installed on it. The Google Toolbar, for example (http://toolbar.google.com/en_GB) not only gives you the joy of Google searching from any web page, but also blocks annoying pop-ups, and fills out online forms to save you time and hassle.

Banishing pop-ups (cont.)

Play around

8 Try and get the program in synch with how you work and play on the internet; it needs to be your buddy, not something that will hack you off. The row of icons at the bottom of the program window is worth experimenting with, to set controls that the program will operate under as you surf the internet.

9 This window is telling you that the blacklist of banned sites is currently empty; this may change, of course, as your surfing time continues and you get used to what annoys you and what doesn't. Don't be afraid to experiment – click Close to close this window and move onwards and upwards to a hassle-free surfing life!

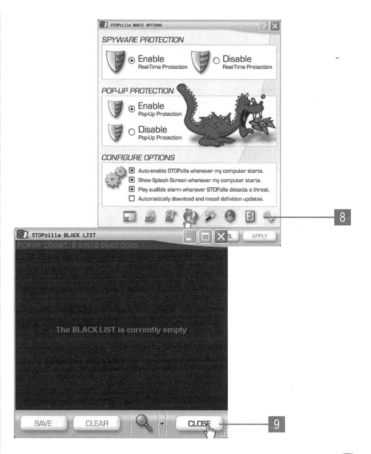

For your information

The requirements for the program, as listed on www.steganos.com, are:
Windows 98, Windows 98 SE, Windows Me, Windows 2000, Windows XP Home Edition or Windows XP Professional.

- Internet access

- 12 Mb of space on your hard drive for installation

- Screen resolution of at least 800 x 600 pixels

- High color (16-bit)

- At least 32 Mb of memory

- At least a Pentium or comparable processor

- A mouse or another Windows-compatible pointing device

It seems like your PC, then, is secretly recording and tracking every move you make across the internet. So just what can you do to protect your privacy online? With all this talk of spyware, spam and pop-up ads floating around, it seems like your privacy is being compromised like never before, which is a scary thought for anyone who really wants to get the most out of the internet.

Thankfully, there are ways to cover your tracks online, whether or not you have something to 'hide' (which, we would hope, none of you reading this book have!). A very, very simple technique is to clear your 'History' in Internet Explorer, of course, but this rather basic solution doesn't really strike at the heart of the problem. Over the next few pages, to conclude our chapter on internet security, we're going to look at a program which aims to let you effectively surf anonymously, removing all traces of your online presence.

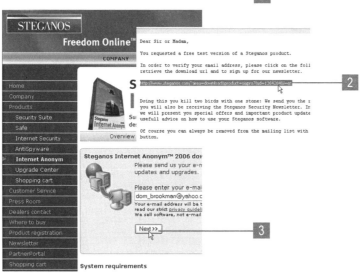

Covering your tracks online

Let Steganos help

1 At www.steganos.com, you'll see some top programs that promise you 'freedom online'. Steganos Safe 8 offers secure protection for your data, AntiVirus 7 is a top antivirus package, and Internet Anonym 2006 lets you surf anonymously (as the name suggests). It's this latter package which we're going to look at here; click on Test Now under Internet Anonym.

2 Enter your email address, read the system requirements and click Next. You'll then need to go to your email Inbox to verify the email address you've entered.

3 Hotmail's zealous spam filter has actually marked this email as junk, which is quite ironic, but never mind. There's a link in the email which you need to click so that you can retrieve the download URL.

4

Covering your tracks online (cont.)

Start download

4. That done, click Start download.

5. Now choose the setup type that best suits your needs – a complete installation or a custom installation. We go for Complete and click Next.

6. You're in day 1 of your test period. Click Next again.

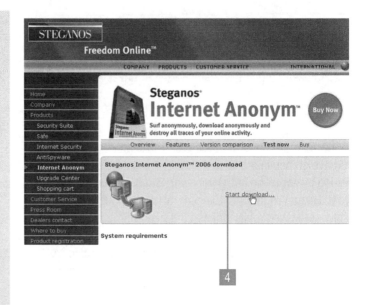

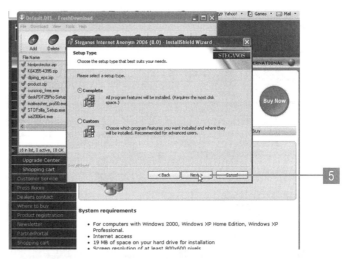

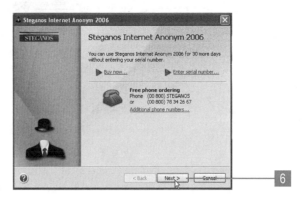

130

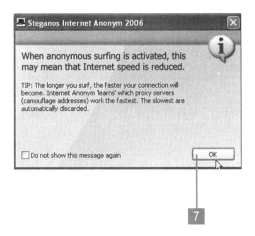

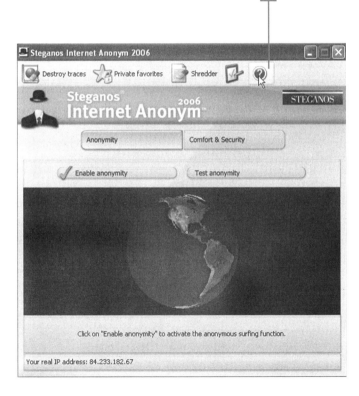

The program in action

7 There had to be a caveat; when anonymous surfing is activated, this may mean that internet speed is reduced. Be reassured, however, that the longer you surf, the faster your connection will become, thanks to the intelligence of the program. Click OK to move on.

8 At the moment, anonymous surfing is deactivated. There are a number of ways to turn it on – the program recommends you click on Enable anonymously to activate the function. If you need some help, click on the '?' to get some information about the program.

4

Timesaver tip

For more on online privacy and the different programs available, try our old friend www.download.com. The Internet section from the list on the left-hand side of the home page has a further sub-section entitled Online Privacy which should give you what you need.

Covering your tracks online (cont.)

The program in action

9 Click on Enable anonymity to put the program to work.

10 Click on Disable anonymity to go back to normal surfing.

For your information

Enter your email address under Security Newsletter on the home page to sign up for regular updates on all the very latest Steganos products and news.

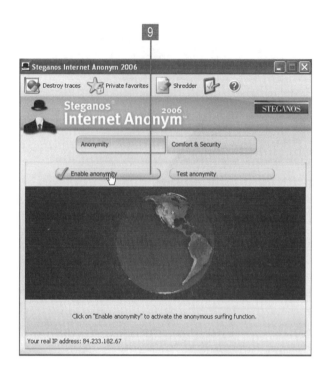

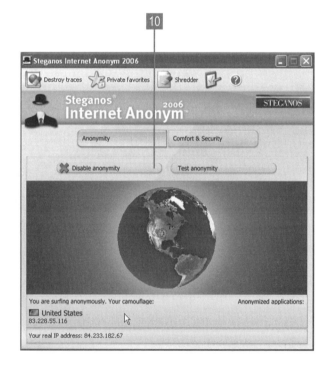

These days, monitoring your children's' access to the internet is more important than ever. It's not being censorious – it's being a responsible parent, concerned about your child's welfare. You can go over the top, of course – there needs to be a degree of trust involved, otherwise your children will just find sneakier ways of accessing prohibited sites. There's an interesting statistic on www.netnanny.com which says that 46%of surveyed youth between 9 and 19 say they have given out personal information on the internet – this is a worrying statistic. Netnanny is one of the best programs out there to keep your children

safe on the internet, helping you stop porn, limiting time online, stopping file sharing and protecting personal info. A free trial is on offer at www.netnanny.com.

Elsewhere, you can try Cybersitter (www.cybersitter.com) and CyberPatrol (www.cyberpatrol.com), both of which take this crucial area of internet safety very seriously. Ultimately, if you mix vigilance with trust, and have an open dialogue with your children about their use of the internet, everyone can be happy and free to enjoy the rich benefits of being online.

Exploring the different security packages online

As we've said, there are plenty of software packages out there for you to try when it comes to online security. Look out for free trials of programs, remember to check back to sites for updates, and stay vigilant. Symantec (www.symantec.com) is one of the leading providers of security products – check www.symantec.com/product/index_homecomp.html for a list of home software. And McAfee's range at www.mcafeestore.com is similarly impressive.

The battle against the nastier side of the internet is unlikely to ever be won completely, but it's nice to know that there's a good few companies out there willing to help you maintain confidence in the internet with simple, fast and often cheap solutions. Don't panic about the viruses and hackers out there – just maintain your own personal security conscientiously and you should be fine.

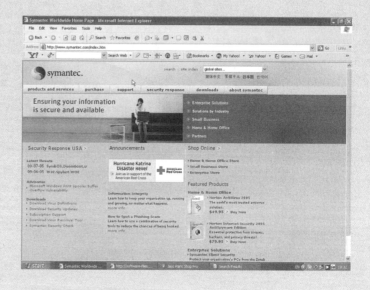

Your life online: work and business

5

Introduction

It may seem like a cliché to say it, but the internet has changed the face of our working and business lives for ever. Job hunting, for example, used to be a matter of trawling through dozens of newspapers, risking serious eye strain as you laboriously sift through thousands of ads, desperate to find something matching your own skills and requirements. You'd need to take a week off work just to get through all the newspapers, by which time you'd be knackered, disillusioned and in no mood to write a killer CV to help you get that all-important foot in the door.

Those days, thankfully, are over. The internet can now help you filter through the thousands of jobs that are out there, tailoring a search to only bring results back to you that are highly relevant – whether in terms of salary, position, level of experience or even geographical location. The ability to get such highly targeted results, so quickly, simply doesn't exist outside the parameters of your computer. And it's not just in the area of job-hunting where the internet excels, of course. In this chapter, we're also going to see how you can sort out your finances from the comfort of your own armchair. This is a mildly controversial issue, after some recent well-publicised security breaches, but one where a modicum of trust and common sense can save you countless hours spent waiting in deathly dull bank queues. People worry about their important finances being open to every Tom, Dick and Harry online, but this simply isn't true – no major bank would risk compromising their customers' faith in them by not having the most up-to-date and state-of-the-art security systems set up. And remember – no bank will send you a poorly worded, grammatically ghastly email asking you to input your account number or update your details – these are scam emails designed to empty your account at the click of a button. Just ignore them, delete them, and report them to your bank, who'll endeavour

What you'll do

Search for a job online with Guardian Jobs

Get jobs via email

Use Guardian Jobmatch

Find some alternatives to Guardian Jobs

Sign up with an internet banking service with Barclays

Find out what Barclays online has to offer

Find some alternatives to Barclays

Recognise and avoid email scams

Get the latest news online with the BBC

Find some alternatives to the BBC

Sign up for email news alerts with Google

Get free phone calls online with Skype

Find some alternatives to Skype

to trace the culprit – admittedly not an easy task in the sprawling environment of the world wide web.

We'll also see how the BBC has revolutionised the way we expect to receive our news – an ever-more important factor in today's uncertain and volatile world. Personalised news alerts are all the rage at the moment, as people realise they can get the news that they want, when they want, without having to be tied to the whims of a national broadcast or the next day's newspaper. Signing up for highly specific news updates is a doddle, as we'll see shortly. And in the spirit of saving money, which we hope pervades throughout this book, we'll take a look at how the internet firm Skype has totally changed the way we make phone calls – you can now make free calls online, which has the potential to save you an absolute fortune. By the end of this chapter, you'll start to get an indication of just how the internet can change your life for the better.

Timesaver tip

If you're still a bit unsure about how best to go about the potentially mammoth task of finding yourself a new job, click on the Help option in the top-right of the screen. You'll then be taken to a page offering you full and frank advice about how to use the browser tools, customising your search, and how to contact *The Guardian* itself.

Jargon buster

eCommerce – a general term for conducting business or transactions online. Commercial eCommerce products help you set up shop online, selling your wares and potentially making money, if you're selling something people want!

The Guardian probably first worked its way into the hearts of eager job-hunters through its famous Media Guardian pages on a Monday, where journalists up and down the country would trawl through the selection of top media jobs, hoping to find the perfect job. There's far more to the paper's job service than media positions, though, as can be seen by the fat supplements of jobs in all areas of industry that seem to accompany the newspaper virtually every day. As we've mentioned before, however, trawling through page after page of jobs, many of which might be totally unsuitable for you, is no fun whatsoever, which is why the paper's internet arm is such a godsend.

Guardian Jobs, at http://jobs.guardian.co.uk, has been through a couple of redesigns in its time, but now offers a comprehensive service that can be tailored to your specific needs and requirements. A powerful search engine, careers advice, free personality tests and the ability to receive the latest positions via your email Inbox are just some of the features on offer here, so let's get cracking and put the service through its paces.

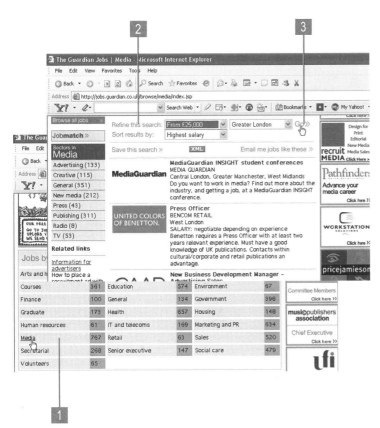

Searching for a job with Guardian Jobs

Basic searching

1. Open your web browser and type www.guardian.co.uk in the Address Bar, to access *The Guardian's* home page. Guardian Unlimited has separate sections for sport, arts, news, science, travel, money and much more – we're just concerned with jobs here, though, so click on Jobs from the menu bar along the top of the screen. We're going to do an example jobs search by category, so click on one of the categories that interests you – we go for Media.

2. Each result found will have a brief description of the job title and requirements, with the option to explore further on a specific position if you wish. You can also use the Refine this search option near the top of the screen to narrow down your results further, which is what we're doing here.

3. Use the pull-down menus to choose what salary bands you're requiring, and also the geographical location you would like. We go for Greater London, then click Go.

Searching for a job with Guardian Jobs (cont.)

Seek out job specifics

1 Having narrowed our search down to a significant degree, we get a list of results for jobs based in London, in the media, paying more than 25K. You'll see a brief description of the job and how much you'll be paid (if that information is available). Click on the heading of the job that interests you – our target is a listing near the bottom of the page.

2 Here's a lengthier description of the job in question, with more detailed requirements and the closing date to get your application in. If you read this far and still want to continue, click on Click here to find out more. You'll then get the chance to send an email to the company, obviously with your completed application and CV.

So you're searching for jobs, but have realised that it's going to be a long process – you don't, after all, just want to take the first thing that offers itself. To tie in the job-hunting process with your busy, everyday life, why not opt to get the very latest positions delivered straight to your Inbox? It's fast, convenient and will save you loads of time and hassle. It might be best to choose a different email address than your work one – your employers might not look too kindly on you reading job emails during office hours! The Guardian has two ways of helping you get jobs via email – we'll look at the second option, JobMatch, in a boxout later on. First off, here's how to sign up for the standard email service.

Getting jobs via email

General alert

1. We're going to set up a quick and general job alert. First of all, carry out a search for jobs by entering your search term in the Search dialog box at the top of the screen.

2. Type In your search term and then click Go.

3. We get 231 vacancies for Editor jobs. To be emailed similar jobs by The Guardian, click on Email me jobs like these.

Timesaver tip

Click on Interviews at the bottom of the Guardian Jobs home page to get vital advice on that all-important part of the recruitment process – the interview. Get this stage right and you'll be almost there, ready to accept an offer for the job of your dreams!

5

Getting jobs via email (cont.)

Final details

4 Now it's just a question of giving Guardian Unlimited your details. If you've signed up for any other services offered by the company, you won't need to enter all your details again – your details will still be on file and you'll just need to make a quick confirmation. If you haven't done anything with the firm before, you'll have to click 'click here to register for the first time' to go through the registration process.

Timesaver tip

If you're getting nowhere fast with job applications, and all the morning post seems to bring is another stream of rejections, your CV may be causing you more damage than good. An eye-catching, mistake-free and truthful CV is vital if you want to give yourself the very best chance of job success, so to see where you may be going wrong, click on CV Surgery from the Guardian Jobs home page. You'll be taken to a very useful mini-site which deals with all the key CV issues, including references, interests and hobbies, and that thorny issue of CV lies.

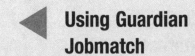
You've seen how you can set up a general, wide-ranging email service from Guardian Jobs. It really does only take a matter of seconds, yet will save you precious hours in the long run, leaving you to concentrate on the things that matter – applying for the actual job itself! There's also a more specific service that we recommend you take advantage of, called Jobmatch. Click on Jobmatch on the home page to be taken to a sub-site which explains clearly what the aims of the service are. Basically, you simply click on an employment sector – such as sales, broadcast, IT, human resources or press and publishing – to be taken to an area specifically dedicated to that employment area. You'll then be asked to fill in a detailed questionnaire, tailored to the job in question – it should take less than 10 minutes to complete, thankfully. The criteria that you set will then help Guardian Jobs send you emails with job vacancies that mirror very closely your demands and requirements, as outlined in the questionnaire. Prospective employers will only see your profile if you decide to apply for the specific job.

So there we have it – a couple of tremendously important email services, to add the icing to an already impressive cake. Give Guardian Jobs a whirl, and it could literally change your life!

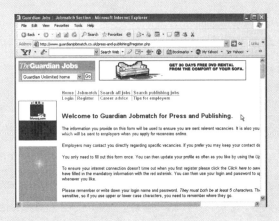

5

Finding some alternatives to Guardian Jobs

Of course, Guardian Jobs is not the only place where you can go online to try and change your employment life. There are too many jobs sites to mention in such a short space here, but one site certainly worth a click is Monster.co.uk (www.monster.co.uk). You may have seen this site advertised on TV, and the wealth of opportunities available here shows that the site has the setup to back up the spend on advertising. The network of Monster jobs stretches throughout Europe and beyond, and touches, like the employer of the week feature, and the chance to get career advice show that the site is serious about finding you work.

Elsewhere, try Yahoo! Careers (http://uk.careers.yahoo.com), Top Jobs UK (http://www.topjobs.co.uk) or the online jobs section of The Daily Telegraph (www.jobs.telegraph.co.uk). Employment is such a huge area that you may even get some limited success by just typing in Jobs into www.google.co.uk, or a more specific search term if you have a particular field in mind.

One final point – there's also stacks of advice online about areas such as job interviews or creating the perfect CV. Although frowned on by some employers, CV templates abound online to try and help you design the perfect résumé – although expect to shell out a fair amount for these in some cases. Try a search at www.download.com if you really want some free CV templates to give you inspiration as you set out on the quest of finding a new job. Good luck!

Important

Ignore all emails claiming to be from Barclays that ask you to follow links to confirm your banking details. These are fake – no matter how closely they are mocked up to look official and important. Key things to often look out for are spelling mistakes in the email – an indication that the mail is fraudulent and has probably been sent with malicious intent from people abroad whose English is not up to scratch.

Jargon buster

Phishing – an internet scam where fake emails are sent to you, often purporting to be from eBay, PayPal, Barclays, etc. trying to con you into revealing your financial information or passwords.

Even the phrase 'online banking' is enough to get thousands of otherwise perfectly sane internet users in a panic, as they conjure up visions of hundreds of pounds disappearing at the click of a button, leaving you bankrupt and with no recourse in the law. The reality, of course, is somewhat different – thankfully so. The Barclays site, which we'll be looking at (www.barclays.co.uk), hosts its online banking on a secure 128-bit encrypted server. Encryption basically means that any information you send over the internet gets coded into meaningless gobbledygook, which will make no sense to anyone with malicious aims.

If you leave your PC and forget to log out of Barclays, the service times out after 10 minutes, giving you further peace of mind. And if you repeatedly log in incorrectly into the site, your online banking access will also be disabled.

Anyway, that's enough of the serious side dealt with. With all this talk of fraud and security procedures, it's easy to forget that online banking is actually fast, powerful and incredibly convenient, allowing you to pay bills at the click of a button, check balances and carry out a number of financial housekeeping tasks that would take an age if you were trying to get them through on the high street. We're going to take a quick scoot around the Barclays site to give you an idea of how a typical online banking operation works.

Signing up with an internet banking service with Barclays

Register with Barclays

1. Go to the Barclays home page at www.barclays.co.uk. There are a number of products and services available here, including loans, mortgages, savings and investments and current accounts. Take a look around to familiarise yourself with the layout.

2. Once you've done that, click on Personal Banking.

3. This screen gives you a list of the products and services, help facilities and useful tools. Click on Online Banking.

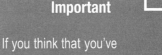

Important

If you think that you've received a fraudulent email that looks like it's from Barclays, forward it to internetsecurity@barclays.co.uk and then delete it from your email account immediately.

5

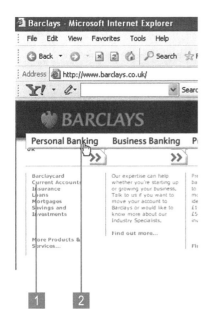

Signing up with an internet banking service with Barclays (cont.)

Fill in the forms

4 The next screen will tell you what you need to sign up for Barclays online banking – a current account and an email address and Connect card. If you're ready to go click on Register now for Online Banking to be taken to this, the first of four registration screens. This first screen takes the form of a series of yes and no questions and answers. Work your way through them, then click on the green next button.

5 Now to enter those all-important details, including your sort code and account number. All information is encrypted for your safety. Carry on clicking next through the final couple of steps, where you'll learn if you've been accepted into the exciting world of online banking.

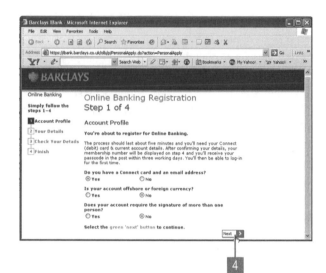

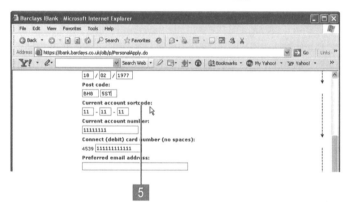

Important

To verify the authenticity of the website that you're on, for example the Barclays site, you can check its security certificate. Do this by double-clicking on the padlock symbol in your browser window.

Important

Do not write down or reveal your Barclays username and password to anyone.

144

Unsurprisingly, we've been concentrating on the security aspects of the Barclays site, to convince you of the inherent safeness in using the site. If you want to find out the kind of thing that you can get up to once your registration has been accepted online, you might want to try and take 5 minutes out to watch the online demo, which goes through everything at a stately pace and makes sure you're up-to-speed with everything. Let's take a look…

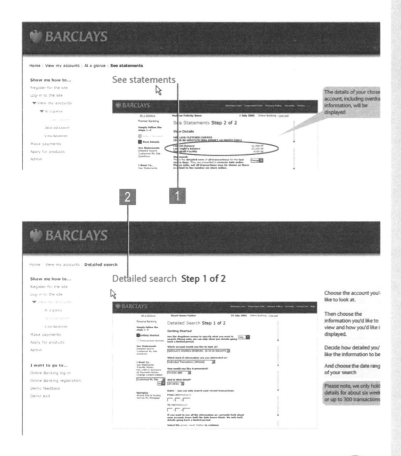

Finding out what Barclays online has to offer

Follow the demo

1 At http://www.personal.barclays.co.uk/BRC1/jsp/brccontrol?site=pfs &task=channelFWgroup&value= 7278&target=_self, click on Online demo to be taken on a tour of the site. One of the most important things you can do online is see a detailed breakdown of your statement, as shown here. All your transactions from the last 60 days can be shown, and you can check your overdraft facilities and any other accounts with Barclays that you might have.

2 You can carry out a detailed search of an account, which is useful, for example, if you're after the details of one specific transaction. Parameters such as the type of information displayed and the date range can all be set from here. Carry on through the demo to see the range of tasks you can carry out, such as paying bills to a company or a single person.

For your information

From the Barclays home page, click on More sites on the right-hand side to see the family of Barclays sites across the globe. Stretching from Africa to Zimbabwe, and incorporating a number of side projects such as the Barclays Premiership, this page of web links leaves you in no doubt as to the strength and breadth of this global financial giant.

5

Finding out what Barclays online has to offer (cont.)

Open an E-Savings Account

3 We've just got space to tell you about one more feature of the Barclays site – the E-Savings Account. This account, which costs just £1 to open, gives you instant access to your money online, day or night, instant online transfers and tiered interest rates. To open the account, or just find out more information about it, click on Personal Banking from the home page, then Open an E-Savings Account, then Log-in to apply.

Finding some alternatives to Barclays

It's no surprise, considering how fierce the competition on the high street is, that the major banks all have a strong online presence. Try Natwest (www.natwest.com), Halifax (www.halifax.co.uk), HSBC (www.hsbc.co.uk), Lloyds TSB (www.lloydstsb.com) or Alliance & Leicester (www.alliance-leicester.co.uk).

There are also online-only banks that you may wish to try, including Egg's at www.egg.co.uk and Smile's at www.smile.co.uk . And a useful site if you're still unsure about online banking security issues is www.banksafeonline.org.uk.

Recognising and avoiding email scams

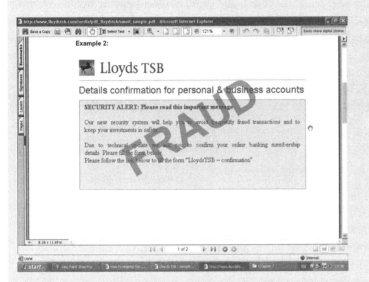

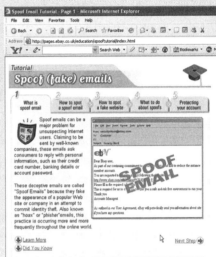

Sooner or later in your time on the internet, you're going to be sent spam masquerading as a real email, asking you to change your bank details immediately due to 'essential site maintenance' or some such excuse. These screenshots show an example of a Lloyds Bank scam and an eBay scam, and you can see further examples on the Barclays site at www.personal.barclays.co.uk/BRC1/jsp/brccontrol?task=articlegroup&value=6454&target=_self&site=pfs.

These lame attempts at conning you out of your cash should be sent straight into the Trash – your bank will never contact you like this. As Barclays says on its site, it will never send you emails asking you for your security or other personal information.

We'll repeat the key fact that if you actually briefly read the vast majority of these emails, you'll see stacks of laughable spelling mistakes, odd English and grammatical errors, which should be enough to get you suspicious and on your guard in the first place. Spotting these bloopers is an even faster way of knowing that what you're being sent isn't for real.

If the worst comes to the worst, your bank should cover you for any financial losses from falling victim to one of these scams, but it's far, far better to take the shortcut, and stay vigilant yourself, rather than have to go the long-winded way of filing a claim and potentially waiting weeks for your missing funds to return.

5

Getting the latest news online with the BBC

Access the headlines

1 There are two ways of quickly getting to the BBC News home page. You can either go direct to news.bbc.co.uk, or do our method here – go to the main BBC launch page at www.bbc.co.uk, and then click on News.

2 Here's the layout of the main news stories – whatever the day is, you'll see an arrangement like this, with the main stories at the top.

3 Under Around the World Now you can see the stories from across the world, showing the depth of the BBC's coverage.

4 Down the left-hand side of the screen are the different sub-categories of BBC News. Click on one that interests you; we click on Business.

It's no exaggeration to say that this whole book could be filled on the BBC website alone. Pop along to www.bbc.co.uk and you'll instantly get a feel of the staggering comprehensiveness of the site, even after management cutbacks – business, entertainment, health, history, learning, lifestyle, music, news, science and nature, society and culture and sport all jostle together on a site that, no matter how much information it is asked to contain, never suffers from being garish or over-crowded.

Budding web designers the world over could take a leaf out of the BBC's book when it comes to providing customers with what they want – which, in the case of the Beeb, is authoritative factual news and opinion, along with the very best local information and key resources such as weather and travel updates.

We're going to be zooming in on the news service over the next few pages, finding out how you can get the very latest headlines on your desktop, in as little or as much detail as you need. We'll also look at some alternatives to the BBC, and draw your attention to the crowning glory of online news – being able to sign up for desktop news alerts, customising how and when you receive the very latest updates. We'll start off with a leisurely stroll through how the BBC online news operation works.

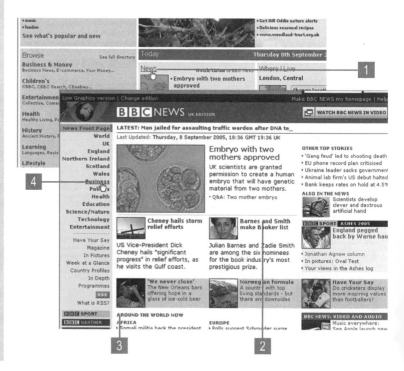

Access extra features

5 Once you've toured all the news headlines that you need, why not branch out a bit? The BBC's Weather Centre is invaluable if you have a pressing need to find out the latest meteorological conditions where you are, or access a long-term forecast. Click on BBC Weather on the bar on the left-hand side of the screen, to be taken to all the weather information you could possibly need. In the dialog box for UK and World Forecast, we enter our home town of Bournemouth, and then click Go.

6 Sports fans are also well catered for online, with not only the latest news and features, but live reports on major events such as the Ashes or The Open. Look out for the yellow bar of BBC Sport, seen here on the right-hand side of the screen, where we're clicking on 'Owen defends Eriksson'.

Timesaver tip

Feeling a bit lost? Then simply click on A-Z Index to get a full alphabetical rundown of what you can expect to find on the Beeb's site.

Timesaver tip

We'll look at Google News Alerts later, but you can also get BBC News Alerts too. From the news home page at news.bbc.co.uk/, simply click on News Alerts on the bar at the bottom of the page, then Download, to start getting the latest breaking news headlines direct to your PC.

Getting the latest news online with the BBC (cont.)

Access extra features

7 Live interviews are now there for us to enjoy; courtesy of the BBC.

8 Note the links at the bottom. Just click on an underlined link to be whisked off to another online destination.

9 The BBC also has a wealth of video news that you can watch from the comfort of your PC – it will obviously help to have broadband for features such as this. Click on Watch BBC News in Video in the top-right of the screen, then choose your preferred media player. The BBC News Player will then open and play you the news of your choice – there's a selection of clips on the right of the player. Choose what size player you want with the three links under the video screen – we go for Double.

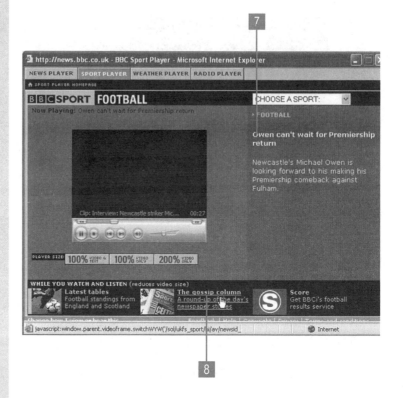

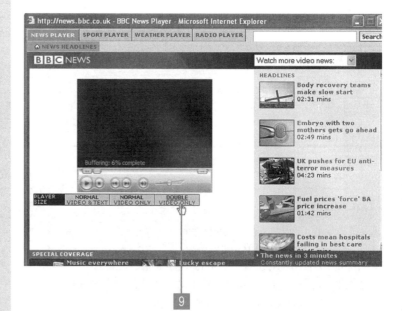

Search the site

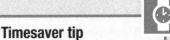

10 Handily enough, the BBC also has a powerful search facility to allow you to access the specific news items that you want. Simply go to the Search dialog box in the top right-hand corner, enter your search term and click Search to carry out your hunt.

Timesaver tip

If you're in a bit of a rush and just want the basic, no-frills version of the site, click on Low-graphics version in the top-left corner of the home page, to access a predominantly text-based version of proceedings.

5

Finding some alternatives to the BBC

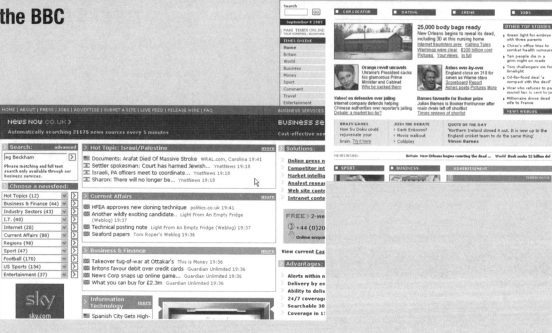

It comes as no surprise to learn that there is a wide selection of other sites online for you to get your news. Obviously it pays to stick with a trusted brand such as The Times (www.thetimes.co.uk), but there are nevertheless a few outsiders who manage to bring their own slant to the online news arena. NewsNow, for example (www.newsnow.co.uk) acts as a kind of news search engine – filtering out the news from over 20,000 different sources every 5 minutes, and grouping them intro topics such as internet, sport and entertainment. Click on the story you want to know more about to be taken to the website where the story originated – very clever. The fact that the site is updated so frequently, after a trawl through so many sites, is an advantage – although you may find an American or business bias grating at times.

We'll also look at Google News alerts, but Google News UK (news.google.co.uk) brings the weight of its mighty search operation to the online news field to great effect, with news again divided into different categories for ease of reference and reading.

As we've said, the traditional print-based papers all have strong online presences, although a few are only just waking up to the possibilities of the internet. Some national papers in the UK are worried – if you can read their news online for free, will you still want to buy the paper version? *The Sun* (www.thesun.co.uk) has tried to combat this problem by giving you snippets of stories online and then telling you to go to the paper to get the full tale, but this is unsatisfactory. We much prefer the approach of *The Guardian* (www.guardian.co.uk), whose site gets hundreds of thousands of hits every day across the world. Its comprehensive news coverage, intelligent debate and often irreverent sporting coverage make it an absolute winner in our books. It's won many awards in its time and shaped what punters demand from their online news.

Signing up for email news alerts with Google

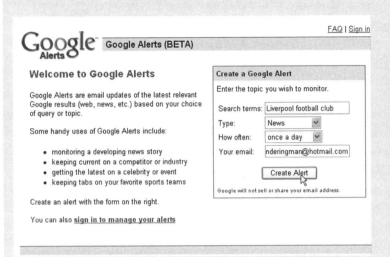

Email news alerts allow you to get updates of certain stories or topics in your Inbox, and are a natural progression of the treatment of news online. Email news digests such as the one offered by Channel 4 News (www.channel4.com/news) have become increasingly popular, letting you get a quick burst of the headlines in an idle minute at work. News alerts take that one step further, and give you an alert every time a topic specified by you crops up in the national news. On the Google News UK home page at news.google.co.uk, click on News Alerts on the left, and then simply enter the topic you wish to monitor, and your email address. Try and be as specific as possible, as if you just type in 'Liverpool' when you mean 'Liverpool football club', you'll be inundated with emails. You can choose the frequency of the email alerts to suit your needs, but it's probably best to use a webmail address anyway, just in case Google starts sending you dozens of emails based on your subject.

5

Getting free phone calls online with Skype

▶

Register with Skype

1 Go to www.skype.com and click on learn about more if you want to familiarise yourself with everything that's going on. When you've done that, click on Download Skype to begin.

2 You'll see some download details on the next couple of screens, letting you know about what the system requirements are for you to be able to run the program successfully. Click on the Download Skype for Windows link at the top of the screen.

For your information

If you want to know the rates for SkypeOut calls, pop along to www.skype.com/products/skyp eout/rates. There, you'll find information about the SkypeOut Global Rate – and, we think, be pretty amazed at its low cost.

Skype (www.skype.com) proclaims its major benefit loudly from its home page. 'The whole world can talk for free', it shouts, continuing: 'With Skype you can talk to anyone, anywhere for free. Forever'. There's little doubt that the prospect of saving tens or hundreds of pounds on your regular phone bill is amazingly enticing. So what exactly is Skype, and how does it work? Well, Skype is a 'Voice Over Internet Protocol' product, which sounds hideously technical and doesn't do the simplicity of the system any favours. You may also hear the technology described as internet telephony. We won't go into the technical details too much, but basically VOIP products use peer-to-peer technology to allow users to contact each other via their PCs, using a simple piece of software. Skype is just one of these little programs that allows you, once downloaded, to make phone calls from your PC – at an incredibly low cost.

Once Skype has downloaded, you choose a username and password, plug in your headset, speakers or USB phone (these vital accessories are available from the Skype shop for you to pick and choose from) and then start calling your fellow Skype friends for free, with excellent sound quality and high security. What's more, there's a subsidiary program called SkypeOut, which allows you to make calls to any telephone number in the world – at local rates. It's not hard to see that you could start to make some serious savings here. You'll need to download Skype to use SkypeOut, and purchase credit, but that's just about all you need to be bothering about. This kind of technology is set to be a massive hit online over the next few years, which is why we're drawing your attention to it in this book. Follow us as we get to grips with the service.

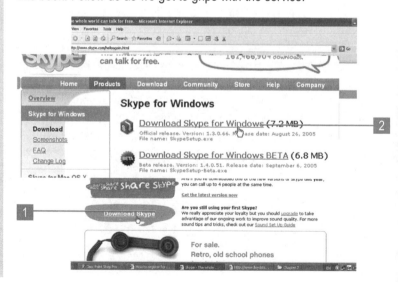

Register with Skype

3 Once you've been through the SkypeSetup Wizard, which should only be a matter of a couple of mouse clicks, you'll need to register a new account. Type in a username, bearing in mind that it must be a minimum of 6 characters, must start with a letter and must not include spaces. If you choose a relatively common name, like we've done here, don't be surprised if, after you've completed the screen, Skype comes back to tell you that the name is already taken, and you must pick again.

4 Carry on filling the boxes until they're all done, then click on Next.

5 Filling in the next set of fields is optional, but will help your friends and family find you on Skype. Enter some geographic and email information, and click Next again when you're done.

5

Getting free phone calls online with Skype (cont.)

Use Skype

1 The main Skype interface is now up and running, and you can see the kind of thing you can do, including adding a contact...

2 ... searching for Skype users...

3 ...and importing your contacts.

4 For the moment, let's search for Skype users who we might know – click on Search for Skype users.

5 Obviously, it's a plus if you already have people you know signed up to Skype – maybe a group of you could sign up at the same time. Type in your Search name term, which may be a mate or a family member, to search for Skype users. To get more info on users, click on the little 'i' icon at the bottom of the dialog box.

Now let's look at the program itself, how to search for users and how to make those all-important phone calls. Don't forget to check out SkypeOut as well for very cheap calls to landlines.

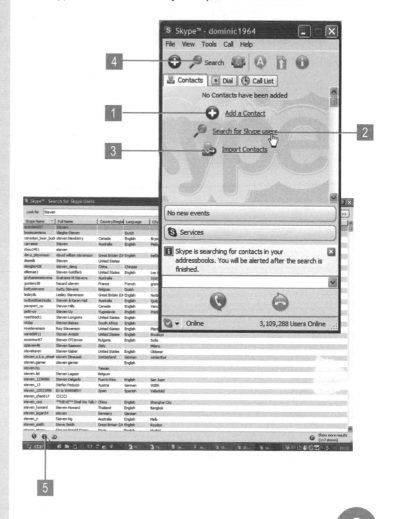

For your information

You may find occasionally that talking on Skype isn't possible – perhaps the person you want to communicate with is offline or busy. When this is the case, you'll be grateful for Skype Voicemail, which at a small cost lets you record messages and send them to mates without disturbing them. You can purchase Skype voicemail from the online store, which you can find at www.skype.com/store.

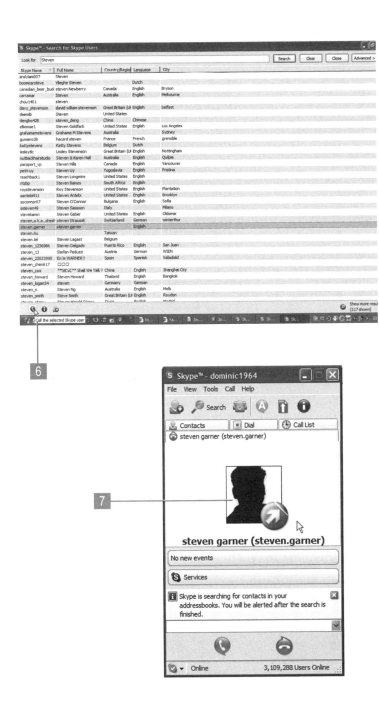

Getting free phone calls online with Skype (cont.)

Use Skype

6 With this full list of selected Skype users, you can highlight a selected user and decide to call them by clicking on the little green phone icon in the bottom-left. We do just that.

7 And we're now calling him, after making sure that we're set up with the correct equipment to carry out the call. Check the help pages and the online store of the site to make sure you have everything you need to carry out a call successfully.

For your information

Unlike some of its rivals in the same field, Skype works on many different Operating Systems, which is a boon if you have friends with Macs. Mac OSX, Linux and PDAs using Pocket PC are all supported, with a 'native look and feel for each platform'.

5

Getting free phone calls online with Skype (cont.)

Use Skype

8 Another way of going about things is just going straight for the Dial option from the main interface, obviously presuming you have the details of the person you want to contact to hand. Click on the Dial icon.

9 Proceedings from then on just work like a normal phone call, expect you're using your mouse to click on the different numbers, which appear in the bottom window. Click the phone icon when you're finished.

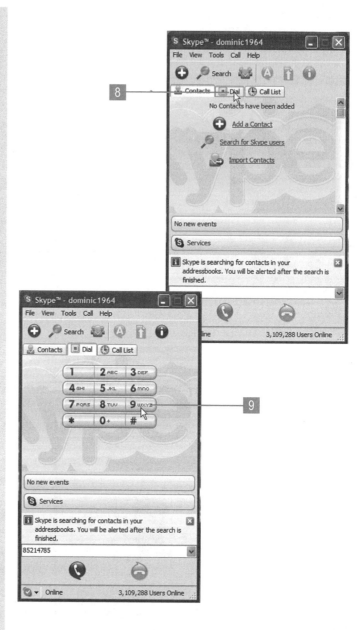

For your information

You can also use Skype to make conference calls, with up to four people speaking to each other at the same time, proving that Skype could become an invaluable tool for business use.

Important

Remember that Skype is not a replacement service for your telephone, and therefore it cannot be used for emergency dialing.

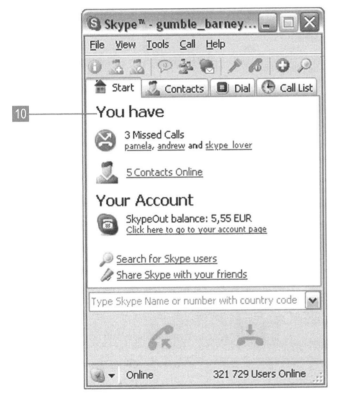

Use Skype

10 Just to round things off, here's a screenshot of a busy Skype interface, taken from the site's examples that are dotted liberally around. Note status details such as your missed calls (3) and number of contacts that you have who are online at the moment (5). Your balance, which comes into play when you have SkypeOut, is also shown, as is the total number of users online.

Finding some alternatives to Skype

So what can you do if you want to enter the brave new world of VOIP, but want to try a different service than that which Skype offers? Well, there are a couple of options. Callserve (www.callserve.com) is a UK-based service that promises savings of up to 90% on your phone calls – again, it's just a matter of downloading the free internet telephone software, registering your details, purchasing call time and then making your call. After the software has booted up you dial as you would do from a conventional phone, from the replica of a mobile phone that appears on screen. Simply click on the numbers and off you go. Yahoo! Messenger, at http://uk.messenger.yahoo.com, now features BT Communicator, which allows you to make voice calls to most landline numbers and mobiles, without the need for a headset or PC phone. Note that you do need to be a PC user and BT home phone customer to access this service – if you're not, you'll have to

use Yahoo! Messenger's Voice Chat function instead. Check the home page for the latest offers – with the weight of Yahoo! behind it, this could prove to be an extremely popular service.

A third service to mention before we go is an intriguing one. CD-WOW! (www.cdwow.com) is most well-known for its amazingly cheap CDs and DVDs (most chart CDs are priced about a fiver cheaper than high street stores' asking price), but now has a subsidiary service called WOW TALK, a free service open to all CD-WOW! members. You'll need to register, download the software and grab a WOW-Talk! headset (the most basic of which is priced less than a fiver) before you can get talking. Once all that's done, talking to anyone in the world through your PC for free is incredibly exciting, which basically sums up the attraction of this emerging technology.

5

Your life online: leisure

Introduction

Over the next couple of chapters, we're going to look at how the internet can increase the enjoyment you squeeze out of what precious leisure hours you have during the week.

The speed at which some of the topics we're going to discuss over the next few pages has been adopted by the Great British public has been staggering. Only a few years ago, for example, video players ruled the roost, with an emerging technology known as 'DVD' being spoken of by those in the know, but seen by the populous at large as a flashy, expensive format that only tech-heads could get any enjoyment from.

Fast forward a couple of years (pun intended), and now VHS as a format is effectively dead, with DVDs in charge. With the expansion has seen a demise in your local high street video store as the place to get your films – you can now rent them online, watch them as long as you like, and send them back in a pre-paid envelope, all for a fee of somewhere in the region of £10 and £20 a month. Which, even if you're just a moderately keen film fan who watches say three films a week, works out at less than £2 a DVD. We'll be looking at one of these immensely popular online stores, LOVEFiLM, later in this chapter.

Any guide to leisure and shopping online simply has to take into account perhaps the biggest online phenomenon of the last 5 years – eBay. This online auction site has had a staggering level of success in the UK and beyond since the turn of the century, to the point where it literally seems that everyone has bought or sold something from the site. We'll be looking in-depth at how to search for items in this giant marketplace, giving you expert buying and selling tips along the way.

What you'll do

Do your weekly shop at Tesco.com

Find some alternatives to Tesco

Buy on Amazon.co.uk

Use Amazon Marketplace to pick up a bargain

Sign up with LOVEFiLM and choose DVDs to rent

Set up a wish list of films

Find some alternatives to LOVEFiLM

Use an auction website: Register with eBay

Search on eBay

Buy goods on eBay

Sell your goods on eBay

Find some alternatives to eBay

Get the latest auction news delivered to your mobile

Find and use a genealogy website: 1837Online.com

Find alternatives to 1837Online

Finally, we'll highlight another online craze – the genealogy boom, as thousands of people up and down the country trace their ancestry for free, with the help of the web. Gone are the days of sneezing your way through the layers of dust in your local library's record section – you can now access millions of family records with a couple of mouse clicks.

For our first task, we're going to look at how Tesco tackles the interesting area of doing your weekly shopping online.

Timesaver tip

In a rush? Then use the Express Shopper option and get Tesco to do all the hard work of picking for you. Type all the items that you want on the notepad on the left-hand side, click Find now and Tesco will come back with what's available.

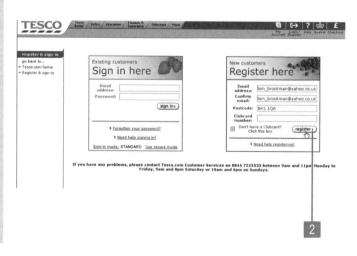

Shopping for food online hasn't, it is fair to say, taken the British public by storm in the way that, say, buying DVDs or items on eBay has. You only need to look at the queue in your local Asda at the weekend, as tired and harassed shoppers battle for the best goods, to see that the weekly pilgrimage to the supermarket is still part of our regular routine.

One of the major reasons for this, we guess, is perhaps the most obvious disadvantage of buying your food online – how can you test that the bananas, apples, melons, etc. are in good condition, without actually being able to see or feel them? In your supermarket, you can be guided by the evidence of your own eyes. When you add on the delivery costs as well, online food shopping looks a less attractive proposition.

This is doing the process down somewhat, however. If you lead an especially busy life, or live in a remote area that is miles from the nearest supermarket, online food shopping could prove to be an absolute godsend. What's more, you can pick up some impressive online-only bargains as well, avoid the sheer bloody-minded hassle of queuing up, and be in and out within ten minutes, without having to carry back-breaking bags, load the car or push a massive trolley around for miles. Looked at this way, the whole proposition starts to become a good deal more attractive.

Tesco offers a whole range of features, including insurance, books, DVDs and even holidays and flights, but we're going to concentrate here on a more conventional grocery shopping list.

Doing your weekly shop at Tesco.com

6

First steps

1 At www.tesco.com, click on Groceries to your door in the top-left corner.

2 If this is your first time at the site, you're going to need to register. First off, enter an email address (we recommend a non-work one), confirm it, enter your postcode and Clubcard number if you have one, and click register.

Doing your weekly shop at Tesco.com (cont.)

First steps

3 The registration process continues with this screen, where you'll be asked to enter vital details such as your name and address. To ensure your online security, Tesco will ask you for a password.

4 After this brief procedure, you should be accepted into the hallowed arena of online shopping. There are a couple of ways to shop, and you may want to take a little tour around the site to see what's what. One option is to use this Search box in the top-right to find what you want.

5 We're instead going to go straight to the Express Shopper option and see what that does for us. Click on the Express Shopper icon underneath Start shopping at the top of the screen.

6 Type the general items you want in the list on the left hand-side. Tesco's tip is that simple specific things work best, such as 'cod fillets' rather than 'a fillet of cod in a mornay source'.

7 Then click Find now.

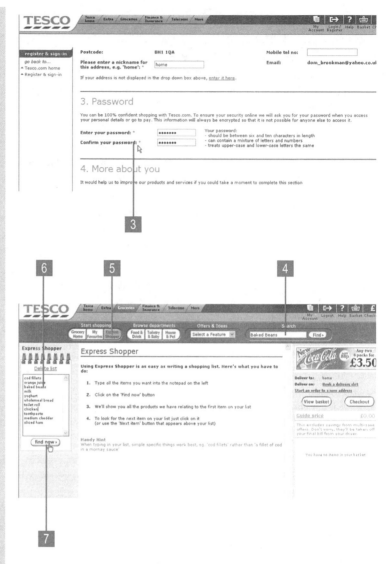

Timesaver tip

Booking a delivery slot is obviously an important procedure. At www.tesco.com/superstore/deliveryslots, you can pick a 2-hour window, such as 17.00-19.00, when you know you're going to be in to receive the goods. You obviously also need to select the day – you can pick one up to 3 weeks in advance. Expect to pay between £3.99 and £5.99 for the privilege of delivery. If you book a delivery time before you shop, it will be reserved for 2 hours.

First steps

8 Click on one of the food items in your list on the left to get Tesco to give you its search results. We click on Chicken.

9 Here you see the relevant results. You can see photos if you wish, choose the weight of a product, write a note about it, select the quantity, view the price and click add if you want it to be added to your basket. It's quite good fun, so don't get carried away, otherwise you'll end up spending hundreds!

10 Selections, their prices and a running total will be added to the bill on the right-hand side of the screen.

11 Carry on selecting what you want, until you're done. When finished, click on Checkout.

Timesaver tip

Not all the products may be available when you choose them, so Tesco asks you to make some substitutions, which you'll be sent in the event of unavailabilities.

For your information

Should things go wrong, which they may well do in the early days of you using the service, use the Contact us link on the home page to access the different ways of registering a complaint or a query. Tesco has email links for technical queries, miscellaneous queries or queries regarding groceries; you'll need to state your problem and enter your details such as your name, address, telephone number and order number, if applicable. If you'd rather speak by phone, try the grocery number on 0845 7225533, 9 a.m. to 11 p.m. Monday to Friday, 9 a.m. to 8 p.m. Saturday and 10 a.m. to 6 p.m. Sunday. If your problems is of a more technical nature, try 0906 301 8000 (8 a.m. to midnight 7 days a week. Calls charged at 50p a minute), or email support@tesco.net

Doing your weekly shop at Tesco.com (cont.)

Choose a delivery time

12 Another important bit coming up – the choosing of the delivery time. Obviously you need to make sure you or a pal are going to be in to pick up the delivery. You'll see a matrix of available times and the prices for those time slots. Choose a time slot and day, and click in its corresponding little box. Our choice is one of the cheapest, at £3.99.

13 Now it's just a matter of confirming your delivery, entering your credit card details, and waiting! Type in your details carefully, and click confirm my order when you're done.

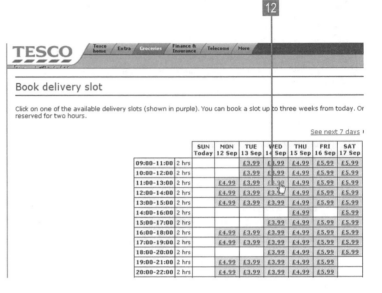

12

TESCO
Tesco home / Extra / Groceries / Finance & Insurance / Telecoms / More

Book delivery slot

Click on one of the available delivery slots (shown in purple). You can book a slot up to three weeks from today. Or reserved for two hours.

See next 7 days ▸

		SUN Today	MON 12 Sep	TUE 13 Sep	WED 14 Sep	THU 15 Sep	FRI 16 Sep	SAT 17 Sep
09:00-11:00	2 hrs			£3.99	£3.99	£4.99	£5.99	£5.99
10:00-12:00	2 hrs			£3.99	£3.99	£4.99	£5.99	£5.99
11:00-13:00	2 hrs		£4.99	£3.99	£3.99	£4.99	£5.99	£5.99
12:00-14:00	2 hrs		£4.99	£3.99	£3.99	£4.99	£5.99	£5.99
13:00-15:00	2 hrs		£4.99	£3.99	£3.99	£4.99	£5.99	£5.99
14:00-16:00	2 hrs					£4.99		£5.99
15:00-17:00	2 hrs			£3.99	£4.99	£5.99		
16:00-18:00	2 hrs		£4.99	£3.99	£3.99	£4.99	£5.99	£5.99
17:00-19:00	2 hrs		£4.99	£3.99	£3.99	£4.99	£5.99	£5.99
18:00-20:00	2 hrs			£3.99	£4.99	£5.99	£5.99	
19:00-21:00	2 hrs		£4.99	£3.99	£3.99	£4.99	£5.99	
20:00-22:00	2 hrs		£4.99	£3.99	£3.99	£4.99	£5.99	

Step 1. Type your code (e.g. 1234-abcd-5678 or save123) in the box below and click 'use code'.

Promotion code: [ ] (use code ▸)

Step 2. Check your discount in the Order Summary above.

If you have more than one code to enter click here

See help on eCoupons and eVouchers

Name on card: Mr Simon Westpot
Card number: 4875648765874
Expiry date: 02 ▾ / 09 ▾
Issue Number:

○ Store my card details for next time
◉ Don't store my card details for next time

5. Confirm your order

By clicking on the 'confirm my order' button you confirm your acceptance to Tesco.com's terms and conditions and product terms and conditions. See Tesco.com's Privacy Policy.

You will not pay anything extra when you pay by credit or debit card. Tesco Merchant Services Ltd processes all card transactions for a 2.5% handling charge which is included in the cost of your shopping.

Our acceptance of an order takes place on dispatch of the order, at which point the contract will be made and your account will be charged.

(confirm my order ▸)

13

ⓘ For your information

Tesco online has a number of promises; your order will be saved even if you don't check out, your payment details will be kept secure, and all in-store special offers are available online as well.

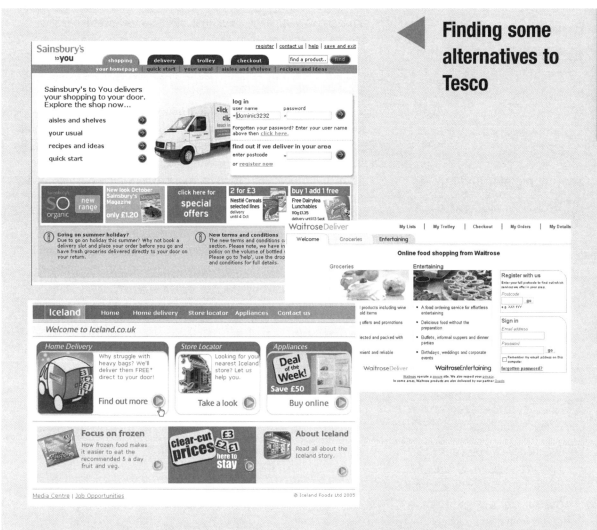

Sainsbury's has fallen behind, some might argue, in the high street battle, but its online presence at www.sainsbury.co.uk shows how seriously it takes the internet. The name of its home delivery service is Sainsbury's to You, at www.sainsburystoyou.com, and its system of home ordering is pretty similar to Tesco's, with the same mix of special offers and deep shelves.

If you're more of a Waitrose fan, you can access their online service at www.waitrosedeliver.com, where there are over 15,000 products for you to choose from. Iceland, meanwhile, has a twist on

proceedings – it doesn't let you actually buy your Iceland food from the comfort of your own armchair, but if you spend more than £25 in its store in the high street, it will deliver your bags direct to your door for free, which can't be bad. See www.iceland.co.uk.

Ultimately, online grocery shopping is a nice option to have, which may come in handy in emergencies, or for people who are housebound. Whilst not changing the face of the internet as we know it, it is yet another useful feature to encompass into our everyday lives.

Buying on Amazon.co.uk

Search, register and buy

1 Registering with Amazon is a little bit of a weird one – the best way is actually after you've chosen what you want to buy. Here we are at the home page of Amazon UK, www.amazon.co.uk, and there's lots to see and do. Product categories such as books and music are tabbed at the top of the screen.

2 And they're also down the left-hand side of the screen.

3 Big money-off deals are often right in the centre, where they can get your attention, such as this summer sale and 'Rent DVDs from only £5.99 per month' deal.

4 Important buttons such as Your Account, Wish List and View Basket are right at the top, near the Amazon.co.uk logo.

Amazon (www.amazon.co.uk) has blazed a trail over the last decade when it comes to safe, reliable online shopping, with the added benefit of saving about 25% on everything you buy as well! It's hard to say why Amazon has been so successful – it must boil down to more than just the fact that it was one of the first major players in the online entertainment shop market. What Amazon seems to do, without you actually speaking to a human being there (even finding a phone number on the site is a notoriously difficult process) is look after the customer – with regular newsletters, on-site recommendations based on your previous buying habits, and a transparently clear buying and distribution process which lets you know the exact state of your order at any one time. Stuff comes quickly, too – you may have to pay for delivery (although the relatively new 'SuperSaver Delivery' option now gives you free postage on any orders over £19, with the trade-off that you may have to wait a bit longer for your goods to arrive), but it's not unknown for you to order something one day, and for it to arrive the next.

Let's look at a simple book selection and purchase on the site.

Timesaver tip

As we've said, postage can add quite a lot on to your final order on the Amazon site, so when you get to the checkout, if your bid is over £19, make sure you choose SuperSaver Delivery. SuperSaver items will take 2–5 days longer to reach you than the same item posted first class, but if you're saving a fiver or so, and are not in any urgent need of getting your item, you may regard this as a sacrifice worth making.

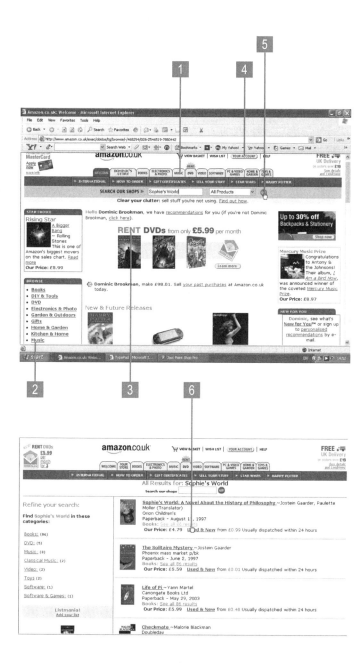

Search, register and buy

5   A good way to start is by using the powerful search engine facility. In the Search box here, we enter the title of a book we're interested in and click Go.

6   Here are all the results, in all formats, for our search term of *Sophie's World*. We're interested in the paperback version of this famous philosophical bestseller by Jostein Gaarder, so we click See all 86 results next to Books.

Buyong on Amazon.co.uk (cont.)

Book hunting

7 Here are the organized results. Look how intelligent Amazon is – it's already populated the left-hand side of the screen with Related Areas to the book in question, even recommending music we may like that is similar to it!

8 The top search result gives us the title, author, publisher, average customer review, dispatch time, and price details. As is usual with Amazon, we're going to save a fair bit of money over the high street if we buy online – some 20%.

9 We want to snap up this deal, so we click on Add to Basket.

10 Here, on the right-hand side, we can see Listmania, where users submit Lists of their favourite books, DVDs, songs or whatever. All these lists that appear here will have *Sophie's World* included in them, so we click on one of them to go off and read more.

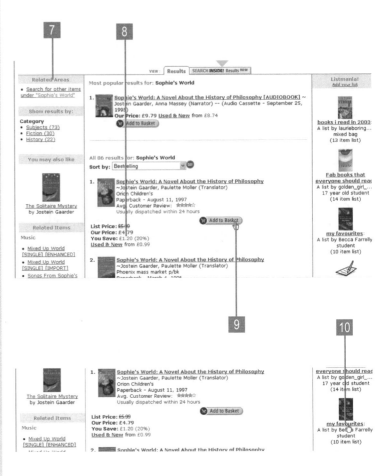

Timesaver tip

Once you've used Amazon a couple of times, when you access the home page, you'll see a Welcome notice, and a message saying 'we have recommendations for you'. These recommendations are based on your shopping choices – if you've bought the book *The Liar* by Stephen Fry, for example, it may recommend another one of his books, such as *Paperweight*, or one of his films, such as *Wilde*. You don't have to do anything with these recommendations, obviously, but they may inspire you to make further buying choices, which will please Amazon. When you get your recommendations you can click on I Own it or Not Interested if you're not impressed with the advice being given.

Becca Farrelly's comments:
an amazing insight into someones imagination and what they think of the world

2. **The Solitaire Mystery**
by Jostein Gaarder
Avg. Customer Review: ★★★★★

Paperback
List Price: £6.99
Our Price: £5.59
You Save: £1.40 (20%)
Used & New from £0.01

Books to change your lif
A list by sotonstu, Studer
(8 items)

For your information

A good way of getting feedback on a purchase is to read
other reviews and comments on them from users, although
bear in mind that these may be a) badly written and b)
planted by unscrupulous PR employees, seeking to get their
product sold as many times as possible.

Timesaver tip

We'll be looking at renting DVDs online later in this chapter,
but Amazon has recently joined the race as well. Join the
service at the rather unwieldy URL of
www.amazon.co.uk/gp/subs/rentals/help/learn-
more.html/026-8491476-1294053 and choose from a number
of subscription models, such as £9.99 for 6 DVDs a month,
or £7.99 for 4 DVDs a month.

Book hunting

11 Just to prove the list system
does work, the list that we
clicked on told us about another
Jostein Gaarder book which we
hadn't even heard about, so we
click on its title to find out more.
The world of Amazon truly is
massive.

12 Our explorations over, we click
the Add to Shopping Basket
button to be taken to this
screen: Customers who
shopped for this item also
shopped for these items. This
feature is a bit hit and miss –
some of what's come up is just
different versions of the same
book. It doesn't hurt to have a
quick browse through what
appears, though.

13 When you're done, click
Proceed to Checkout on the
right.

Buying on Amazon.co.uk (cont.)

Registering

14 Ordering may be quick and easy on Amazon, but we're going to need to register first, as this is our first purchase from the site. Enter your email address and click in the circle next to I am a new customer.

15 Then click on Sign in using our secure server.

16 Time to enter your address details; where you want the book to be sent. Double-check for errors, then click on Continue.

Timesaver tip

Clicks you make on the site, as you work your way around, are memorised by Amazon, with many of them going on something called 'The page you made'. This page is totally editable by you, and stands as a good record of your tastes and general online entertainment requirements.

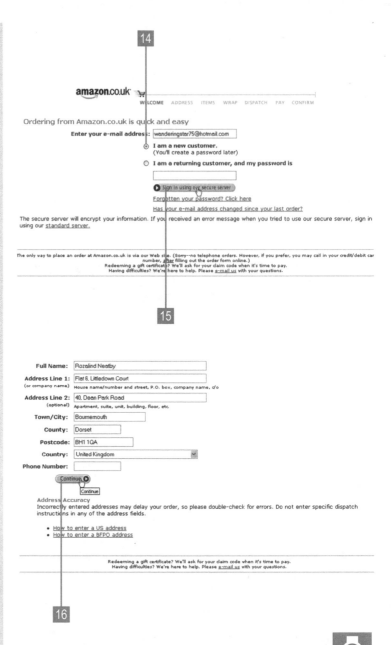

Timesaver tip

If you're a bit short on money, but like tantalising yourself with the prospect of buying something in the future, when you see an item you like, click on the Add to Wish List button. You can then come back later, perhaps when you're feeling a little bit more flush, and treat yourself.

full credit card number (why this is safe).
If you prefer to give the number to us by phone, enter only the card's last five digits. After you have completed your order, we'll
e-mail you the phone number to call to provide your full credit card number. You may also pay by cheque (why this takes longer).

Continue ►
(you can review this order before it is fina

Paying with a credit card?

Payment Method	Credit Card No.	Expiry Date	Cardholder's name
⊙ Visa/Delta/Electron ▾	4758975947850■■■	01 ▾ 2011 ▾	Mr D M Brookman
(Maestro/Switch only) Issue Number: ☐ OR Start Date: – ▾ – ▾			

○ Pay by cheque or postal order
(or check funds on account)

Do you have a gift certificate or promotional claim code?
If you have more than one gift certificate, click the "Enter another" button. If not, click the Continue button below.

Enter code: ☐ Enter another

If your gift certificate or promotional claim code doesn't cover the cost of your order, we will use the card you enter above for the balance. (You may not pa
by cheque in this case.) Find out more about gift certificates.

Registering

17 You now need to select a payment method and create a password. It's all 100% secure. We enter our credit card details here.

18 After choosing your password and clicking Continue, you should be ready to go! This order screen is the crux of the whole order. A summary of what you've asked for, with the relevant pricing details, can be seen down the right-hand side of the screen.

19 Payment details can be seen towards the bottom-right.

20 Delivery details are on the left. We want to change the despatch address, so click on Change.

For your information

Shopping with Amazon is totally secure, so you can be as confident as possible that your details are not being picked up by criminals as you use the Amazon site.

Jargon buster

Password – many websites ask you for a password, known only to you, to access their services. Passwords are often a combination of words and numbers; when you're setting yours, try to have a few different passwords that are not easily guessable – for added peace of mind.

Buying on Amazon.co.uk (cont.)

Final steps

21 Enter the new address that you want to use, and then click Dispatch to this address.

22 With everything sorted and double-checked, simply click Place your order and you're done!

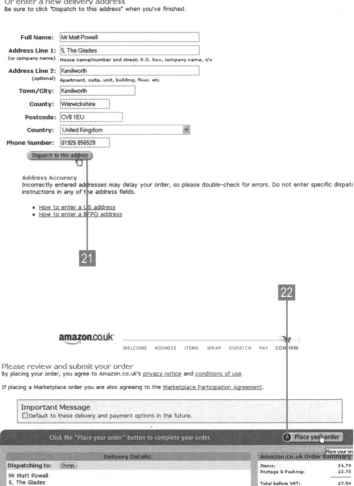

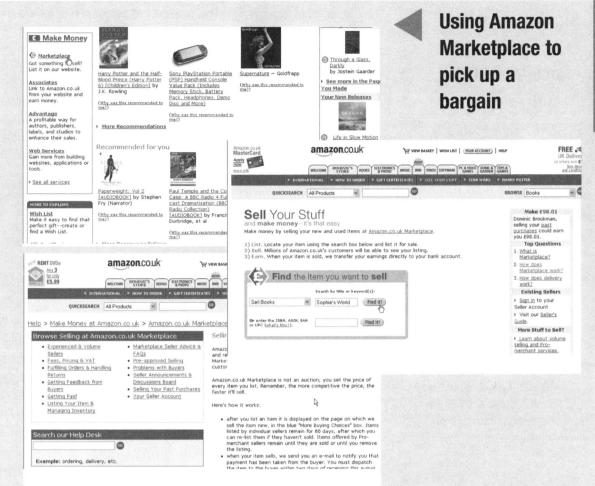

Using Amazon Marketplace to pick up a bargain

On the Amazon home page, halfway down the screen on the left, you should see something called Amazon Marketplace. Click on the link to find out how you can make money from your old DVDs, books, CDs and the like.

Basically, the Marketplace procedure is split into three sections – List, Sell and Earn. You locate your item using the powerful Amazon search facility, get a 'used price guideline' from the bods at Amazon, and then set the price that you want it to go for, and state your delivery methods.

When people search for stuff on Amazon, they'll then see a Used option which will include how they can

get the item second-hand, and your submission should be in there, once you've registered it. They can then basically buy the item from you, with Amazon taking a nice commission for being the middleman in the process. You get the address of the buyer and have to post the package, with your buyer being automatically charged a delivery fee on your behalf.

Obviously if you price your item too high, you're unlikely to get anyone buying it. Price it low, however, and you could get a sale, and gradually build up enough money to buy lots of shiny new stuff from Amazon. So everyone's a winner.

Signing up with LOVEFiLM and choosing DVDs to rent

Register for films through the post

 First-time users of the site will get to this screen when they first go to www.lovefilm.com. You'll see that there's a free trial for you to take advantage of, so you can work out whether the site is for you. Click on Start your free trial right now.

 You'll enter the registration process. Type in a password, email address and delivery information, then click on Continue.

Timesaver tip

LOVEFiLM has recommendations for you to take advantage of, should you so desire. These recommendations are based on the marks out of seven you give every film you watch, so mark carefully, and you should see some useful tips come up when you click on Recommendations from the home page.

The speed at which renting DVDs online has taken off has surprised even seasoned observers of the internet. However, when you look at the benefits, perhaps it shouldn't be that much of a shock. From the comfort of your armchair, you can pick from over 30,000 DVDs in a typical online store – way more than you can find down the local high street emporium. Basically everything that's ever been released on DVD can be found in these virtual stores. Overheads are low, so you'll typically only be paying about the equivalent of £1 or £2 a film once you've worked it out over the period of a month. So you'll save lots of money. And there are no postage charges normally, either – you just watch the film, stick it back in its pre-paid envelope, seal it up and send it back to the company. The most work you have to do is make your way to the nearest postbox. You can keep DVDs for as long as you like, although this isn't a very cost-effective way of using the sites – we reckon it's good to try and watch three films a week or so, which shouldn't be too hard, to get your money's worth.

There are a number of players out there, but we're going to see what LOVEFiLM (www.lovefilm.com) has to offer.

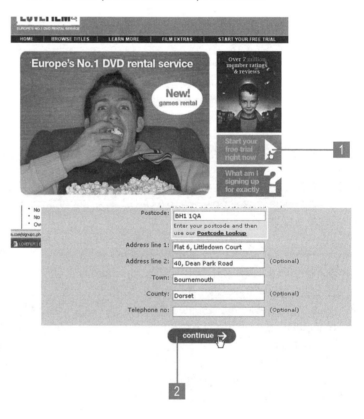

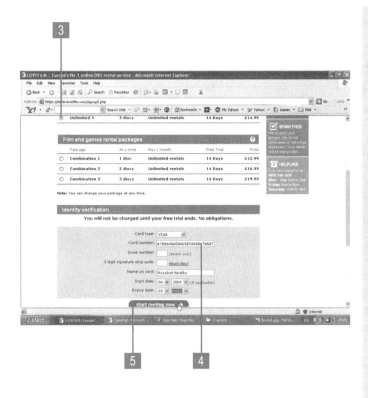

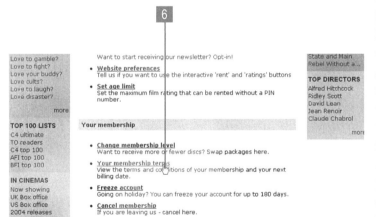

Signing up with LOVEFiLM and choosing DVDs to rent (cont.)

6

Register for films through the post

3 What package do you want? It depends on how enthusiastic a film-lover you are, and how many films you reckon you're likely to watch in the course of any one month. Click in the little circle next to the package you'd like.

4 Enter your credit card details.

5 Then click Start renting now.

6 There's a whole host of options to play with on this screen, which can be accessed by clicking Your account in future visits. Click View membership terms if you'd like to check just what you've signed yourself up for.

Timesaver tip

Click on the Your account link in the top-right-hand corner of the home page to access vital customisation options, such as changing your delivery address, changing your membership level, or signing up for the regular newsletter.

Signing up with LOVEFiLM and choosing DVDs to rent (cont.)

Register for films through the post

7 Here are your details. Not happy? Click on change to alter things.

8 At last! The main screen you'll be working from every time you click back to the site. In the middle are all the special offers, deals and features.

9 Down the right-hand side are the new releases, and letters and decades for you to click on to access a particular time period or film.

10 On the left are links to the charts, the recommended films... and the Search box, which is as good a place as any to look for a film. Type in your film selection and click Search.

Timesaver tip

LOVEFiLM has a nifty feature on the left-hand side of its home page known as Moods, which aims to match your own personal mood with a selection of films. So, if on a particular day you feel like crying, or dancing, or watching sport, or laughing, or getting all slushy and romantic, the site will come up with some suggestions to match your feelings. Just click on the particular Mood on the left to get some relevant suggestions.

Signing up with LOVEFiLM and choosing DVDs to rent (cont.)

6

Rent it!

11 You'll see a list of films matching your criteria. Click the film title to see a mini review and its average mark from users – DVD watchers are encouraged to rate everything they rate out of seven, for the benefit of other users of the site. If you like what you see, click Rent Now and it will be added to your list of films awaiting to be sent out by the site.

SEARCH

Search all

Search

GENRES

Select...

see all genres

QUICK PICKS

UK top 50 chart
New releases
Coming soon
Editors choice
Top rated
Most popular
Indie films
Soundtracks
PSP films NEW!

GAMES NEW!

PS2 games
PSP games (UMD)

RECOMMENDED

Harvey
Sleepers

HEAT (DISC 1) (1995 - DVD)

TimeOut REVIEW Investigating a bold armed robbery which has left three security guards dead, LA cop Vincent Hanna (Pacino), whose devotion to work is threatening his third marriage, follows a trail that leads him to suspect a gang of thieves headed by Neil McCauley (De Niro). Trouble is, McCauley's cunning is at least equal to Hanna's, and that makes him a hard man to nail. Still, unknown to Hanna, McCauley's gang have their own troubles: one of their number is a volatile psychopath, while the businessman whose bonds they've stolen is not above some rough stuff himself. Such a synopsis barely scratches the surface of Mann's masterly crime epic. Painstakingly detailed, with enough characters, subplots and telling nuances to fill out half a dozen conventional thrillers, this is simply the best American crime movie - and indeed, one of the finest movies, period - in over a decade. The action scenes are better than anything produced by John Woo, Quentin Tarantino; the characterisation has a depth most American film-makers only dream of; the use of location, decor and music is inspired; Dante Spinotti's camerawork is superb; and the large, imaginatively chosen cast gives terrific support to the two leads, both back on glorious form.

RENT NOW

Recommend to a friend

		Average Rating
Director:	Michael Mann	5 Click to rate
Starring:	Al Pacino, Robert De Niro, Tom Sizemore, Diane Venora, Amy Brenneman, Ashley Judd, Mykelti Williamson, Wes Studi, Ted Levine, Jon Voight, Val Kilmer, Natalie Portman	
Year:	1995	
Runtime:	164	
Certificate:	15	

11

Did you know ?

You can have three films on the go at any one time – watch one, send it back, and it'll be replaced in the post within the next couple of days by another film from your priority list.

For your information

Special offers are a big deal on the site, and help you get extra credit if, for example, you get a friend to sign up with the site and remain with it. Click on Special Offers from the home page to see what potential money-saving or money-earning delights the store has for you.

Setting up a
wish list of films

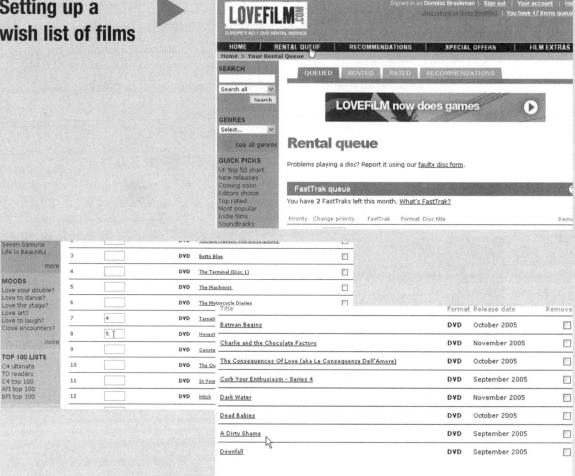

As we've seen, selecting a film that you would like to rent is easy on LOVEFiLM. All you have to do is click on Rent Now, and it then gets added to a big, long list of films known as your Wishlist, or Rental Queue. Click on Rental Queue from the LOVEFiLM home page to access the list of films that are imminently on their way to you. When you've got a list, they'll be in order of Priority – the ones nearer the top are, theoretically, the ones that will come to you first (subject to availability).

So if you've got a film on your list that you're really desperate to see, but it's languishing at no. 56 on your list, click in the Change Priority column and box next to the film, and type in a number that should get it seen by the LOVEFiLM bods – in the top 10 should do it. Should you have loads and loads of films, and gamble on getting what you really want over something you're not too fussed about, or just populate your list with stuff you're mad keen on? It's up to you, and part of the game.

From the list, you can also choose to buy the film at RRP, delete it from your list, or remind yourself what it's actually about by simply clicking on its name. And then just pray that your most wanted films come to you first!

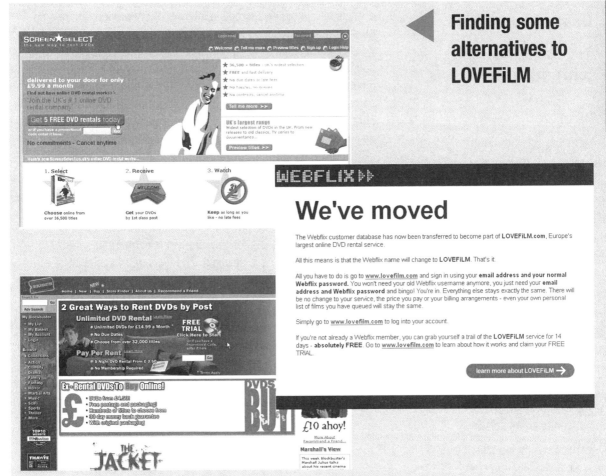

Joining the battle for your wallets in the DVD rental arena have been a number of alternatives over the past couple of years. Prices vary from site to site, so we won't include specific prices, but remember that you're unlikely to get a deal that's massively different from any of the others – these sites have to make their money too, of course, and any significantly cheap deal is likely to be copied by rivals. ScreenSelect (www.screenselect.co.uk) is a big player, with way over 30,000 titles to choose from, the almost-obligatory free trial, free postage and the ability to cancel anytime. Blockbuster (www.blockbuster.co.uk) brings with it the cachet of its well-known high street branch, and has a suitably busy rental operation, as well as the chance to buy

ex-rental DVDs online. Webflix, meanwhile (www.webflix.co.uk), has just been absorbed into LOVEFiLM, showing the way the market may go – a couple of the big guys snapping up the smaller ones.

Ultimately, the choice is yours – and you can even have a few free trials to work out which service is the best, although bear in mind it can be difficult to unsubscribe yourself sometimes from sites, once you've given them your details. Apart from this caveat, online DVD rental is a good thing, and all you have to hope is that there's not a series of postal strikes over the next few years, to spoil your viewing fun!

Using an auction website: register with eBay

First steps on eBay

1. Here we are at the home page of eBay UK, www.ebay.co.uk. It's worth stopping here and showing you what's what before we start our registration. The register link is at the top of the screen.

2. There's a nice big Search bar at the top, through which you can do a general search, under Welcome to eBay.

3. Great Products Now is in the centre of the screen.

4. Browse through the favourite categories on the left.

5. Get help about eBay with 'eBay Explained'. Ideal for newcomers who feel a bit lost.

6. PayPal is the commonest way of carrying out your financial business on eBay. Find out all about it here.

eBay is an absolutely incredible internet phenomenon. There's no other phrase to describe how an auction site which was more of a word-of-mouth kind of thing only a couple of years ago, has suddenly exploded into the national consciousness. It's been like a massive chain reaction, helped by incredible bargains, a friendly community-like feel to the site, and acres of press coverage, not only in the computer press, but the national media as well. Barely a day seems to by at the moment without the latest controversy or eBay craze hitting the news; the phrase to be 'an eBayer' has entered our language.

One of the reasons for eBay's success is simply the fact that everything seems to be on there, no matter how obscure it is. Whatever you're looking for, you can virtually guarantee that someone, somewhere is selling it. The flip side of this coin, of course, is that if you want to sell all that stuff cluttering up your house or garage, the chances are that there'll be someone willing to pay for it and help make you a tidy little sum.

So, both buying and selling on eBay are massively popular, and we'll look at both these areas over the next 20 pages. To kick off, however, you're going to need to know how to register with the site, so that's what we'll deal with first.

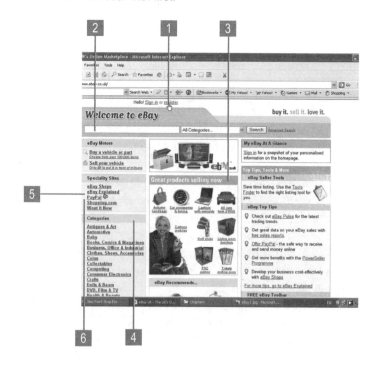

Important: A working email address is required to complete regis

Email address

dominicb@paragon.co.uk | 7

Examples: myname@aol.com or myname@yahoo.com

Re-enter email address

dominicb@paragon.co.uk

9

eBay's User Agreement and Privacy Policy
In order to use eBay, you must first read and agree to eBay's Use
and conditions that apply to your use of eBay eBay's User Agree
by clicking here.

You should also read eBay's Privacy Policy to learn about the wa
your personal information. The Privacy Policy can be viewed and p

By checking the boxes below, I confirm the following:
☑ I have read and accept the User Agreement and I have read th
☐ I agree to receive communications from eBay and understand
   preferences at any time in My eBay.
☐ I must be an adult (18 years old) to trade on eBay and I certif
   into this Agreement.

Security Meter
The darker the bar appears, th
secure your password is.

8 ── Continue >

Secret answer
Hewitt
n if you forget your password.

10 ── Continue >

Did you know ?

eBay has over 150 million users, spread over 30 countries.
It's the UK's most visited eCommerce site, with some 30
million items going through the auction process at any one
time. The amount of transactions being completed at any
one time is staggering – a mobile phone sells every minute
and a car every 4 minutes on eBay.co.uk. A very general
overview of eBay and what it does can be found at
http://pages.ebay.co.uk/help/ebayexplained/newtoebay/index.
html.

Timesaver tip

An excellent place to start getting to grips with the eBay
website is in the community forums, which you can find at
http://hub.ebay.co.uk/community?ssPageName=h:h:over:UK.
Here, you can access discussion boards, chat groups and
an answer centre, where you can find some excellent
answers to common queries.

Registration

7 The first registration screen
asks you to enter your address
and email details. A working
email address is required to
complete registration. If you use
a common, free webmail
address as your email address
(such as Yahoo! or Hotmail), a
couple of steps down the line,
eBay will also require you to
enter credit card details as
further proof of your identity.
Don't worry – eBay won't
charge anything to your card.

8 Confirm the legal stuff by
clicking in the boxes, then click
Continue.

9 Time to choose your username
and product. If you're going to
sell a specific product, you
might want your username to
reflect it – 'cardshark' if you're
selling playing cards, for
example. Choose a password
that's easy for you to remember,
but hard for others to guess. A
combination of letters and
numerals is often a good bet.
Note the security meter – the
darker the bar, the more secure
your password is.

10 Choose a secret question and
answer, then click Continue.

Using an auction website: register with eBay (cont.)

Registration

11 Up pops the Confirm your Identity screen. Read the warning that says because we entered a Yahoo! address, a credit card process is necessary to further confirm our identity.

12 You could, however, try a different email address if you don't want to enter your credit card details. Click Enter a different email.

13 Otherwise, enter your credit card details in the space provided. The information you provide is totally secure.

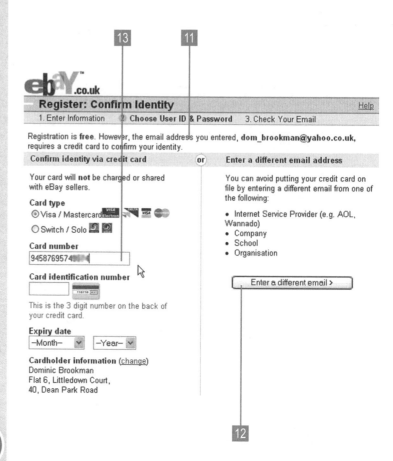

Register: Confirm Identity   Help
1. Enter Information   2 Choose User ID & Password   3. Check Your Email

Registration is **free**. However, the email address you entered, **dom_brookman@yahoo.co.uk**, requires a credit card to confirm your identity.

Confirm identity via credit card   (or)   **Enter a different email address**

Your card will **not** be charged or shared with eBay sellers.

Card type
◉ Visa / Mastercard
○ Switch / Solo

Card number
94587695740

Card identification number

This is the 3 digit number on the back of your credit card.

Expiry date
–Month–   –Year–

Cardholder information (change)
Dominic Brookman
Flat 6, Littledown Court,
40, Dean Park Road

You can avoid putting your credit card on file by entering a different email from one of the following:

- Internet Service Provider (e.g. AOL, Wannado)
- Company
- School
- Organisation

[Enter a different email >]

For your information

Want to know more about the rules and regulations that govern eBay and help it to run so smoothly? Try going to http://pages.ebay.co.uk/help/pol icies/index.html. Here, you can find rules for sellers and buyers, which items are prohibited on eBay, terms regarding alcohol and general official terms and conditions.

For your information

One thing people are very worried about on eBay is online security. How safe are your credit card details? What do you do if you don't receive your items? How do you report a problem? These questions and more can be dealt with at the eBay Security Centre, which you can find at http://pages.ebay.co.uk/safetycentre/index.html.

eb𝐚Y.co.uk

Registration: Enter a Different Email Address

Hel

1. Enter Information   2 Choose User ID & Password   3. Check Your Email

Enter an email address from one of the following:

- Internet Service Provider (Wannado, AOL, etc.)
- Company
- School
- Organisation

If you don't have this type of email, please place your credit card on file instead.

Email address

simonjones@paragon.co.uk

Important: A valid email address is required to complete registration.

Re-enter email address

simonjones@paragon.co.uk

Continue >

You may still have to place a card on file if the email address you entered is not accepted by our system.

14

Different email address

14 Just to show the system in operation, we opt to enter a different email address to our initial Hotmail entry. An email address from an ISP, company, school or organisation should fit the bill here, although you might not want your work email address to become clogged up with messages from eBay (and your employers might not be too keen with you using the address for those purposes, either.) It's a bit of a matter of crossing your fingers and hoping whether the email address will be accepted by the system, but as we've said, it's not the end of the world if it isn't. Click Continue once you've entered your new address, and that should be the registration process done and dusted with.

!

Important

If you get an email purporting to be from eBay or PayPal (eBay's partner which deals with the vast majority of transactions carried out on the site), asking for your credit card details, username or password, don't answer it and forward it to eBay (the address is: spoof@ebay.co.uk). eBay and PayPal will never ask you for these kinds of details. Read more about spoofs and what to do about them at http://pages.ebay.co.uk/safetycentre/spoof.html.

Searching on eBay

Get the hang of searching on eBay and you'll find yourself on a shortcut to picking up some fantastic bargains, and getting into the thick of the auction action. We'll mention eBay-specific third-party search engines in a bit, but for the moment let's look at doing some general and advanced searching through the mighty world of eBay.

Basic searching

1. Our registration accepted, we're now free to explore the site, and the millions of items online. Getting the hang of searching is vital, if you're not to drown in a sea of items. We're going to look at some of the options available to the casual and not so casual searcher. First off, we get a clear idea of what we're looking for – a computer called the Commodore Amiga, from way back in the 1980s. One thing we could do is click on the Computing link from the Categories link on the left.

2. However, we're going to take a different tack, and instead enter Commodore Amiga in the Find what you're looking for box, then under the Welcome to eBay box, click Search.

3. We get a good list of results in the middle of the screen. The title of the auction, its price, how many bids there have been, whether PayPal is accepted by the seller and how long is left in the auction are all shown. Click on an auction's name to access it.

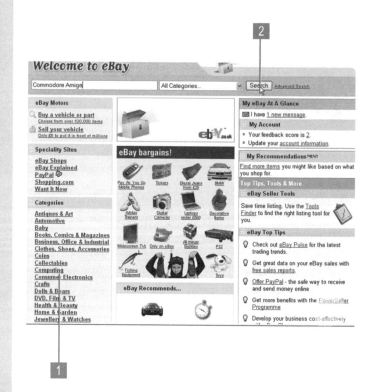

Basic searching

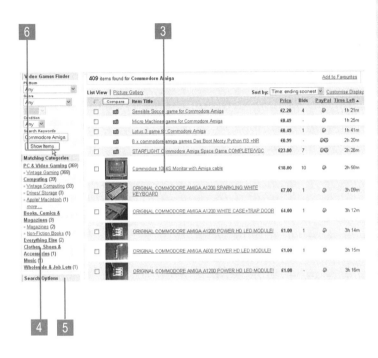

4 It's the bar down the left-hand side of the screen that interest us, however. First of all, you can see the different categories that your search fits into. Click on a category to access its relevant results. Note that this may throw up some bizarre results – quite why 'Clothes, Shoes and Accessories' has featured for what is basically an old computer is a mystery. That's likely to be the seller's fault, however, not eBay's.

5 The Search Options let you set some more parameters for your search.

6 You can set the location where you want to search, and opt to show only listings that are buyable with PayPal, available as Buy It Now items (where you sidestep the auction process and just buy at a set price), in listings that are about to end… and more. Obviously the more demands you set, the less results you're likely to find. Click Show Items when you're happy.

Timesaver tip

A useful utility to download is the eBay Toolbar, at http://pages.ebay.co.uk/ebay_toolbar. This handy little device gives you quick, easy access to eBay from your desktop, keeps track of any items which you have bid on and alerts you when auctions are about to end. The toolbar also comes with AccountGuard, which helps protect your account information and warns you when you are on a potentially fraudulent site.

Searching on eBay (cont.)

Deeper searching

 We didn't get any search results back, so more fine tuning is required. It goes on to list some options of results that match some, but not all, of your criteria; we click on the 15 items listed which satisfies two of our four criteria.

8 Success! At the bottom of the screen is what we're looking for – a model which stands at just £39.99. Click on the auction title to access it and put a bid in.

Timesaver tip

Third-party eBay search engines now exist to help make the process of trawling through eBay even easier. Take a look at www.snapsearch.com, which describes itself as 'the world's first eBay search engine'.

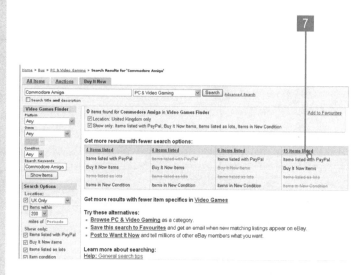

9

Items in Shops
· Find Shops

Members
· Find a Member
· Find Contact
  Information

All of these words

Exclude these words

Exclude words from your search

Items Priced
Min £ [   ]   Max: £ [   ]

From specific sellers (enter sellers' user IDs)
Include ∨
Search up to 10 sellers, separate names by a comma or a space.

Location
⊙ Preferred Locations   on eBay UK ∨
○ Items located in   United Kingdom   ∨
○ Items available to   United Kingdom   ∨
Learn more about search locations

Items near me
☐ Items within 75 ∨ miles of
    ZIP or Postal Code BH2 5ST   or Select a popular city... ∨

Currency
Any currency ∨

Multiple item listings
At least ∨ [   ]   ☐ Items listed as lots
Search for a group or collection of similar items (also called lots).

10

eb**Y**.co.uk

home | pay | services | site map

| Buy | Sell | My eBay | Community | Help |

Hello, cat_dog_weasel! (Sign out)

Search: Items by Seller

Search

Items
· Find Items
· **Items by Seller**
· Items by Bidder
· By Item Number

Shops
· Items in Shops
· Find Shops

Members
· Find a Member
· Find Contact
  Information

Enter seller's User ID
dynamiccoins
Find items offered by a particular seller.

☐ Include completed listings   Last 30 days ∨

☐ Include bidder's email addresses
(Accessible by seller only)

☑ Show close and exact User ID matches

Sort by   **Results per page**
Time: ending soonest ∨   50 ∨

[Search]

11

Deeper searching

9 Back at the home page on www.ebay.co.uk, click on Advanced Search to bring up this screen, where you can find items by seller, by bidder, by item number, by shop... there's a host of options here. In the centre are fields where you can include or exclude words, set minimum and maximum prices, and do more regarding the location of where you want the seller to be based.

10 One seller has been recommended to us by a friend, so we click on Items by Seller.

11 Enter the seller's User ID in the box provided, set some of the subsidiary options, then click Search.

Timesaver tip

The eBay toolbar, which we mentioned earlier, helps significantly when it comes to searching listings. It lets you do everything, from a simple title search to a highly specific title and description hunt through a particular category.

Searching on eBay (cont.)

Final searching options

12 You can also search through eBay Shops, which is an ever-growing area of eBay, where people set up their own shops online, often to sell a particular item such as video games or jewellery. Click on Items in Shops to dive into the Shops area.

13 You'll then need to enter however many details you have; keyword or item number, category and anything else you have to hand. Then click Search and hope for the best.

14 Lastly, if you want to find a member who you believe to be on eBay, you can do a member hunt by clicking on Find a Member from the left-hand side. Enter their user ID or email address in the box provided, then click Search. Note that if you only have their email address, only a limited amount of info will be given to you, for security reasons. With all this searching info available to you, you can be relatively confident that despite the size of the site, you're not going to be helplessly lost.

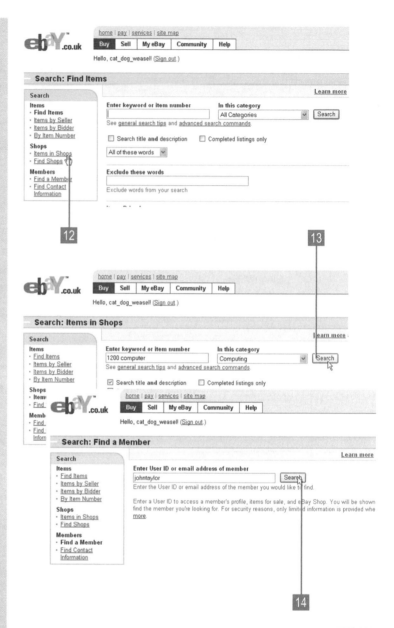

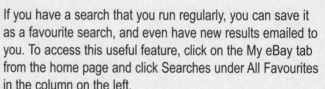

Timesaver tip

If you have a search that you run regularly, you can save it as a favourite search, and even have new results emailed to you. To access this useful feature, click on the My eBay tab from the home page and click Searches under All Favourites in the column on the left.

Let's now get to the crux of the matter – buying and selling on eBay. Selling is perhaps the most exciting element, as this is what offers up the chance of making lots of money. Buying shouldn't be neglected, though, as you can get a real adrenaline rush taking part in auctions and bidding against fellow users, not to mention some superb goods at rock-bottom prices. The key to eBay, perhaps, is the feedback system – when you buy something on eBay, you can give the seller feedback as to how well they handled the whole process of getting the goods to you.

This feedback gradually builds up for a regular user of the site, and anyone who has consistently very high feedback from users should be a good bet to deal with in a new auction. There's a whole minefield of tactics and things to watch out for in the eBuy buying arena – remember, some people make a living out of the site. We'll go through a sample process of looking for an item and deciding whether or not to bid for it. If you win an auction, the process is then down to you and the seller to get in touch and arrange the specifics of the deal. Remember, hundreds of thousands of deals go through without any fuss or problems whatsoever on eBay – the vast majority of sellers out there are trustworthy and honest. There are a couple of bad apples out there trying to spoil people's fun, but that is true unfortunately in every walk of life. We'll give you a few tips along the way, as we enter the bidding arena.

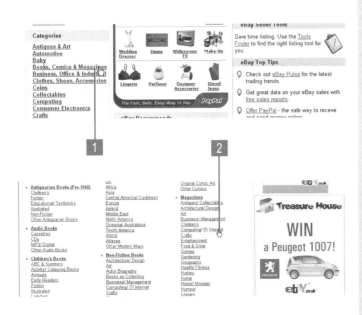

Ready to go?

1 You can browse through eBay for ages – nothing's stopping you just window-shopping for hours on end. Sooner or later, though, you're going to want to join the action. Again, there are a number of ways to get bidding, but we're going to show you just one of them. We've decided that we're after a rare spectrum computer magazine called *Crash* from the 1980s, so we click on Books, Comics & Magazines from the left-hand side.

2 Just look at all the categories that open up. One of eBay's massive strengths is the sheer volume of items that are on sale in the marketplace. We plump for the Computing/IT/Internet sub-category.

Buying goods on eBay (cont.)

Narrow it down

3 The results aren't quite what we want, so we bite the bullet and type in 'Crash magazine' in the top search box. The ability to be flexible, and not give up if you come up against one brick wall, is vital on eBay. What you want is probably out there – you just have to be patient and try a few different avenues occasionally. Click Search.

4 Success! Thirty-eight results match what we want. We knew eBay wouldn't let us down! Click on a title that interests you the most – we go for 4 Crash magazines Sinclair ZX Spectrum 65 66 67 68.

Timesaver tip

Whether you buy from someone with poor or average feedback is up to you, of course, but it's common sense to try and stick to people with excellent feedback. Everyone you buy from on eBay will have a feedback rating and a series of comments left by fellow users; in an auction, click on Read feedback comments to have a squiz through what other people have been saying. Many negative comments should set alarm bells ringing, and convince you to look elsewhere. There are more than enough reliable, trustworthy sellers out there for you to have to risk doing business with someone dodgy.

Auction specifics

5 Auctions on eBay generally look like this, although there is fair scope for personal customisation. The title of the auction is at the top.

6 A picture of what's on offer should be below.

7 On the right of the picture are the bid details, including starting bid, time left, start time, history, item location and postage costs.

8 To the right is the crucial Seller information box. Who is the seller? What's their feedback like? Click on the links here to find out all about them, and read what other users have been saying about them.

9 Below all this, you'll get a detailed description of what's on offer.

10 We click on the seller's name in the Seller information box, to be taken here. You get a full breakdown of the seller's history – he has 100% positive feedback, which is a good start. Scroll down to read fellow user's comments who've done deals with him in the past. Very impressive!

Did you know ?

Anyone with even the slightest passing interest in cars and motor vehicles in general should make their way immediately to the hugely popular and busy eBay Motors subsite, at http://motors.ebay.co.uk/. eBay Motors has over 2 million unique visitors every month – incredibly, a vehicle sells every 2 minutes. This could really be the place where you pick up a fantastic auto bargain.

Buying goods on eBay (cont.)

Shall we bid?

 Looking again at the bid, remember that people's postage details can sometimes send the prices spiraling, which is a bit cheeky. So we click on Postage, payment details and returns policy to be on the safe side. Looking at this now stops any nasty surprises once, perhaps, the auction is over and you've won.

12 Read the relevant terms and conditions. The seller offers PayPal, and will post worldwide.

![!]

Important

This piece of information is worth repeating, as it is very important and can lead to misunderstandings and confusion. So remember – when you click Confirm Bid, you are entering into a legally binding contract to purchase the item from the seller, should yours be the winning bid.

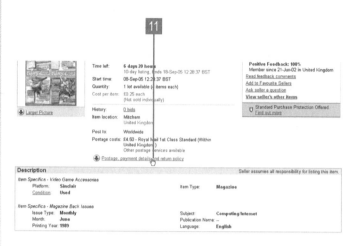

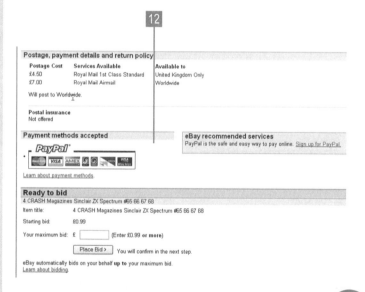

For your information

Want to get the latest gossip on what's hot and what's not on eBay right now? Then you need to read the regularly updated eBay Pulse, which you can find at http://pulse.ebay.co.uk. This great little area tells you what the most popular searches are at any given time, plus further useful info, such as the largest shops (by number of active listings) and the most popular motors at eBay Motors.

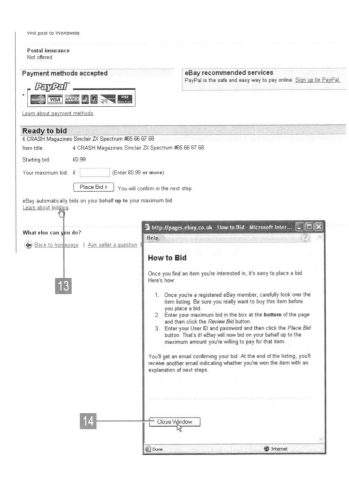

Buying goods on eBay (cont.)

6

Let's bid

13 Scrolling down the screen, you get to the Ready to Bid box. Before setting what would you like your maximum bid to be, click on Learn about bidding.

14 Continuing eBay's excellent policy of holding your hand through the vaguely scary (at least at first) world of online auctions, a How to Bid box pops up, with lots of info about how the bidding process works. As you can see, it's really just a matter of entering your maximum bid, clicking Review Bid, entering your user ID and password and clicking Place Bid. Easy! Click Close Window when you've read the mini-guide.

For your information

The easiest way to buy your items on eBay is by using PayPal, an online money firm that was snapped up by eBay a while ago. eBay describes PayPal as a company that 'enables anyone with an email address to send and receive online payments safely, easily and quickly'. PayPal is free, has no set-up fees and basically means that your financial information is never shared with the seller, which gives peace of mind. As a buyer, you pay for goods using your debit or credit card, bank account or PayPal balance. The seller receives payment immediately; sellers can then withdraw these funds to their bank account or use the PayPal balance to pay another seller. To open a PayPal account, go to https://www.paypal.com/uk/ and click Sign Up.

Buying goods on eBay (cont.)

Final steps

15 So we enter our maximum bid, and click Place Bid. eBay will automatically increase your bid incrementally up to your maximum bid, depending on whether or not there are more bids in the auction.

16 When you click Confirm Bid on the next screen, you are entering into a legally binding contract to purchase the item from the seller, should yours be the winning bid. This is very, very important, so remember it! Click the button and sit back and wait… you could be well on your way to your first eBay purchase! As we've said, if you do win, expect to hear back from your seller pretty promptly, and enter into a polite, clear email dialogue to get the loose ends sewn up nice and promptly. And if the goods come on time and in the correct state, don't forget to leave good feedback on the seller.

Will post to Worldwide.

Postal insurance
Not offered

Payment methods accepted

Learn about payment methods.

eBay recommende
PayPal is the safe and e

Ready to bid
4 CRASH Magazines Sinclair ZX Spectrum #65 66 67 68

Item title:	4 CRASH Magazines Sinclair ZX Spectrum #65 66 67 68
Starting bid:	£0.99
Your maximum bid:	£ [£5.99] (Enter £0.99 **or more**)

Place Bid > You will confirm in the next step.

eBay automatically bids on your behalf **up to** your maximum bid.
Learn about bidding.

15

16

198

Selling stuff on eBay is great fun, and could make you lots of money – that's the good news. It's not for the faint-hearted, however. It would be as well to browse the site and take part in a few auctions from a buyer's point of view before plunging headfirst into the world of selling. If you have an item in mind to sell, browse through similar items on the site to see what the going rate is.

To sell, you need to open a seller's account, which we'll take you through here. You then need to devote a lot of time to your listing – how it will look, what you'll write, the pictures you'll take, the price you'll set... there are a lot of considerations to bear in mind. And even after all that, once your auction is up and running, you'll need to start thinking about how you're going to get the item out to your buyer, and all sorts of issues to deal with after-sales care. That's all in the future, however – here, we're going to deal with the basics behind selling one item, or at least getting the item listing in a decent shape for other people to see.

Selling your goods on eBay

6

First selling steps

1. Keen on selling on eBay? First of all, click on the Sell tab at the top of the home page.

2. Click on How to Sell on the right-hand side if you want eBay's guide to how to set about doing things.

3. Then click on the Sell Your Item button at the top of the screen to get going.

4. Read the blurb about what you're going to have to provide.

Important

When you list items for sale, eBay charges listing fees – it has to make its money somehow! Prices start at 15p. Check back to the site to find out the latest prices.

Selling your goods on eBay (cont.)

Account details

5 The first thing you have to do is enter your credit or debit card details, as eBay charges for every listing you put up. Type in your details, including the name and address in the boxes on the right-hand side. Then click Continue.

6 Your bank details are next. Entering these assures eBay of your identity. Then select how you want to pay your selling fees. The first question you'll then be asked is: how do you want to sell? In an auction, or at a fixed (Buy It Now) price? Make your decision – we go for Sell at online auction.

7 Then click Continue.

8 Here you need to make a decision about the category your item needs to be placed in. You can choose from the selection of main categories you're given, or enter an item keyword to find a category. We're selling a magazine, so we enter 'Magazines' and click Search.

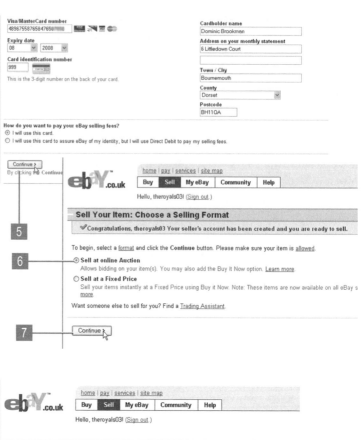

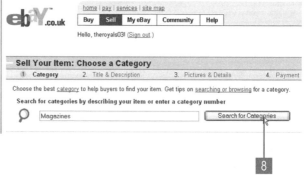

For your information

eBay has prepared a seller's checklist for you to tick off as you go through the selling process; you can find it at http://pages.ebay.co.uk/help/sell/checklist.html. A step-by-step guide to selling on eBay is at http://pages.ebay.co.uk/help/ebayexplained/selling/index.html?ssPageName=UKEEX:howtosell.

9

Sell Your Item: Choose a Category

| | Category | 2. Title & Description | 3. Pictures & Details | 4. Payment & Postage | 5. Review & Submit |

Choose the best category to help buyers to find your item. Get tips on searching or browsing for a category.

Search for categories by describing your item or enter a category number

Computer Magazines

[Search for Categories] | Browse for categories

Categories: Select one for your listing	Item match
⊙ Books, Comics & Magazines > Magazines > Computing/ IT/ Internet	78%
○ Musical Instruments > Pro Audio/ Equipment > Computer Recording/ Software	13%
○ Books, Comics & Magazines > Non-Fiction Books > Computing/ IT/ Internet	9%
○ Computing > Books & Manuals > Other Books & Manuals	9%

Second category (additional fees apply)
♀ Reach more buyers, boost bids by 18%, and increase final sale price by 17% on average.

To add a second category you must first select a category above.
○ None
○ PC & Video Gaming > Vintage Gaming > Commodore > Commodore 64/ 128 > Games
○ Books, Comics & Magazines > Magazines > Entertainment > Video Games
○ Choose your own second category on the next page

10

Second category (additional fees apply)
♀ Reach more buyers, boost bids by 18%, and increase final sale price by 17% on average.

To add a second category you must first select a category above.
○ None
○ PC & Video Gaming > Vintage Gaming > Commodore > Commodore 64/ 128 > Games
⊙ Books, Comics & Magazines > Magazines > Entertainment > Video Games
○ Choose your own second category on the next page

[< Back] [Continue >]

11

Category checks

9 'Magazines' gives us a few too many results to be comfortable with, so we modify our search to 'Computer Magazines'. This brings back four category results, with the top result of 'Books, Comics & Magazines < Magazines < Computing/IT/Internet' being the most relevant. We click in the little circle next to that category heading.

10 We then choose a second category to reach more buyers – Books, Comics & mags, entertainment, video games'.

11 That done, we click Continue.

Did you know ?

As eBay makes clear at http://pages.ebay.co.uk/what-to-sell/index.html, just about anything in your house can be sold to make money online. Start at the top of your house, in the loft or attic, and go through all the bedrooms, living rooms and kitchen areas to see what could make money. Toys and games, coins, stamps, antiques, clothes, jewellery, DVDs, furniture... the list is basically never ending. Do your research online and see what similar items are selling for on eBay before you plump for a price that you want your lot to go for.

Selling your goods on eBay (cont.)

Item description

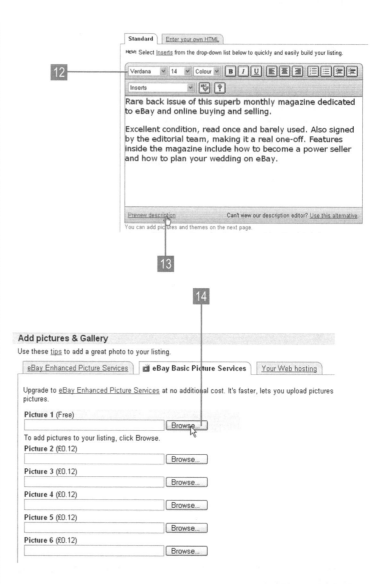

12 Categories sorted out, you can now concentrate on the important specifics of writing about your item. After entering important info such as the condition of the item, you enter the important 'Item Description'. You'll see a Microsoft Word-like window open with space for you to write all about your item. What are its features, benefits and condition? What is its background history? Is there anything unique or significant about the item? All the usual formatting options are available, allowing you to change font, color, font size, how it's indented, whether you want words bold, italic or underlined… a whole wealth of options.

13 If you're unsure about how things will look, click Preview description.

14 Next, enter your location details, and move on to the all-important aspect of providing photos or images of your item. eBay has some tools to help (cont.)

Timesaver tip

eBay has a selection of seller tools, at http://pages.ebay.com/sell/tools.html, which will help you get the perfect listing for your item. eBay's tool Turbo Lister, at http://pages.ebay.com/turbo%5Flister/, is a listing tool which can help you upload items in bulk and make your listings look impressively professional. The utility is free to download, and well worth it.

15

Select a theme
eBay Shops (12)

None
Stores Curves-Blue
Stores Curves-Fuschia
Stores Curves-Gold
Stores Fireworks-Green
Stores Fireworks-Orange
Stores Fireworks-Purple
Stores Metallic-Blue
Stores Metallic-Bronze

Select a layout
Standard
Photo on the left
Photo on the right
Photo on the bottom
Photo on the top

Preview listing

Increase your item's visibility

☐ Remember my selections in the section below.
Selections will be saved for the next time I list.

Preview your listing in search results

	Item Title	PayPal	Price	Bids	Time Listed▾
	This is an example with Gallery	⊘	£x.xx	-	11-Sep 16:51
>>	eBuyer and Online Seller magazine Exclusive copy signed by the editorial team	⊘	£0.50 £1.99	- *Buy It Now*	11-Sep 16:54
	This is an example with Bold		£x.xx	-	11-Sep 16:57

☑ Subtitle (£0.35)
Add a subtitle (searchable by item description only) to give buyers more information. See example

16

14 (cont.)
you out here. Getting this part of the process right is crucial – if the photos are too small, blurry, indistinct or generally poor, people will turn off your auction in droves. To find photos that you've taken of your item, click Browse to browse your PC for the relevant files.

15 You'll move on to more options for how you want your listing to look, as you scroll through theme and layout options provided for you by eBay. Do you want your listing to be posh and ornate, or functional and basic? Should the design border reflect what it is you're selling? Remember, you can play around to your heart's content here.

16 More options towards the bottom of the screen ask you to think about using Bold on your listings to attract attention – this will cost you an extra 75p. You can also think about highlighting and subtitles, which will give your buyer even more information.

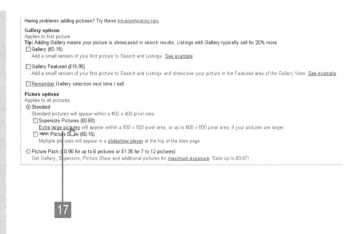

Final steps

17 We're coming to the end now, but there are still plenty of chances to change things. Take a careful look at the picture options to see what's suitable for your listing.

18 Now it's the all-important payment and postage options. Choose your payment methods very carefully.

Timesaver tip

Taking decent photographs of your item is an absolute must if you're serious about selling on eBay. A decent-quality digital camera (not necessarily one that has to have cost you hundreds of pounds, though) is a must, as is giving the buyer a selection of photos of your item, from different angles in decent light, to browse through. Remember, the more you give the buyer, the more likely they are to be tempted into joining your auction and placing a bid.

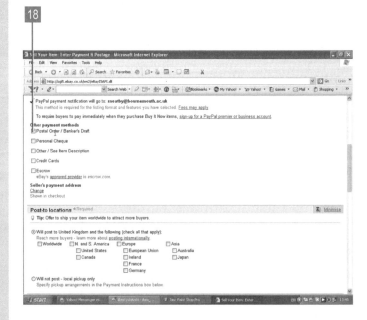

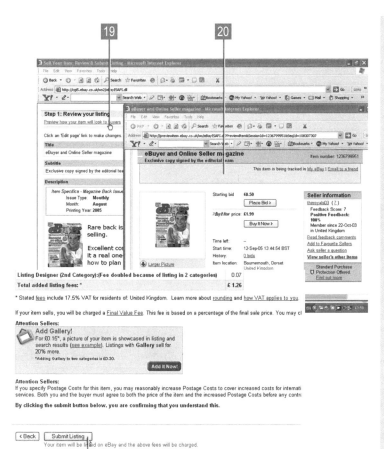

Auction time!

19 It's the final straight now, as you review and submit your listing, checking over everything involved, including your words, pictures and payment details. Even here, you can still preview things to see how it'll look to potential buyers – click on Preview how your item will look to buyers to see a new window open on the right.

20 This is exactly how the auction will look, with all your details and seller information. We're a bit disappointed about our picture, actually (though there is a larger picture further down the screen), so we may change and adapt before it's too late. Changes here could be the difference between your auction being a flop and a massive hit!

21 With everything checked, one more click of Submit Listing and you're done. Now sit back and get engrossed in the complexities and excitement of online auctions – fingers crossed, people will come flocking to your item and start a bidding war!

For your information

The holy grail of eBay selling is to become a PowerSeller – an elite band of top-quality merchants. To be given PowerSeller status at eBay, you must meet certain conditions as to how many sales you've made and what feedback you get – the criteria is at http://pages.ebay.co.uk/services/buyandsell/powerseller/criteria.html. You're basically looking at a minimum of 98% positive feedback, and a minimum feedback rating of 100 that you reach and maintain. There are even different PowerSeller levels, from bronze through to platinum and titanium. Basically, if you're dealing with a PowerSeller online, you're dealing with a highly respected, trustworthy member of the eBay community.

Finding some alternatives to eBay

Finding decent alternatives to eBay is, to put it bluntly, a difficult task. eBay is so far ahead of the field that it's untrue; its rivals are pretty much forced to try and adopt different strategies and pricing structures to try and make themselves stand out from the number one player in the game. Ultimately, it's a race for number 2, being run primarily by CQOut (www.cqout.co.uk), eBid (http://uk.ebid.tv) and QXL (www.qxl.co.uk). Many of these offer lower prices and better customer service than eBay – eBay, after all, is famous for making it virtually impossible to find a phone number for the company, or successfully managing to speak to a human being from its Customer Service Department.

Often the best way to see if these auction alternatives are worth a punt is to see how many

items are on sale at any one time; if there are thousands and thousands, then that's an indication that the site is in good health. Click on Forum of many of the site homepages to see how many people are about, chatting about the service – you'll pick up loads of info that way.

One final trend to bear in mind is the relatively unique phenomenon of reverse bidding, where the lowest unique bid wins the item in question. You can pick up expensive goods at rock-bottom prices this way, although it's a bit of a gamble to bid, and you're often charged a lot for the privilege of entering the auction. Sites like http://www.auction-air.com/ offer this service.

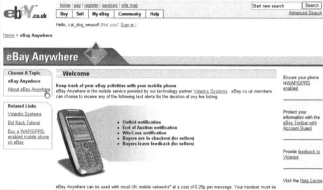

The amount of extra tools that eBay offers you to get the most out of your auction life is impressive, and one of the best is eBay Anywhere, which allows you to receive text message alerts on your mobile phone about the progress of an auction that you're involved in. You should see banner ads promoting the service dotted around eBay, or you can go straight to http://pages.ebay.co.uk/ebay_anywhere/ to find out all about the service. At 25p per message, you can get Outbid notification, End of Auction notification, Win/Lose notification and more. Registration is free, and the only real requirement is that your phone is GPRS-enabled.

Jargon buster

GPRS – stands for General Packet Radio Service, and is a technology fairly new to mobile phones, that allows very fast transmission of data and a new raft of interactive facilities. Find out more about GPRS at http://ebay.volantis.net/anywhere/public/GprsSetup.do.

Finding and using a genealogy website: 1837Online.com

Registration

1 Here we are at 1837online.com. Take a look around to familiarise yourself with everything. Look at the Site Benefits to see what's on offer.

2 A free trial of the site is also provided. Click on the free trial link on the left to find out all about it. Records available in the free trial include births in England and Wales during July, August and September 1868, deaths in England and Wales during January 1984, and births, marriages and deaths overseas during 1870.

3 Click on Register to begin.

4 Enter your personal details and click Submit when you're done.

5 A sample image will appear on screen, and if you can't see it (as we can't), you need to download a little piece of software known as the DjVu viewer, free of charge. Click the underlined link to download it, going on to choose your computer version.

Tracing your family tree online has taken off hugely in the last few years. People have been quick to cotton on to the fact that what once used to be a massively time-consuming, dusty, troublesome task, as you trooped down to the local library or public records office to try and get a glimpse into your family's past, has suddenly become brilliantly easy and fascinating, thanks to the internet.

Many companies have spent a lot of money uploading thousands of records onto the internet and into publicly accessible databases for you to search through – centuries of history, suddenly unlocked for everyone. Just to give you an idea of the figures, at www.ancestry.co.uk, there are some 275 million names to go through. That's a lot of data! Obviously the bulk of the data comes from events such as the 1861 and 1901 censuses in the UK, but, as is common with many genealogy sites, you can also trawl through marriage indexes, parish and probate records and civil registration lists (in July 1837, the civil registration format for births, marriages and deaths was introduced to the UK and Wales).

Many genealogy sites exist as massive portals, pointing you off in all sorts of directions to get to the information you need – even with the power of the internet, this is not a pastime that you're going to be able to complete within a few hours.

Many of the records you can access are free, although some sites operate on a system of credits that you need to buy up before you can get to all the data. If you're serious about genealogy and tracing your family's past, you shouldn't mind too much paying a little bit for the privilege.

We're going to focus on one site, 1837Online.com, to give you a first understanding of how a typical example of this genre works.

County/State:	
Postcode/ZIP code: *	BH1 1QA
Country: *	United Kingdom
Telephone:	
Mobile:	
Alternative Email address:	

You can change these details later using the **My Account** section of the site.

About 1837online.com

Where did you find out about this site? *	Internet Made Easy
Which of the following best describes your reason for using the Birth, Marriage and Death indexes? *	- Other -

Click submit to confirm changes.

4 ———————— SUBMIT

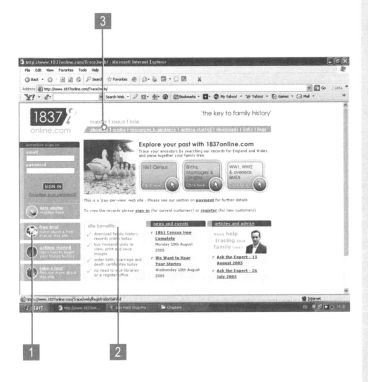

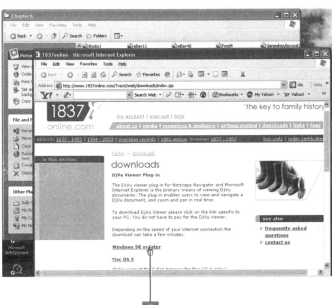

Timesaver tip

If you need a bit of help as you make your way around the site, click on the resources and guidance link from the top of the screen. You'll then be taken to advice about all sorts of things you'll be doing on the site, such as finding surnames, accessing adoption records, looking at parish registers, tracing living relatives, finding divorce records and general tips about the births, marriages and deaths data. Invaluable!

Finding and using a genealogy website: 1837Online.com (cont.)

Starting to search

6   We click on search above 1861 census.

7   We then opt for a person search.

8   If you're a novice to the whole genealogy online game, you may want to click on search tips to get some useful pointers as to what you should be doing.

For your information

1837Online.com has six payment plans for you to choose from. The more units you buy, the cheaper they become, so it may be worth buying in bulk. You can choose up to the £120 price plan, which buys you 2,400 units – this is probably more suitable for the genealogy fanatic!

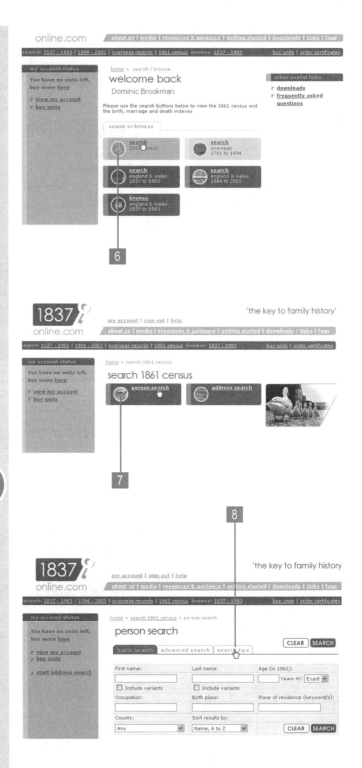

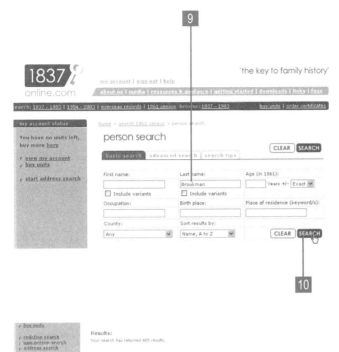

Search results

9 We're doing a basic person search, so just enter the surname we're concerned with.

10 We then click Search.

11 Here are the results. Click on View under View Household Transcript to dig further.

12 To be able to view the details, you need to have credits. Click on buy units to do just that.

For your information

If you want to get in touch with 18370nline for further information, its contact details are as follows:

Postal address:
1837online.com
24 Britton Street
London EC1M 5UA
UK

Telephone:
0870 777 1837

E-mail: info@1837online.com

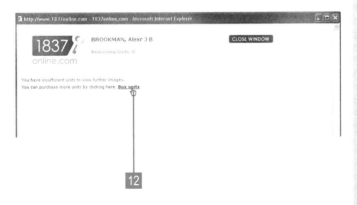

Finding and using a genealogy website: 1837Online.com (cont.)

More browsing

13 Payment costs and details will be outlined here. Click in the green circle next to the plan you want.

14 Enter your credit card details and click Submit.

15 Once your credits have been accepted, how you go about things is obviously up to you. We'll just point out a couple more features. If you like, you can browse English and Welsh records from 1837 to 1983, so we click on that option back on the home page of www.1837online.com.

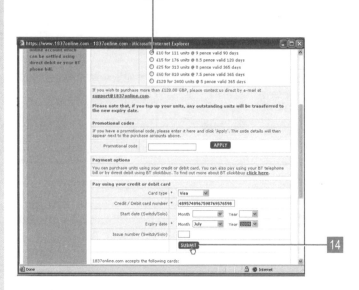

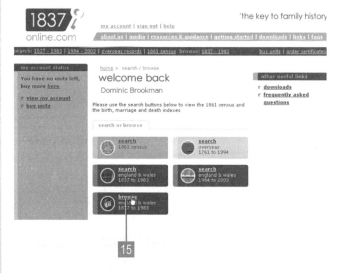

Timesaver tip

Click on Links on the home page to get a series of further useful genealogical links, including the 1901 census for England and Wales.

Timesaver tip

Click on Getting Started for a whole host of useful tips for the beginner. We especially liked the section on organising your records, which is tremendously important if you're taking things seriously. A methodical, accurate approach to logging, recommends the site, can save you hours of time and hassle in the long run.

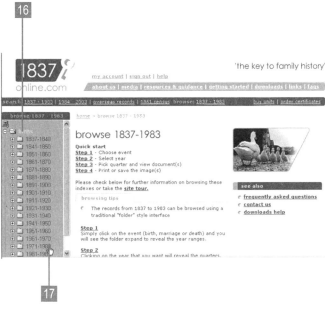

Final steps

16 Select whether you want to browse through births, marriages or deaths.

17 Then choose the year period you want. We go for 1971–1980.

18 Clicking on the 1971–1980 folder on the left-hand side gives you the years from that decade. Clicking a folder next to a year opens further sub-folders, where you can choose on a specific set of months from the year in question.

Did you know ?

Alex Haley's 1976 book *Roots* is generally credited with having made the pursuit of genealogy popular.

Finding and using a genealogy website: 1837Online.com (cont.)

Final step

 The list of records from the year and month period in question will be shown. Again, you can click on View and access further details, providing you now have sufficient credits.

Timesaver tip

Ask the Expert articles, available from the home page, can give you many useful pointers as to the direction which you should be taking.

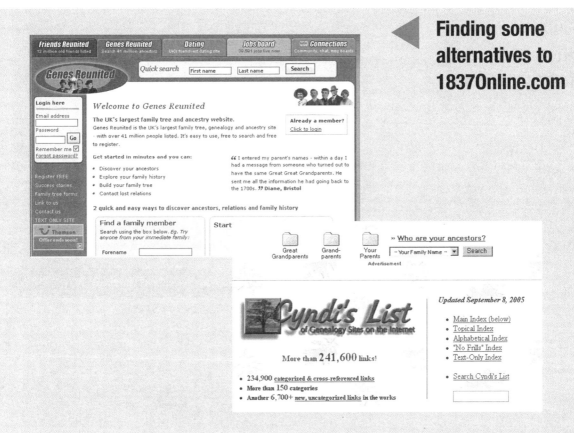

As we've already mentioned, finding alternatives to 1837Online is not a difficult task. The hard part is which site to use, so we recommend a healthy dose of experimentation, having a day or so just looking around the countless sites that are on offer.

We've already mentioned Ancestry.com, which has a healthy selection of records for you to access. Pretty much everyone has heard of the internet smash hit Friends Reunited, which lets you trace old school chums – but did you know that, along with its dating site (www.friendsreuniteddating.co.uk), it also has a genealogy arm? Genes Reunited (www.genesreunited.co.uk) describes itself as the UK's largest family tree and ancestry website, with over 37 million people listed. It's free to search and free to register, so you could get some vital information about your ancestors here, start building

your family tree and even contact lost relations. Very impressive.

Moving on, the curiously named Cyndi's List (www.cyndislist.com) acts as a portal to other sites, with over 240,200 links and 150 categories. GENUKI (www.genuki.org.uk) has stacks of UK and Irish records, including church history, military records, court records and maps. And the 1901 census for England and Wales can be accessed at www.1901census.nationalarchives.gov.uk, letting you search over 32,000,000 people.

Obviously this only scratches the surface of the world of genealogy online, but part of the joy of the hobby is discovering sites and new links and information yourself. Have fun as you dive into the fascinating world of the past.

Finding some alternatives to 18370nline.com

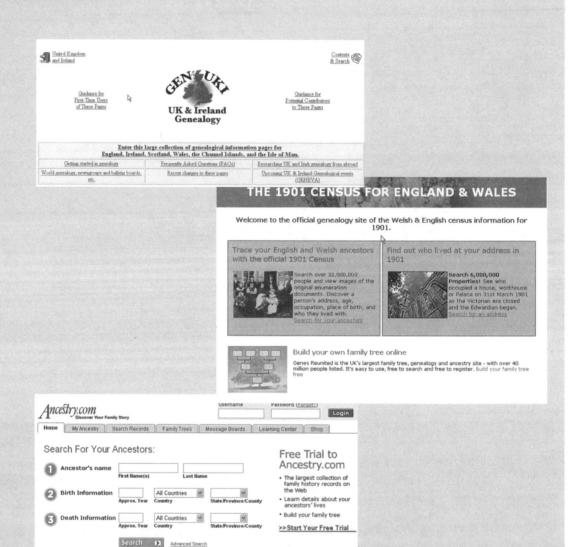

Your life online: travel and health

Introduction

One of the major plus points of the internet is how it opens up a whole world of exciting travel possibilities, with just a few mouse clicks. Whereas before a holiday abroad involved months of planning, a trip to the local travel agents and collecting a bewildering array of brochures and leaflets for your chosen sunspots, now you can decide where you want to go, pick a couple of powerful, easy-to-use websites and have your booking done and dusted within a matter of minutes. Amazing. And not only that, but the prices quoted by some online firms for flights, hotels and package holidays can be absolutely staggering – no longer is worldwide travel the sole provision of the elite rich. Obviously you need to exercise a healthy degree of scepticisim if deals seem too good to be true – some online travel firms have come in for fierce criticism recently for unleashing a series of 'hidden' charges on your basic holiday rate, which mean that your dream bargain vacation suddenly turns into a wallet-busting nightmare. Nevertheless, you really can save hundreds of pounds with the help of the internet when it comes to holidays, which leaves you more time to spend on treats when you're actually away!

As well as helping you jet off to far-flung destinations, the internet can also help significantly with domestic-based travel, which is why we'll also look at snapping up UK train tickets in a flash. And the practicalities of travel shouldn't be ignored, either. It's all too easy to get horrendously lost when you're out and about, which is where map and directions sites such as Multimap really come into play. From the initial holiday planning stages, all the way through to finding the quickest way to where you're going, we've got it covered over the next few pages.

What you'll do

Register with Multimap

Find directions with Multimap

Explore some of Multimap's other features

Find some alternatives to Multimap

Register with The Trainline

Buy a train ticket online with The Trainline

Find some alternatives to The Trainline

Use Expedia to plan a flight and hotel

Find some alternatives to Expedia

Get the latest health information online with NHS Direct

Find other health information online

Finally, we'll take time out from all this hectic globetrotting and find out about how to look after ourselves properly, with the help of online health sites. This is a mildly controversial area, in so far as there's a lot of charlatans and quick-fix merchants out there, eager to play on people's health paranoia to make a quick buck with so-called 'miracle' cures and remedies. The level of mis-information and scaremongering when it comes to medical websites can be seriously off-putting. There are, however, plenty of dedicated, professional, honest and trustworthy health sites out there, so we'll point you in the direction of some of the very best UK resources. And, of course, the crucial fact to remember is that if you're seriously worried, you should book an appointment with your real-life GP as soon as possible. When it comes to your health, the internet should be used as a valuable background information tool, and nothing more.

Let's kick off by planning a long journey in the UK, with the help of the renowned and popular Multimap site.

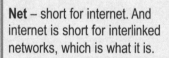

Important

If you're worried about Multimap giving your personal information to all and sundry, there's no need. None of your details will be disclosed without your consent, and if you want further written proof of this, take a look at the site's privacy policy at www.multimap.com/static/priva cypolicy.htm

Jargon buster

Net – short for internet. And internet is short for interlinked networks, which is what it is.

The motto of Multimap (www.multimap.com) is 'online maps to everywhere', and this is no lie. It may seem an obvious service to provide – directions between any two given points in Great Britain – but you'd be surprised just how many sites manage to make a mess of what should be a flexible, intuitive process. Multimap adds the icing to an already extremely impressive cake with a wealth of extra features, such as an hotel search, aerial photos and tube maps, but for the moment we're just going to concentrate on registering with the service, a five-minute (tops) procedure which will save a good deal of time and hassle in the long run.

Registering with Multimap

Multimap registration

1 Open your web browser and type in www.multimap.com into the Address Bar at the top of the screen. You'll be taken to the Multimap home page. Click on the Register link, which you'll find at the top-right of the screen.

2 You'll now be asked to enter some of your personal details, including name, postcode, date of birth and mobile number. When you enter your username and password at the top of the screen, try and pick something memorable that you're not likely to forget. Not all of these fields are compulsory – just those with red stars next to them. When you're done, click on the Submit Now button at the bottom of the screen.

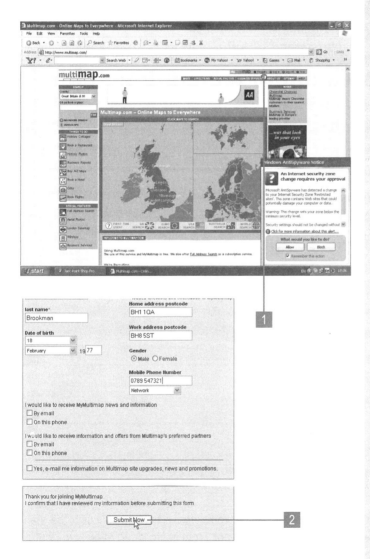

Finding directions with Multimap

Get directions

1 You should now see that you're registered, and you'll even be provided with a nice full-color map at the bottom of the screen of your surrounding area, taken from the postcode you entered at the registration process. The first thing you now need to do is click on the Directions tab at the top of the screen.

2 This is the simple bit, really. You basically just need to enter the postcode of the place you're starting off from, and the postcode of the place you wish to go to. Before you get directions, you need to check Multimap understands the location, so click the Verify address button every time you enter a postcode.

So we've registered with the site, and now it's time to get our directions, which should take only a matter of a few minutes or so. The directions will be presented in a format ideal for printing out and having with you in the car as you drive – try and get a passenger to read them rather than yourself, of course! Note that the directions you do get are split up into different sections – if you're going on an especially long route, Multimap will give you a couple of reminders to take a break, as recommended by all motoring organisations. Basically, every 2 hours you should be thinking of having a stretch of your legs or a stop at a service station.

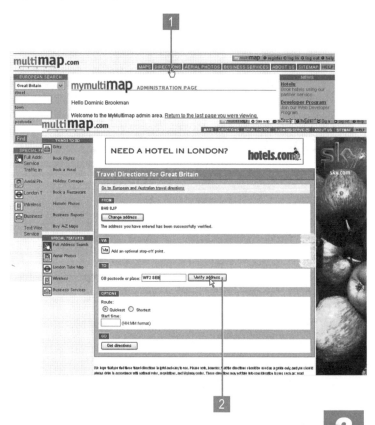

Did you know ?

If you're keen on being very specific about your journey, and maybe need to factor in a stopping-off point to stretch your legs or carry out an errand, you can choose to go via a specific place on your route from A to B. Simply click the Via button after entering your From postcode to make sure that Multimap sends you through a specific place.

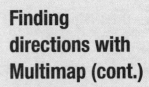

Travel Directions for Great Britain

Go to European and Australian travel directions

FROM

BH8 8JP

[Change address]

The address you have entered has been successfully verified.

VIA

[Via] Add an optional stop-off point.

TO

WF2 8EB

[Change address]

The address you have entered has been successfully verified.

OPTIONS

Route:
◉ Quickest ○ Shortest
Start time:
10.00   (HH.MM format)

GO

[Get directions]

3 ———————— 4

ROUTE

#	Instruction		Map	Distance so far	Time
1	Depart on Wellington Road	for 0.1 miles	Map	0 miles (0 km)	10:00
2	Turn left onto Beechey Road	for 0.2 miles	Map	0.1 miles (0.2 km)	10:00
3	Turn right onto Lowther Road	for 0.2 miles	Map	0.3 miles (0.5 km)	10:01
4	Turn left onto Bennett Road	for 0.5 miles	Map	0.5 miles (0.8 km)	10:01
5	Turn right onto A3049 Richmond Park Road	for 0.1 miles	Map	0.9 miles (1.5 km)	10:02
6	Turn left onto Queen's Park South Drive	for 0.4 miles	Map	1.1 miles (1.7 km)	10:03
7	Bear left onto Slip Road	for 0.1 miles	Map	1.4 miles (2.3 km)	10:04
8	Turn left onto A338 Wessex Way	for 7.6 miles	Map	1.5 miles (2.5 km)	10:04
9	At the roundabout, take the third exit onto A338 Ringwood Road	for 1.3 miles	Map	9.2 miles (14.8 km)	10:15
10	At the roundabout, take the second exit onto Slip Road	for 0.3 miles	Map	10.5 miles (16.8 km)	10:18
11	Continue straight ahead onto A31	for 10.2 miles	Map	10.7 miles (17.3 km)	10:19
12	Continue straight ahead onto M27 (M27/J1)	for 8.5 miles	Map	20.9 miles (33.7 km)	10:31
13	Continue straight ahead onto M3 (J4)	for 1.3 miles	Map	29.4 miles (47.3 km)	10:39
14	Exit onto M3 (M3/J13)	for 8.9 miles	Map	30.7 miles (49.4 km)	10:40
15	Exit to the left onto M3 Slip Road (J9)	for 0.2 miles	Map	39.6 miles (63.7 km)	10:58
16	At the roundabout, take the second exit onto A34 Winchester By-pass	for 29.3 miles	Map	39.8 miles (64 km)	10:59
17	At the roundabout, take the second exit onto A34	for 33.3 miles	Map	69.1 miles (111.2 km)	11:23

That's around 2 hours of driving, it's time for a break.
Be sure to find a safe place to stop.

Your instructions

3 There are a couple more co-ordinates to set before you can get your prized series of concise directions. Once you've verified the addresses, you get to the Options – do you want the shortest route, or the quickest? There is a difference between the two, so think carefully. Then you can set a starting time if you wish, before clicking Get directions.

4 And here are the directions for our journey from Bournemouth. Note how they're cleverly divided up into different stages – basically every time you need to go on a new road or make a new turn, you'll be given a new command. You're also given the estimated mileage between each step, the completed mileage and how long you've been going – all the stats a driver could need! If one particular step puzzles you, click on the Map link to see a detailed drawing of what you're being expected to do.

7

Timesaver tip

In the unlikely event that you found Multimap's directions not good enough, why not click on the Please use our feedback form link at the bottom of the directions screen? You can then air your grievances and maybe lead to a change in the designated route that will benefit legions of drivers for years to come!

Exploring some of Multimap's other features

Other Multimap features

1 Out and about in the capital? Then you might need a tube map to help you go speedily from one area of London to another. Back on the home page of www.multimap.com, all you have to do is scroll down and click on London Tubemap to get your very own guide to the famous underground system. Very useful.

2 You can even start sorting out your accommodation, as well. On the home page of Multimap again, click on Book a hotel. You'll then be taken to this screen, which tells you that Multimap runs a hotel service in conjunction with its partner, Active Hotels. Select a placename or postcode in the dialog box at the top of the screen, give your check-in date and how many nights you want to stay, then click Search to get a list of available hotels. Easy!

One of the most interesting ways that the consumer has benefited over the last couple of years, in regards to the internet, is the fierce competition that's out there. With so many websites jostling for your time, money and attention, the days of a site offering the one basic service seem long gone. Just look at Google, for instance – once a humble search engine, it's now diversifying into all kinds of interesting avenues, such as email, internet acceleration and, yes, maps. So it should come as no surprise to you to hear that Multimap does more than just print out directions for you – here are a couple more juicy features for you to get your teeth into.

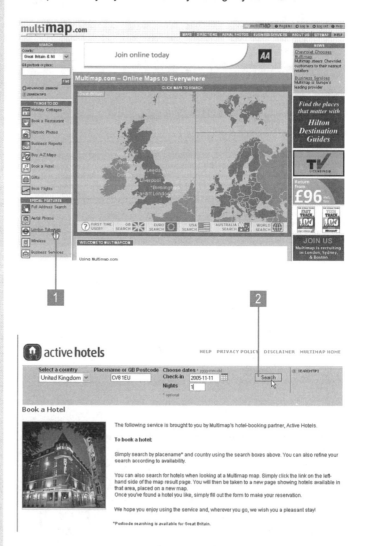

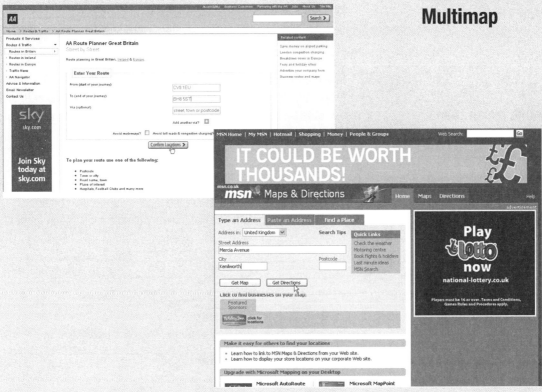

Multimap isn't the only option when it comes to looking for the very best, concise directions, of course. As we've mentioned, Google has leapt to the fore recently with Google Maps (maps.google.com – note you'll need IE 5.5 or above, 7.1 or above of Netscape and 7.5 of Opera or above to get the service to work), which brings the famous search engine's clarity of thought and speed to giving you the very best in clear, detailed maps.

The AA's route planner, which you can find at http://www.theaa.com/travelwatch/planner_main.jsp has a simple journey finder for you to get to grips with, with added options, such as being able to choose to avoid motorways, toll roads of congestion charging, proving a welcome bonus. MapQuest

(www.mapquest.co.uk) gives excellent driving directions, and don't underestimate the concise way that MSN Maps & Directions (http://maps.msn.co.uk/) presents its findings, either.

Ultimately, the point of using these kind of sites is to make your life easier and save you time getting lost – although no map site can foresee all the major traffic incidents that seem to occur on our roads almost daily. Occasionally, you may find a few eccentric suggestions from some of these sites as to the best way to go, but in general you should find that all these sites mentioned make getting from A to B a good deal easier, helping you arrive at your chosen destination in a positive, fresh frame of mind. Happy motoring!

Registering with The Trainline

Trainline registration

1. Here we are at the home page of The Trainline (www.thetrainline.com). You can dive straight in and book tickets first if you like, but if this is your first visit to the site, and you're planning on using it regularly, it's a good idea to register first. Down the menu bar on the left-hand side of the screen, you'll see the Register link. Click it.

2. As is usual with these kinds of sites, you'll be asked a few simple questions so the site can find out a little about you. Try and enter a memorable username and password, but one that isn't the same as what you're using on other internet websites. Decide whether you want to be sent further useful information by the people behind the site, view the privacy policy if you wish, and click the box at the bottom to say that you've read and understood the terms and conditions. Then click Register Now. And that's it!

You can hardly have failed to see some of the adverts in the national press over the last couple of years, promising cross-country travel on the train at rock-bottom prices. To take advantage of such low deals, you need to know what your journey is well in advance (often about a month or so in some cases, which is not much use if you're more of a spontaneous traveler), get online and then basically just cross your fingers that there's a value or saver return ticket for where you want to go. Virgin Trains' website (www.virgintrains.co.uk) is one of the best train sites around to snap up some great deals, but the different permutations and offers can get a tad confusing at times, so we're going to take a look at The Trainline (www.thetrainline.com) instead. Whilst you may not strike gold with an especially low price here, you can get times and tickets here very quickly, saving you the hassle of aeons spent hanging on the telephone or queuing up at the local station's ticket office. To kick off, we're going to look at the very simple registration process.

Timesaver tip

Still in a mess about what's going on, and unsure about what to do? There's a highly useful 'help' link on the left-hand side of the screen which gives you some Frequently Asked Questions (FAQs) – twenty-two pages of them, in fact. These should sort you out.

Over the next couple of pages, we're going to look at snapping up a ticket from The Trainline, for a journey from London Waterloo to Bournemouth. You don't have to use the site to buy tickets, of course – you can just use it to get a quick timetable of trains, and sort out the payment later. It's a quicker and less time-consuming process, however, to get times and tickets at the same time, leaving you free to concentrate on the journey and not having to worry about that desperate last-minute queue for tickets. Recent regulations have meant that many train providers are getting very strict on people not having a valid ticket when they board the train – the excuse that you were 'just going to buy one on board' doesn't really wash any more, and could land you with a hefty fine. So it really is worth sorting it all out as early a time as possible, from the comfort of your home PC.

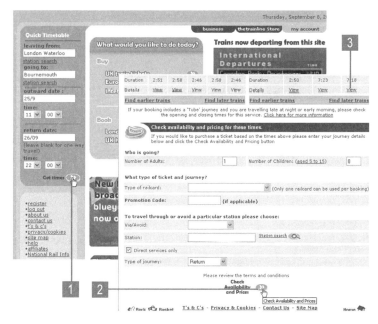

Timesaver tip

You can even use The Trainline to plan a day or evening of entertainment or cultural events, such as top West End shows or a trip to Disneyland Paris. The Trainline's sister sites often have some great travel+hotel+show ticket deals going on, so check out the dialog box on the right-hand side of the home page entitled UK & European Shortbreaks from The Trainline for more info.

Get the times of trains

1 First things first – we need to set the parameters of our journey, so The Trainline can go off and do its business. You need to enter, in the dialog box on the left-hand side of the screen, where you're going from and your destination, the outward date and the return date, and the times you'd like to go and come back. When you're done, click on Get times.

2 The times for your specified journey will appear at the top of the screen, with the duration stated as well. If you want to see a journey in more specific detail, click on the View link.

3 Scroll down the screen and you can set some further ticket details – whether you have a railcard or a promotion code (these are sometimes found in the national press, or if the site itself is running any special deals for members), and whether or not you want to go via any specific stations (this is unlikely, unless you're picking someone up along the way). When you're happy, click on Check Availability & Prices.

Buying train tickets online with The Trainline (cont.)

Get pricing details

1 Once you've decided on the broad range of times when you want to travel, you can start the all-important process of finding out how much it's all going to cost. Because we're booking in advance, we're being offered a return fee of under £39.00 from London to Bournemouth – quite a bargain.

2 Just see how the prices vary – we've got everything from £39 for a network away day, all the way up to £119.20 for a first open return. Being poor, impoverished types, we click inside the circle for a network away break, leaving at 11.35 and returning 22.11 the next day.

3 Here, you can opt to get this journey texted to you if you like.

4 Once you've set all those parameters, as a further time-saving tactic, ask yourself this question: are you likely to do this journey often? If you are, you can choose to nominate it as a favourite journey, give it a name, and save it, so that the site remembers it on your next visit. Very convenient. Click Save if you want to do this.

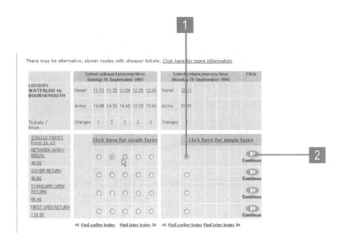

Did you know ?

There's a number of different delivery options that you can choose from when you're looking to pick up tickets. Choose between first class post, a 'Fastticket' machine (located at many stations), next day special delivery, or same day delivery. Unless you're really paranoid or in an incredible rush, first class post should be fine, and won't cost anything extra. Expect them to arrive 3 to 5 days before your journey.

Buying train tickets online with The Trainline (cont.)

Get pricing details

5 On the next screen, click in the box to say that you understand the terms and conditions, and that the terms of the booking are correct. Choose how you want the tickets delivered, before entering this screen, where you need to enter the relevant address details. At any time if you make a mistake or want to go back a few steps, just click on the Back button at the bottom-left. Click Continue when you've entered the relevant details.

6 We've reached what the Trainline describes as Step 6 out of 7 of the whole process – and it's only taken a matter of minutes. Here, you're given the train times for the final time, the ticket type and the cost... all you need to do now is pay for it! Click Continue to payment.

?

Did you know ?

Before you go to the payment page, click on Printer Friendly Page to get a printout of your booking. This gives you added peace of mind, and can come in useful in the unlikely event that there's a problem.

Buying train tickets online with The Trainline (cont.)

Make your payment

1 And now it's time to fork out the necessary readies. Many people, especially those new to the internet, are worried about the security of online payments – there's been loads of scare stories in the national press which have put people off. The truth is, however, as long as you look for cast-iron indications that a site is secure, such as a little padlock icon in the bottom-left of your browser window, you'll be fine. All the reputable websites you've learned about in this book, such as Amazon, Tesco or The Trainline, offer rock-solid online security. There's a big padlock icon on this payment screen to tell you that payments are secure – click the link underneath it for further details if you wish. Otherwise, enter your card type, number, expiry date and security code, then click on Buy ticket. And that's it!

Total Cost of Ticket(s) :	39.00 GBP
Total Travel Essentials Charges :	2.00 GBP
Credit Card fee:	1.50 GBP
TOTAL PRICE	42.50 GBP

A fee of £1.50 is applied to all Credit and Charge Card transactions. Debit Cards are free.

All payments are secure.
Click here for further details

Enter your payment details below...

Card type:	Visa Credit	Update
Card number:	I56565656565656565565	
Card expiry date:	February	2008
Card issue number:		(Switch only)
Card start date: (Switch only)		
Card Security Code:	545	

(In all cases, except AMEX, we require 3 digits - click here for more detail)

Please click 'Buy Ticket' and we'll confirm receipt of your order.

Buy ticket
Buy Ticket

Please wait for confirmation. If you experience any problems please call 0870 010 1296

Back   Basket   **T's & C's** - **Privacy & Cookies** - **Contact Us** - **Site Map**   Home

1

For your information

Another indication that this is a secure site is the BT Secure Site by Verisign icon on the home page. Click on the icon to view more information about this scheme, which describes itself as 'the sign of trust on the net'. Look out for it on your internet travels as an added indication that things are as they should be when it comes to online security.

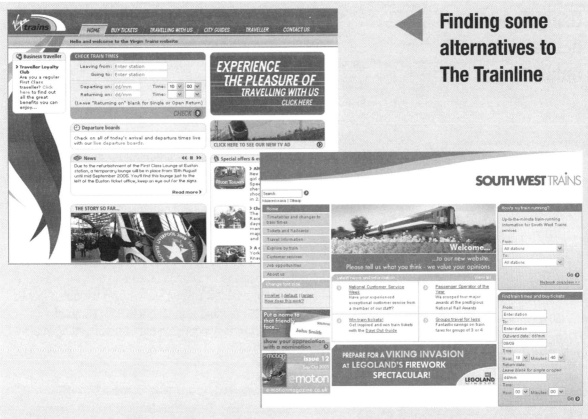

As we've already mentioned, The Trainline isn't the only site you can turn to when it comes to getting your train tickets online. One of the most heavily advertised sites is the Virgin Trains site (www.virgintrains.co.uk), which allows you not only buy tickets for Virgin trains, but also any journey across the UK. The site has had a number of redesigns over the years and is currently in its best incarnation, with a host of added extras, such as special offers and events, news updates and city guides, adding to the experience. The Buy Tickets link allows you to chance your arm with Virgin Value, which takes you to a separate sub-site where you can see if you strike it lucky with cheap tickets. When Virgin actually releases its cheap tickets is a closely guarded secret that no investigations at numerous ticket offices by this author managed to uncover, so there's more than an element of pot luck about this process, but as a general rule, the earlier you start

browsing, the better. If the Value option doesn't come up trumps, you can go through a similar-looking process to The Trainline's to get tickets for any UK train, and choose from a variety of postage options as usual.

You can also look online for the website for your own local train operator – there's a good chance that there will, at the very least, be some sort of online presence. Here's the site for SouthWest Trains (www.swtrains.co.uk), which operates the southwest lines of the UK (unsurprisingly). The actual train ticket buying aspect of this site actually takes you back to The Trainline, funnily enough – showing just how highly that site is regarded. You can also get some great ideas for days out, and find out the usual timetable and engineering works details. Happy travelling!

Using Expedia to plan a flight and hotel

Setting your options

1   So let's set about creating our 'perfect trip'. We're off to the stunning Canadian city of Vancouver, and we'd like to sort out a flight and a hotel from Expedia's comprehensive directory. There are six options available here – you can go for flight only, hotel only or car only, or mix and match to save. We click in the circle next to Flight + Hotel.

2   We're departing from London Heathrow, so enter that underneath Departing from. We then set our departure date and the time of day which we'd like to go – morning.

3   We enter Vancouver in the Going to box, then enter our return date and the time of day we'd like to come back.

Expedia (www.expedia.co.uk) must rank as one of the best travel websites out there. You may have seen the site advertised on national TV over the last couple of years, but the sheer depth, efficiency and professionalism of the site means that it speaks for itself in many respects. The key to the site's success lies in its flexibility, and the fact that it puts so many of the travel decisions in the hands of you, the user. Just want to get the best deals on flights? No problem. Want to get everything sorted out in one visit, from flights to hotel reservations to car hire and sightseeing suggestions? Easy. Expedia's intelligent way of sussing out what you need from your holiday means that you can create a tailor-made holiday where all the important parameters have been set by you – there's none of that 'you must do this, this and this' approach so beloved by inferior websites. The attention to detail is mightily impressive – little touches like getting the occasional email before you fly out with suggestions for what to do when you land are much appreciated. Over the next few pages, we're going to book a flight and hotel in one fell swoop, and also take a look at some of Expedia's rivals and how they approach the issue of getting you away in style.

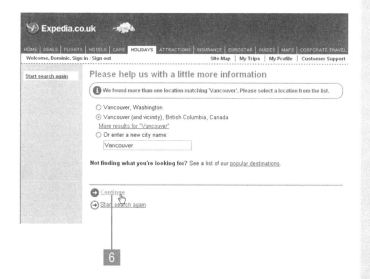

Using Expedia to plan a flight and hotel (cont.)

Setting your options

4 Now select the number of adults and children going.

5 And click Search to set Expedia off looking for relevant holidays.

6 Expedia now just needs us to clear up whether we mean Vancouver, Washington, or Vancouver, Canada, so we click in the circle next to the latter option and then click on Continue.

Timesaver tip

If you want to get regular holiday news and details of special offers delivered straight to your Inbox, simply enter your email address in the dialog box on the left-hand side of the home page, underneath where it says Sign up for email. Then click Submit. Your email address won't be passed on to any third parties, and you'll soon be getting exclusive email travel offers in your mailbox.

Using Expedia to plan a flight and hotel (cont.)

Vancouver decisions

7 Let's get our London to Vancouver search results into some sort of order. The Sort by bar at the top of the screen lets you sort by price, hotel name, hotel class and more. We click in the Price circle to sort by price, so the cheapest option appears at the top.

8 Each result is blocked off from the next one, so you can clearly get a handle on what's being offered. Inside each result, you'll see a picture and brief description of the hotel, and how many stars the hotel is.

9 You'll also see the logo of the flight operator who is getting you there, and details of the outbound and return legs of the flight.

10 If this particular deal strikes your fancy, click on Choose and continue.

11 Things are starting to take shape now, but we've realised that, as we're not the best flyers in the world, we'd like to see if there's a shorter flight. So we click on Choose a different flight for this trip.

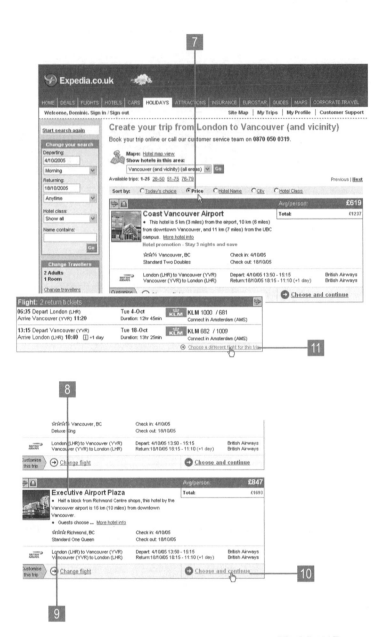

Timesaver tip

In conjunction with reading this tutorial on Expedia, find out even more information by clicking on Expedia User Guide on the bar that runs across the top of the screen. You'll be taken to a series of How do I? examples, which will make everything clear.

Trip details

Book your trip online or call our customer service team on **0870 050 0319**.

Sub-total for this trip:	£1,692.98	Included:
Average price per passenger:	£846.49	▪ Items selected, taxes, & fees for flight.
Insurance for all travellers:	£90.00	Insurance was added for benefit when travelling. **You can**
Total price for this trip:	£1,782.98	**remove the insurance option below.**

Flight: 2 return tickets

13:50 Depart London (LHR)	Tue 4-Oct	BRITISH AIRWAYS	British Airways 87
Arrive Vancouver (YVR) **15:15**	Duration: 9hr 25min		Direct flight
18:15 Depart Vancouver (YVR)	Tue 18-Oct	BRITISH AIRWAYS	British Airways 86
Arrive London (LHR) **11:10** ⓘ +1 day	Duration: 8hr 55min		Direct flight

➔ Choose a different flight or airport for this trip.

`12`

Travel insurance

Select Insurance Options - We strongly recommend you buy insurance before travelling.

Insurance Options	Price - for all travellers
◉ Single trip - Cancellation, Medical, Baggage & Other _Details_	Included
○ Annual Multi Trip Worldwide - Cancellation, Medical, Baggage & Other _Details_	+ £66.00
○ No thanks, I already have travel insurance.	- £90.00
☐ Add Winter Sports Option to my policy	£90.00

Total:	£1,782.98	Included:
Avg/person:	£891.49	▪ Items selected, taxes, & fees for flight.
		Insurance was added for benefit when travelling. **You can**
		remove the insurance option above.

Re-price Made changes? Calculate the new price with selected upgrades.

`13` ➔ Continue booking this trip.

➔ Search and view other trips.

Timesaver tip

Despite the introduction of the Euro in many countries over the last couple of years, working out currency requirements can be a bind – and of course, the further you travel, the more likely you are to have to deal with a totally foreign currency. So, as part of your pre-holiday preparation, it's a good idea to know exactly where you stand when it comes to your finances, and what a certain amount of English sterling converts to overseas. Expedia has a currency converter, which will help you get a grip on what the score is, money-wise. Simply click on Currency Converter under Traveller Tools on the left-hand side of the home page to be taken to a simple, but highly useful, tool which lets you select the currency to convert from, and the currency to convert to. Type in the two parameters and then simply click Display Currency Converter results.

Using Expedia to plan a flight and hotel (cont.)

`7`

Choose a flight

`12` For £846.69 per person, we now have 14 nights in a hotel in Vancouver and a return British Airways flight – a direct flight as well, which saves the hassle of having to stop anywhere for a changeover. Click on Choose a different flight if you're not happy.

`13` The good thing about Expedia is that it sorts out all the little details of a holiday that are so easily forgotten – such as insurance, which could prove vital if you get yourself into any kinds of scrapes whilst you're away. Here, we're given some travel insurance options, and you can do as you please whether to take Expedia up on its suggestions. Note the running total at the bottom of the screen, so you're always aware of just how much this is all costing you. Click Continue booking this trip to carry on.

Using Expedia to plan a flight and hotel (cont.)

Further activities

14 Expedia certainly knows its onions when it comes to presenting you with a variety of possible activities for your holiday, so you'll now be presented with some mouth-watering possibilities for your trip. You may be perfectly happy to make your own entertainment while you're there – all these things cost extra money, of course, and it's hard to vouch for the strength of an event on the basis of just a few screenshots and lines of text. If something is recommended by Expedia, however, you can at least be fairly sure that the extra won't be rubbish. We've been tempted by the Trolley Tour so we click on that to glean some more information.

15 After making choices for a range of Vancouver activities, our last thing to do is read and accept the rules and restrictions. Having done that, check the box at the bottom of the terms to continue.

16 Then it's time to select a booking option. We go for Review preferences, then purchase.

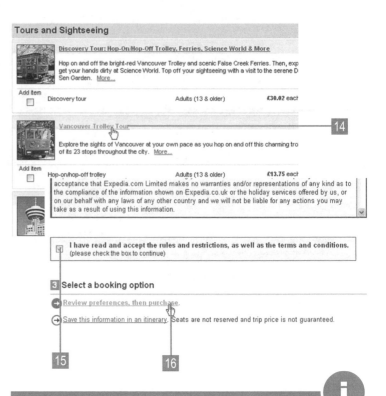

For your information

When it comes to your holiday, you may fall into one of two camps. You may like the thrill of traveling 'blind', knowing very little about your destination, and finding out everything by yourself or with your family and friends. This spontaneous approach can be exciting, but how do you know that it won't cause you to miss out on a fantastic restaurant, a stunning castle, a fascinating local custom or a gorgeous little side-street packed full of boutiques and unique market stalls? If you fall into the camp of wanting to get the full lowdown on a place before setting foot there, Expedia's city guides will be just the ticket. Spanning places all across Europe, Asia and America, taking in stunning slideshows and time-saving tips, the guides serve as an excellent aperitif to the main course of your holiday. To access them, simply click on Guides from the menu bar that runs across the top of the screen. Then sit back and start soaking up the atmosphere of your chosen destination – or just read open-mouthed about that area of Paradise which you've always promised yourself you'd visit, but just haven't got round to seeing yet.

18

Using Expedia to plan a flight and hotel (cont.)

Expedia.co.uk

HOME | DEALS | FLIGHTS | HOTELS | CARS | HOLIDAYS | ATTRACTIONS | INSURANCE | EUROSTAR | GUIDES | MAPS | CORPORATE TRAVEL

Site Map | My Trips | My Profile | Customer Support

QUESTIONS?

* Having trouble signing in?
* Microsoft Passport FAQs

Expedia.co.uk sign in options

Already a registered user?

User name:

Password:

Forgot your password or user name?

☑ Save this password on my computer for automatic sign in.
Note: Recommended for use on private machines only.

⊕ **Sign in to Expedia.co.uk**

⊕ Sign out

New Expedia.co.uk user?

⊕ Create an account

.Net Passport User?

Sign In

Registration and payment

17 Here we are at the sign-in options. If you've used Expedia before, you can simply enter your username and password in the boxes provided, and then click on Sign in to Expedia.co.uk to continue.

18 If this is the first time you've used the site, however, you'll need to go through the brief process of creating an account so that the site can know who you are. On the right-hand side of this screen, click on Create an account.

19

17

Supply email address

We'll use this address to confirm your travel purchases or notify you of a reservation change.

Current email address:

wanderingstar75@hotmail.com

☐ Email me travel deals, special offers, and information about my trips.

Review membership agreement

By continuing on you agree to the following terms and conditions:

```
AGREEMENT BETWEEN CUSTOMER AND EXPEDIA, INC.

This Web site is offered to you, the customer, by Expedia,
Inc., 3150 139th Avenue SE, Bellevue, WA  98005, USA.,
conditioned on your acceptance without modification of the
terms, conditions and notices contained herein.  Your use of
this Web site constitutes your agreement to all such terms,
conditions, and notices. If you do not agree with these terms
and conditions then you are not authorised to use this Web site

PERSONAL AND NON-COMMERCIAL USE LIMITATION
This Web site is for your personal and non-commercial use. The
```

⊕ Sign up and continue using Expedia.co.uk

Note that account creation may take a minute or two.

20

19 Time to enter your details now, including the usual username, password and email address. In the Current email address box, it's probably best to use a webmail account, rather than your work address. We enter our Hotmail address.

20 Review the membership agreement before clicking on Sign up and continue using Expedia.co.uk.

7

Using Expedia to plan a flight and hotel (cont.)

Passenger details

21 You can then enter the passenger details for you and your companion, making sure you don't make any mistakes with the phone numbers or passport information. Once you've done all that, all you need to do is click on Proceed to booking, where you just need to enter your credit card details in the secure payment environment, and set about getting ready to enjoy your Expedia holiday!

! Important

Make sure the website you are visiting offers a secure online booking service!

We will forward your preferences and requests to the airline, but we cannot guarantee that they will be honoured. Please confirm your requests directly with the airline before departure.

Hotel: Executive Airport Plaza, Richmond

To book the reservation, the hotel requires the name of an adult for each room.

Room contact (adult)

Select from the list ▾ **or** Add a new traveller   Guests: **2 adults**

Insurance

Travel insurance has been added for travellers whose names are specified for the flight.

Single trip - Cancellation, Medical, Baggage & Other

---

2 Select an option

➡ Proceed to booking

➡ Cancel and view saved itinerary

21

236

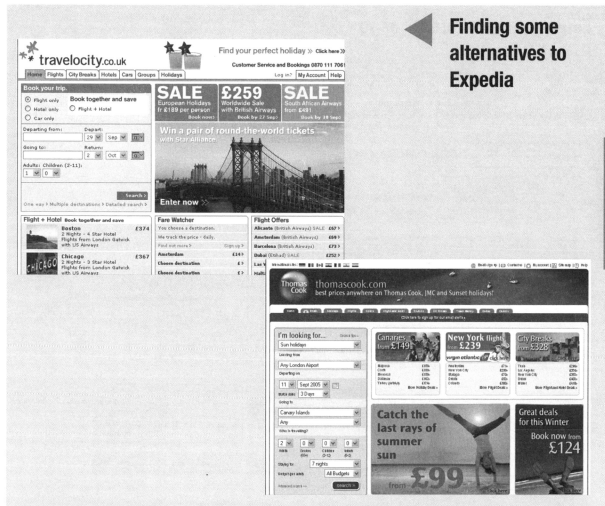

There are, of course, hundreds of alternatives to Expedia when it comes to sorting out your holiday. You may find one site simply fits your needs the best, and stick with that one no matter where you go. This is unlikely, however, and you may even find yourself using one site for cheap flights, one for finding a hotel, and one for finding out all about a place. Some sites go for the 'all-in-one' approach, whilst others specialise in aspects such as, say, finding you the very cheapest flight. Travelocity (www.travelocity.com or www.travelocity.co.uk) goes down the Expedia route, with airfares, hotels, cruises and destination guides all helping you sort out where you want to go.

The website of popular travel company Thomas Cook (www.thomascook.com) deals in cheap family holidays and last-minute deals, with bright, garish banners on the home page serving to get your attention nicely. And when it comes to cheap deals, the price comparison directory available at www.cheapflights.co.uk makes sure that you can suss out how to save as much money as possible on your flight abroad. Sites like these are well worthwhile if you're keen on saving a few pounds (and who isn't?) – you'd be surprised just how much different airlines' prices can differ. Cheapflights also offers an email service where you be alerted to the very latest deals and discounts.

Finding some alternatives to Expedia (cont.)

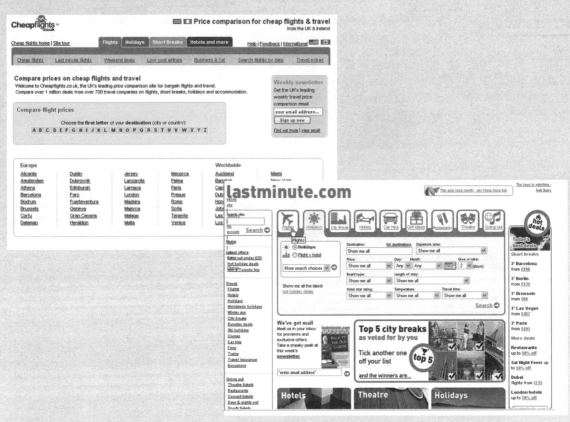

On a similar cheap theme is the famous site at www.lastminute.com – one of the most recognisable internet brand names from years gone by is still going strong, and now also lets you get deals on restaurants, the theatre and special entertainment events. The site design here can be a tad hectic at times, but it's a great place for people whose lives are so busy that they simply can't plan a holiday months in advance.

Ultimately the range of holiday options out there online is staggering, and to a certain extent your own personal preferences will hold sway. Make sure the site offers secure online booking, and don't just go for the first deal you see – shop around and you could end up saving yourself an absolute fortune. Then you can spend the spare money enjoying yourself when you actually arrive!

The amount of health websites that even just a casual internet search can unearth is staggering. Such a level of choice may initially be seen as a good thing, and to many extents it is. Knowledge is power, after all, and when it comes to your health, getting the facts behind some medical symptoms can be a good thing. Local GPs, indeed, have even been reporting that patients have been coming in to their surgeries with a marked increase in their knowledge levels about symptoms, illnesses and cures. Problems arise, of course, when people take everything they read online as gospel, and get dangerously wrong information from a health site purporting to tell people about their health, but ultimately only concerned with making a quick buck, or scare-mongering. So picking the right health site to get safe, reliable health information is vital, as is remembering the basic fact that your doctor should always be the person you go to when you're concerned about a health issue – the internet should just be seen as a useful background tool, and nothing else.

Nevertheless, when a health site does get it right, it really does, and the NHS Direct site (www.nhsdircct.nhs.uk) really impresses with its no-frills, comprehensive approach to health information and facts. We'll go for a run through the site now, and also look at some trustworthy alternatives to the NHS way of doing things.

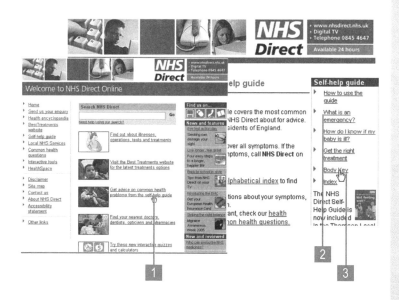

Getting the latest health information online with NHS Direct

Browsing through NHS Direct

1 Type www.nhsdirect.nhs.uk into your web browser. You'll see the home page is pretty crammed – you can find out about illnesses, see the latest treatment options, get advice on common health problems, and find your nearest doctors, dentists, opticians and pharmacies. We're going to look at some common-sense advice for regular health problems, so click on Get advice on common health problems from the Self-help guide.

2 The Self-help guide's intention is to answer the most common health problems that people have. On the right-hand side is a number of useful links, including what to do in an emergency, and what constitutes an emergency – this could be potentially life-saving advice in the future. Click What is an emergency? for the lowdown.

3 You need to decide how you're going to progress through the Self-help guide – whether through the alphabetical index, or the pictorial body key. We go for the latter option, so click on Body Key.

Getting the latest health information online with NHS Direct (cont.)

Looking at the Body Key

4 Here's the pictorial representation of the body, broken up into head and neck, chest, arms abdomen, urinary, genitals, hands, legs, skin and feet. Click on the relevant area of the body where you're experiencing symptoms – we click on Head and neck.

5 Under Head and neck, you can see a list of common problems, including toothache, headaches sore throats. If what you're after isn't there, you'll need to click on Can't find the information you want? to go hunting deeper.

6 Otherwise, simply click on the relevant problem that's been bugging you. We click on Headache in adults.

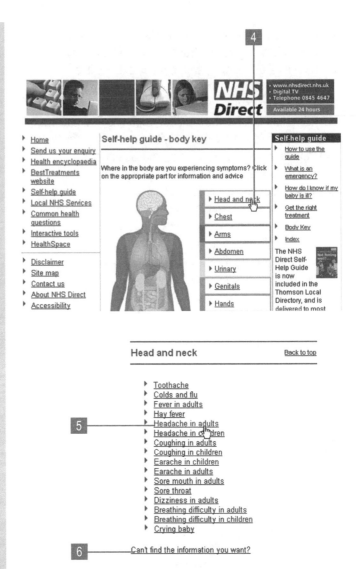

For your information

One of the most useful features of the NHS Direct website is its Health encyclopaedia, which has its own link on the menu bar on the left-hand side of the home page. These days there's a bewildering array of diseases and health problems, and it's good to get no-nonsense explanations of what everything means, so you can nod your head sagely next time you see your GP!

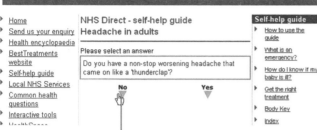

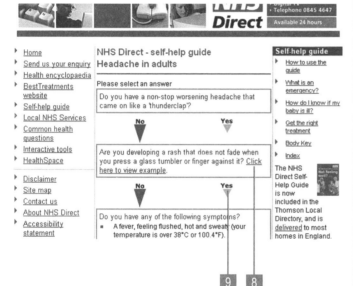

7

9 8

For your information

The interactive tools that the site provides, again accessible from the menu on the left-hand side of the home page, are a fine touch, giving you information about such aspects of life as smoking, drinking and eating the right balance of fruit and vegetables in a highly visual way. There's more than one way of presenting important health information than in boring reams of text, as these interactive tools and games show.

Getting the latest health information online with NHS Direct (cont.)

Questions and answers

7 Here comes the nice and direct questions and answers section of the site, as it endeavors to get to the bottom of the headache problem. You're asked a question about your illness, and need to click No or Yes as an answer. Our intense, feverish headache doesn't come on like a 'thunderclap', so we click No to this particular question.

8 Carry on answering the questions as required. Some of them even have examples to let you know what exactly they're getting at, which is a nice touch.

9 The site hits the mark with a description of feeling flushed and hot, so we click Yes. You'll then get a review of your answers, and the suggested courses of action, which range from ringing NHS Direct to and, in serious cases only obviously, calling 999.

Getting the latest health information online with NHS Direct (cont.)

Search through the Best Treatments website

1 We've been through the Self-help procedure, so let's now look at another trick that NHS Direct has up its sleeve – the Best Treatments zone of the site. From the home page, click on BestTreatments website to be taken to this screen. The purpose of the site is to use evidence, taken from medical research to help you decide which treatments are the best for your ailments. Under Patients, click on the condition that's troubling you.

2 Now, you can look at the key points about treating hay fever, laid out in easy-to-understand bullet points.

3 Click on the underlined links to access an additional pop-up window that serves as a glossary for complex terms.

4 If you want to know more about the symptoms of hay fever, the What are the symptoms? link on the left-hand side of the page will tell you all that you need to know.

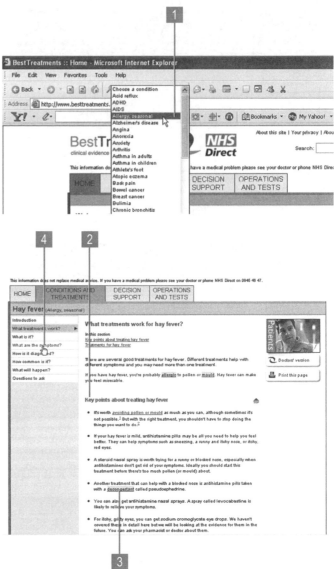

Timesaver tip

Climate in the UK seems to be getting even weirder – summer 2005 has seen heatwave conditions one week, then flash floods and massive thunderstorms the next. NHS Direct has some useful Health Alerts that can advise on the best precautions to take to deal with the vagaries of modern day life. Simply click on Health alerts in the menu bar on the right-hand side of the home page to get the full lowdown.

Welcome to NHS Direct Online

- Home
- Send us your enquiry
- Health encyclopaedia
- BestTreatments website
- Self-help guide
- Local NHS Services
- Common health questions
- Interactive tools
- HealthSpace

- Disclaimer
- Site map
- Contact us
- About NHS Direct
- Accessibility statement

- Other links

Search NHS Direct

[   ] Go

Need help using our search?

Find out about illnesses, operations, tests and treatments

Visit the Best Treatments website for the latest treatments options

Get advice on common health problems from the self-help guide

Find your nearest doctors, dentists, opticians and pharmacies

Find us on...

News and features

Eye test action day

Smoking can damage your sight

Live longer, feel great
Four easy steps to a longer, happier life

Back to school in style
Tips from NHS Direct on your TV

Introducing the EHIC
Get your European Health Insurance Card

Striking the right balance
Migraine Awareness Week 2005

1

NHS Direct
- www.nhsdirect.nhs.uk
- Digital TV
- Telephone 0845 4647
Available 24 hours

- Home
- Send us your enquiry
- Health encyclopaedia
- BestTreatments website
- Self-help guide
- Local NHS Services
- Common health questions
- Interactive tools
- HealthSpace

- Disclaimer
- Site map
- Contact us
- About NHS Direct
- Accessibility statement

Find your local NHS Services

This page allows you to search for your 5 nearest Doctors, Opticians, Dentists and Pharmacies. If you still cannot find what you are looking for, there is a fuller search available here

From here you can find your five nearest:

- GP surgeries,
- opticians,
- dentists, and
- pharmacies.

Please enter your postcode in the box below. Tick the box next to it if you would like your postcode to be remembered for your next visit.

Please enter your postcode [BH8 9JP]

Set this to be my home postcode: [✓]

[Search]

Look for other NHS services near you, including walk-in centres and A&E departments, or find services in Scotland and Wales.

3 **4** **2**

For your information

The NHS Direct phone number is available 24 hours a day, to provide confidential information on what to do if you or your family are feeling ill, or have particular health conditions and local healthcare services. Call 0845 4647; all calls are recorded, and calls are charged at BT local rates.

Getting the latest health information online with NHS Direct (cont.)

Find your nearest doctors

1 There's still some mileage left in the site to explore – proving that it's one of the best health sites around. It can always be handy to know where your nearest medical outlet is, especially if you're new to an area. From the home page, click on Find your nearest doctors, dentists, opticians and pharmacies.

2 You can now find your nearest medical stations. Enter your postcode in the box provided.

3 If you would like to be remembered on your next visit to the site, thus saving valuable time, check the box next to Set this to be my home postcode.

4 Then click on Search to set NHS Direct off on its business.

7

Getting the latest health information online with NHS Direct (cont.)

Open your own Health Space

1 We've just got time to mention one final useful aspect of the site – HealthSpace. This handy resource basically acts as a kind of online diary, where you can jot down all your relevant health information – all your medications, favourite health links, local services and general jottings. Very useful, and a real time-saving device if your medical history is complicated and full of different treatments. All you have to do to access this personal corner of the web is click on HealthSpace on the left, and then follow the links to start filling your very own health journal. An excellent final touch.

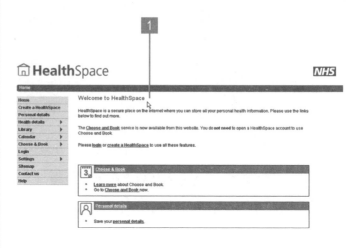

Important

We've said this already, but it really is worth repeating, as it's such an important factor. If you are worried about your health, you must make an appointment with your local GP as soon as possible. Regard medical websites as useful tools that act as informational resources, and nothing more. And don't do digging up all the obscure health websites, either – many of these will have something to sell and could well end up whipping up an entirely false scare just to get you to part with some cash.

Finding other sources of health information online

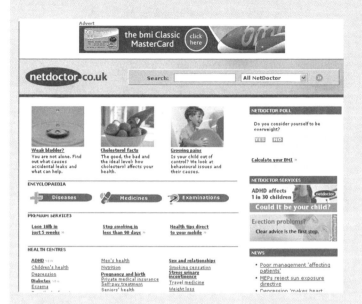

As we've mentioned, there is an absolute plethora of health websites out there – some good, some bad. Here's a small taster of some of the most reputable resources.

One of the most impressive UK sites is www.netdoctor.co.uk, an independent site which scores highly not only on the quality of the information imparted, but also in the novel way of presenting details, with the use of online polls, discussion forums, health centers and support groups. Important, so-called 'embarrassing' health areas such as sexual problems, eczema and incontinence are covered without fuss, and there's a focus on programmes to change your life, such as losing 10 lbs in 5 weeks, or stopping smoking in less than 90 days. You can even sign up for health tips direct to your mobile (at a charge – check the specific section for details).

Unsurprisingly, considering its highly impressive online track record, the BBC's approach to health at www.bbc.co.uk/health is packed to the gills with useful info. With messageboards, newsletters, fitness tips and no-nonsense information on common

problems, there's enough here to see you through the year.

The BUPA website (www.bupa.co.uk) fills you in on exactly what this leading provider of healthcare services can do for you, and covers important issues such as health assessments, insurance and the very latest health information.

The popular men's magazine *Men's Health* has a strong online presence at www.menshealth.co.uk. There does seem to be somewhat of an over-emphasis on sex and dating here, which presumably springs from its real-world 'lad's mag' tag, but there's still plenty here for health-conscious blokes to focus on, as there is at www.healthofmen.com/. Men are notoriously bad at looking after themselves or visiting the doctor's, so maybe these sites will act as motivation to make that surgery visit.

So you should now be armed with the information you need, ready to consult your GP if something's up. A healthy lifestyle is a happy lifestyle, so start using the health resources that the internet has to offer today.

Finding other sources of health information online (cont.)

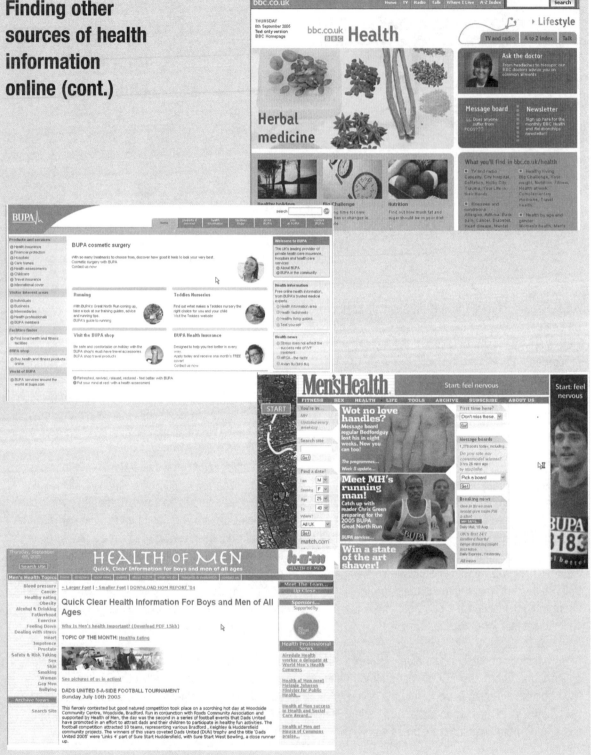

Your life online: multimedia

8

Introduction

Say the word 'multimedia' and you may get blank looks at yet another example of technical-sounding internet jargon. For the purposes of this chapter, however, we're just using the term as a generic banner for the exciting audio and visual features that the internet brings with it. Listening to streaming radio ('streaming' is a data transfer technique commonly associated with audio or video files, which lets you access them without having to go through the rigmarole of lengthy download times), downloading MP3 music files and playing graphically rich online games are just some of the things you can do online to stretch your PC to the max, and it's these fun tasks which we're going to be concentrating on in this chapter.

It goes without saying that to get the most out of the tasks here, you'll need a broadband-enabled PC; in theory you should be able to do everything described with a bog-standard dial-up computer, but you may find the slowness a tad frustrating and dispiriting. Downloading music from the internet, in the form of MP3 files, has been a massively controversial internet topic in the last decade. When the boom first started, dozens of illegal sites sprung up, which got artists and record companies extremely worried – their livelihood was being threatened by free, illegal distribution of their client's work. Napster (www.napster.co.uk) was at the forefront of the controversy, but it's recently bounced back, like many of its rivals, with a completely legit online presence, which is a real boon for any genuine fans of music. The free and legal download market is now holding sway online, and the fuss is dying down, which is good news for all concerned.

Our look at internet games may seem frivolous at first, but why shouldn't you enjoy your time online, and take a break from some of

What you'll do

Find and listen to an internet radio station with Live365.com

Create your own broadcast

Explore Live365.com add-ons

Find the best online radio stations

Explore the Epitonic MP3 site

Download music from iTunes

Find alternatives to iTunes

Explore the online games site www.miniclip.com

Dig out the very best online games

the more serious-minded tasks? Games have improved leaps and bounds since the rather primitive efforts of yesteryear, and now you can enjoy some challenging, highly addictive games through your browser.

We'll kick off proceedings by looking at the world of internet radio.

Timesaver tip

Make good use of the powerful search engine, which you can find at the top of the home page. Its Advanced option lets you search by artist, station info, genre, location and audio quality, and the Advanced Search Tips link puts you in the right direction if you're not getting the results that you want.

Jargon buster

Streaming – a technique for transferring data such that it can be processed as a steady and continuous stream. Streaming technologies are becoming increasingly important with the growth of the Internet because most users do not have fast enough access to download large multimedia files quickly. With streaming, the client browser or plug-in can start displaying the data before the entire file has been transmitted.

Jargon buster

Multimedia – the use of computers to present text, graphics, video, animation, and sound in an integrated way. Long touted as the future revolution in computing, multimedia applications were, until the mid-90s, uncommon due to the expensive hardware required. With increases in performance and decreases in price, however, multimedia is now commonplace. Nearly all PCs are capable of displaying video, though the resolution available depends on the power of the computer's video adapter and CPU.

Music fans should be in absolute heaven online. Before you even get to the prospect of listening to MP3s downloaded from the internet – some of which are online exclusives that will never see the light of day in the high street – you can take part in thousands of messageboards, get the very latest news on your favourite artists (virtually all major singers now have their own websites), and get acres of scurrilous gossip from online newspapers and magazines. We'll be looking at the ever-popular MP3 download market soon, but for the moment we're going to take a look at internet radio. Just type those two words into Google and you'll get thousands of links, with a staggering depth and range. We're going to look at Live365.com (www.live365.com), which not only has thousands of free online radio stations for you to explore, sorted by genre, but also lets you set up your own station, at a price. Let's put it through its paces.

Finding and listening to an internet radio station with Live365.com

First steps

1 There's a variety of different ways to get into the action at Live365.com, but we're going to dive straight in and search through the stations by genre. Look at the choice on offer – not bad, huh? Reggae, Latin, Irish, Jazz and Reality all get a look in (quite what Reality music is, we're not sure), but we opt for Pop.

2 A superb collection of stations comes to light. Each station has a brief description so you can get an idea of what kind of music it'll be playing in your chosen genre. We click on the ninth station suggested in the search results.

8

Finding and listening to an internet radio station with Live365.com (cont.)

Listen in

3 The station loads. Take a look at Now Playing to see what tunes are on the jukebox…

4 And click Play to play the track that's on at the moment.

5 The Live365 Player Window opens. If you want to buy one of the tracks being played, click on Buy.

6 Otherwise, just settle back and listen to the streaming radio! The volume bar is just below the main song window, if you want to change the sound levels.

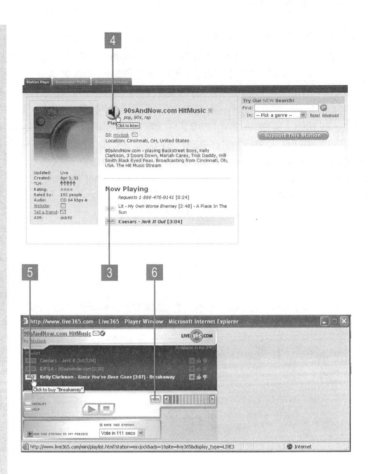

For your information

What do the guys and gals at Live365.com reckon is hot when it comes to online radio stations? Pay a visit to http://www.live365.com/cgibin/directory.cgi?genre= Recommendations to see the list of recommendations, with full rundowns on the kind of music that each signposted radio station plays.

Hopefully by now you've seen just how to listen to an online radio station – pretty easy, isn't it? Experiment with the different genres to see all the stations that are available, and try and find a couple or so that match your tastes most closely.

There's plenty more to do on the site – you may want to sign up with the site to get special member privileges and benefits, or you may want to set about creating your own broadcast. Getting set up for this fun feature is what we're going to look at next.

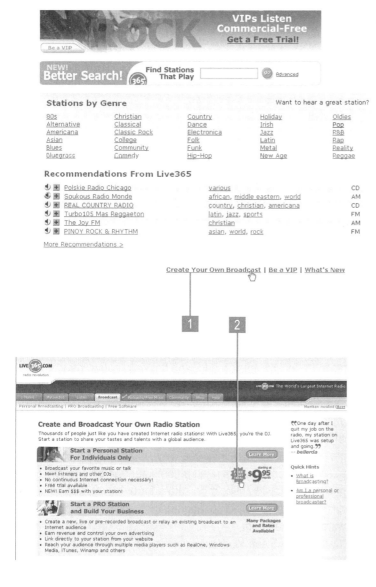

Creating your own broadcast

Signing up

1 From the home page of Live365.com, click on Create Your Own Broadcast.

2 Starting your own personal station is probably what you want to do at this stage, rather than starting a pro station and building your own business. There's a free trial available when you start your own station, which is handy if you just want to experiment. Remember to cancel the free trial, however, at the end of the 7 days, else you could find yourself forking out for a service that you're not actually using. Have a read of the benefits on offer, then click Free 7-Day Trial.

8

Timesaver tip

The help site at http://help.live365.com/ has a series of FAQs (Frequently Asked Questions) which you can read to find solutions to any problems on the site that you may be having.

Creating your own broadcast (cont.)

Signing up

3. There's a number of packages on offer, so if you're a bit confused as to the pricing structure and what you can expect, click on the ? Learn More icon on the far right.

4. Then compare packages and click on Free Trial next to the deal which you want to subscribe to.

5. If you haven't registered with the site previously, now is the time to. Enter your username and password, plus your age and gender, then click Next.

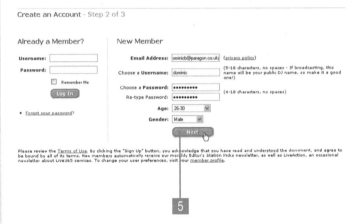

Timesaver tip

Change the technicalities and settings behind how you listen to Live365.com music at www.live365.com/cgi-bin/personalize.cgi. From here, you can answer a few simple questions to make sure that you listen to the kind of music you want, how you want.

For your information

You may be puzzled as to what the Podcast link on the home page lets you do. Podcasts are one of the latest crazes in the online music world, and basically allow you to download specially recorded audio shows, to listen to either on your computer or your MP3 player – your iPod, for example (the iPod is Apple's portable MP3-playing device which has taken the music world by storm over the last couple of years. For more info, see www.apple-shop.co.uk). To receive a podcast, you'll need a computer and an internet connection (which you should be sorted for by now!), and podcasting software called an 'aggregator'. Download the software you need from http://www.live365.com/podcasts/xml/live365_spotcast_of_the_week.xml, and find out more info on the Live365 site itself.

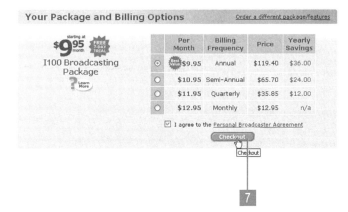

Signing up

6 It's worth pointing out that, like so many sites these days, the username you chose may already be taken. There's absolutely no need to panic if it is, however: Live365 will tell you so, and give you some alternative suggestions which are close to what you originally wanted. Click Next when you're done.

7 Now it's time to go to the checkout to buy your package, which will enable you to start broadcasting. Once you've paid, you'll be able to broadcast your favourite music or talk, meet listeners and other DJs, and take charge of your music. You basically upload your favourite music MP3s from your computer to the site, arrange them in a playlist, and hit Play! Your station will then be broadcast around the world, with a potential audience of three million listeners per month. Click Checkout and then go on your way, remembering that Live365 has step-by-step pointers to make sure that the process of uploading your tracks is as swift and painless as possible.

8

Exploring Live365.com add-ons

What else is out there?

1 Like so many internet sites, one of the best ways to find out what's going on, and how to make the most of the seriously cool features lying around, is to access the messageboards and have a good old natter. Click on Community followed by Message Boards to meet fellow 'radio revolutionaries' who can help you on your way.

2 The Live365/com shop also has some gear well worth snapping up, including package deals, T-shirts and gift certificates. Simply click on Shop from the home page and dive in.

Before we leave Live365.com, we've got time to highlight a couple more features which will help you get the most from the site.

Online radio fans will be delighted to find out that there's a wealth of ways to listen to your favourite tunes online. In fact, there are so many internet radio stations around, playing a bewildering array of different styles, that it can be very hard to find your way around to something which you really, really want to listen to – which is why Radio Locator (www.radio-locator.com) is so useful. This invaluable site acts as a comprehensive radio search engine, letting you hunt through over 10,000 radio station web pages from the US and across the world. Which should be enough for even the most demanding music fan!

BBC Radio, at www.bbc.co.uk/radio, is as huge as you'd expect from such a major broadcasting player. Quite aside from all the info and links on your favourite national stations and artists, you can launch the BBC Radio Player to listen to shows live – and, crucially, 'Listen Again' to programmes that you may have missed due to pressures of time and work, for up to 7 days after the original transmission. This service is an absolute godsend and has proved massively popular – so, for example, you could listen to the Chris Moyles breakfast show at six in the evening, through your computer. Brilliant.

RadioTower (www.radiotower.com) is very good for beginners to the online radio game, and Yahoo!'s LAUNCHcast feature (http://music.yahoo.com/launchcast) scores highly on the personalisation approach, letting you build up your very own preference list and playlist.
The internet has been a real shot in the arm for radio enthusiasts – long may the boom continue.

Exploring the Epitonic MP3 site

Get to grips with Epitonic

1. Let's take a look at the Epitonic home page, at www.epitonic.com. Different genres are down the left-hand side.

2. Today's featured music is in the middle of the screen.

3. Scroll down the screen and you can see all the new-to-Epitonic tracks.

4. Or, this box in the top-left contains quick links to all the major areas of the site. We go for Top downloads.

5. Use this search box to search for artists.

When it comes to online music and legally downloading tracks, it's a massive world out there. The choice currently on offer is staggering, and whilst the main battle is often whittled down to one between iTunes (http://www.apple.com/uk/itunes/) and Napster (www.napster.co.uk), there is plenty more for the savvy music hunter to get their teeth into. That's not to say that these two services aren't superb – the renowned Napster, for example, promises you 'Unlimited access to 1,000,000+ tracks', allowing you to 'listen to and download an unlimited amount of music' with its 'fast, safe and legal' service (the 'legal' part is an important word, after the trouble Napster has been in over the past). And there's a free trial to get you started as well.

We'll explore the famous world of iTunes in a little while, but for the moment, we're going to concentrate on a music download site that you may not have heard of – Epitonic (www.epitonic.com). The music on offer here may be slightly eclectic, but it makes a change from the mainstream offerings provided by many of the big players, so it's well worth a look.

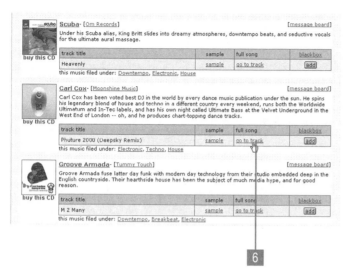

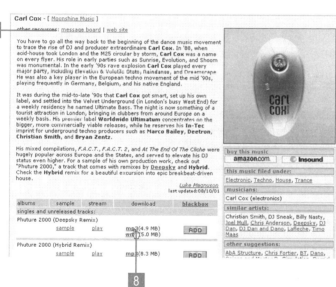

Picking a track

6 Here are the top downloads currently on Epitonic. Each item has an option to buy the CD, listen to a sample, go to a track or add it to your blackbox. Click on anything that interests you.

7 You'll get loads more info on the artist that you clicked on – very impressive. Note the links to a relevant messageboard and website for the artist.

8 We choose to download one of the tracks, so click on the MP3 link.

For your information

The Epitonic Blackbox, at www.epitonic.com/blackbox, lets you create your own playlists, made up of your favourite songs from the site. The playlist can then be sent to your mates, to impress them (or otherwise) with your music taste. The Blackbox basically acts as an extremely handy storage facility for all your music. First-time users will need to register at www.epitonic.com/blackbox/bb_register.jsp

Did you know ?

At www.epitonic.com/radio.jsp, you can select songs and musical styles of your choice, and then click Play Epitonic Radio. You'll then be able to listen to the chosen tracks through your music player while you work.

Exploring the Epitonic MP3 site (cont.)

Download it

9 You may be prompted to download a music player, if you don't already have one – we're asked to download the excellent Winamp 5. Click Download.

10 The song is now playing in the background – it's a shame this page doesn't come with audio capabilities as well! Obviously, now you can carry on hunting for decent MP3s, making good use of the search facility in the top-left to get to what you want as quickly and efficiently as possible. Epitonic brings excellent music to your PC, with the minimum of fuss – just what the doctor ordered.

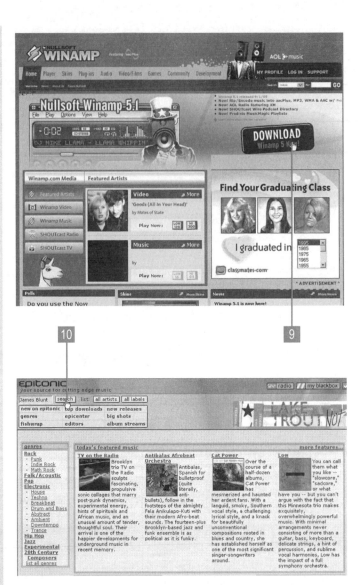

For your information

Everyone loves the iPod, don't they? Well, certainly even more people do, now that the funky color iPod is doing such brisk business. Get the full lowdown on the huge range of different iPods – there's a massive family to browse through now – at www.apple.com/uk/ipod/color/

For your information

You'd have to be a bit of a music nut to be up for this, but there's even an Epitonic newsletter that you can sign up to, at http://www.epitonic.com/newsletter, to get the full lowdown on what's happening in Epitonic-land. You can also access back copies of newsletters to browse through at your leisure as well.

We're now going to look at the world-famous iTunes music player and music store, where you can download songs to your heart's content (if you have a fat wallet). You just have to look at Apple's home page at www.apple.com/uk/itunes to get an understanding of just how phenomenally successful iTunes is – in the relatively short period of its existence, over half a billion (!) songs have been sold and legally downloaded on the site. That's pretty impressive! Many people see iTunes as Mac-based, of course, but iTunes is also available for the PC. You're basically getting one of the world's best jukeboxes, combined with the number one music download store inside it – which can't be bad. The download is free, and you can get on with looking at a legal music download catalogue of more than 1.2 million tracks. There are plenty of exclusive and pre-release tracks online, and the best part is that many tracks allow you a 30-second preview before you download, so you can see if you really want to splash your cash before making the plunge. Brilliant.

And don't forget, if you have an iPod, iTunes becomes even more important, acting as the buffer between your favourite music and actually getting it uploaded onto your funky portable player.

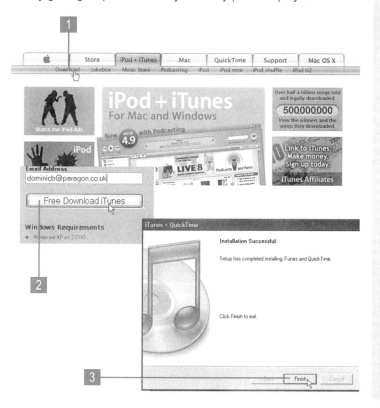

Downloading music from iTunes

Download iTunes

1. Here we are at www.apple.com/uk/itunes, with plenty of stuff going on. Read all the blurb about the wonderful world of Apple, then click on Download to start the process of downloading iTunes to your PC.

2. You'll now see just what you can expect from the latest version of iTunes for your PC – a staggering array of tracks. Choose your operating system by clicking in the relevant circle on the left-hand side, then click Free Download iTunes.

3. The download will take place, and eventually you should reach this screen, informing you that installation has been successful. Click Finish to exit.

Downloading music from iTunes (cont.)

Track time

4 Thumbnails of featured tracks currently doing the business on iTunes will appear – whether it's new releases, exclusives or pre-releases. Options down the left-hand side let you choose different sections, or you can head for the charts on the right, which is what we go for. Under Today's Top Songs click Top 100 Songs if you want the full rundown, or just click a title of a song if you want to download it. We go for the number 7.

5 Lots of information about the chosen song appears, plus a window underneath which tells you the name of the track, its duration, the artist, and the all-important price. We want to buy it, so we click on Buy Song.

6 To download music from the iTunes Music Store, you need to sign in. If you already have an iPod, for example, you'll have an Apple ID and Password, but if you're a first time curious user, you'll need to click on Create New Account.

Did you know ?

The iTunes music store has more than 1.2 million songs, 9,000 audiobooks and 3,000 podcasts. It works brilliantly with the iPod, letting you build a music collection with just a few clicks of the mouse. Remember to keep an eye on your wallet, though, as all these downloads can get a bit pricey!

Downloading music from iTunes (cont.)

Final steps

7 It's a three-part process to create an Apple account, and it shouldn't take too long. Follow the on-screen prompts, decide what newsletters (if any) you want to sign up for, and click Continue to make your way through the steps.

8 Once you're in, you can set about using the site to its full potential, getting full album information, as we're doing here with Coldplay, (click Buy Album to buy the whole album) looking at an artist or band's full download list, creating playlists, setting up artist alerts, telling a friend about some great new music you've heard... the choice is yours. Sit back and enjoy one of the best music download sites there is – Apple truly has revolutionised what we expect from an online music store.

For your information

Get the latest scoops hot from the Apple factory (well, lukewarm, anyway) by signing up for the newsletter. Fill in the relevant fields at http://registration.euro.apple.com/storenews/uk/index.html to become one of the people in the know.

Your life online: multimedia 261

Finding some alternatives to iTunes

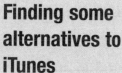

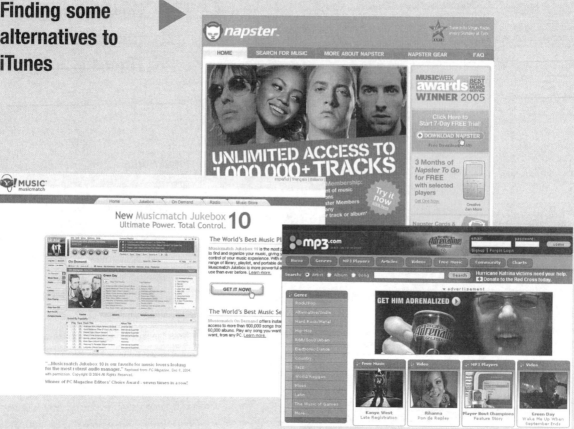

When it comes to downloading music from the internet, you really are spoilt for choice. The only thing to look out for, obviously, is the legality of the site – people have found themselves on the wrong side of the law for illegal downloading in the past, so it's well to stick with a big, legal site which you know and can trust. We've already mentioned the fantastic Napster in passing (www.napster.co.uk) – this giant has really spread its wings over the last couple of years or so, to offer a comprehensive, legal music service that won't see you get in any difficulties with the law.

The Musicmatch Jukebox, at www.musicmatch.com, is a very powerful way of organising your music, and goes hand-in-hand with Musicmatch On Demand, which you can find and download at www.musicmatch.com/download/ondemand_intro.html. Musicmatch On Demand promises you instant access to more than 800,000 songs (at $4.99 a month), and there's a free trial for you to preview the service on offer as well.

Playlouder (www.playlouder.com/downloads) lets you buy new releases or old favourites at 99p per track and £7.99 or less for albums, and allows you to listen before you buy as well. And don't forget MP3.com (www.mp3.com) as well, and even the service offered by supermarket giant Tesco, at www.tescodownloads.com. Tesco has over 400,000 tracks, with single tracks only 79p.
Again, we've just touched the tip of the iceberg here, so don't be afraid to experiment and see, and listen to, the masses of music out there.

At last! It's time to kick back and unwind, and explore the world of online games. The good news is that what once was regarded as, perhaps, a rather geeky or nerdy pastime is becoming more and more acceptable as a fun source of entertainment – for kids and for adults.

Your first experience of online games may have come from an email forwarded to you by a friend – many games these days are based around popular real-life events, such as the World Cup or The Ashes. Individual games are dotted around pretty much everywhere you look on the internet, as a cursory glance at Google will tell you, but perhaps the best way for a newcomer to join the arena is to access a site which has dozens of different games – which is what we're going to do here, with Miniclip.com.

Many of these game sites require you to have what are known as 'plug-ins' on your computer. The commonest plug-ins for games sites are Shockwave and Flash; both are widely used applications which you can download without any worries about safety or reliability.So let's put our feet up and have some fun, as we look at the kind of games you can find on Miniclip.com, and on the internet in general.

Exploring the online games site www.miniclip.com

Important

You may laugh at this warning, but the fact is that many internet games can be very addictive, so be warned! Obviously, it's not a good idea to while away 10 minutes at work by playing internet games – your bosses won't be too impressed, and you could end up getting yourself the sack. Especially when that 10 minutes turns into an hour! So try and make internet games part of your everyday surfing life, and a little vignette to enjoy, rather than the main course. Otherwise hours could go by and you won't have achieved anything, except perhaps a new high score on a funky new version of Space Invaders!

8

Jargon buster

Plug-ins – are simple little utilities that you download to your computer and which expand the capabilities of your browser, allowing you, for example, to view certain kinds of graphics and video.

Exploring the online games site www.miniclip.com (cont.)

Home page fun

1 Here we are at www.miniclip.com, and what a host of options is on offer. Across the top of the screen are links to useful features such as the toolbar and the forum.

2 Down the left-hand side is the chart of the most popular games.

3 In the middle are all the various games – or, at least, a selection of them. Click on More under a category to see the full list in a particular genre.

4 For the moment, we click on Join to register.

5 Simply enter your email address to register. Use a secondary or webmail address, rather than a work one.

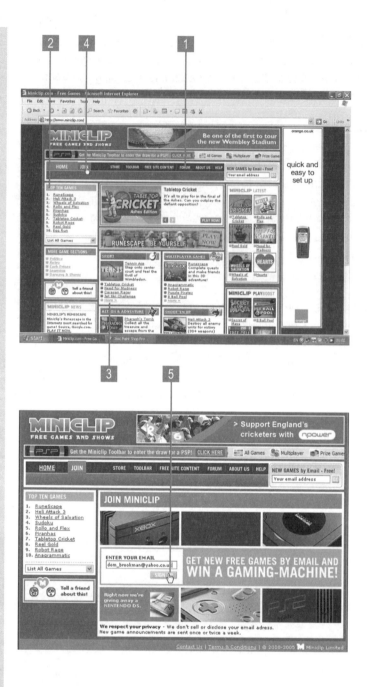

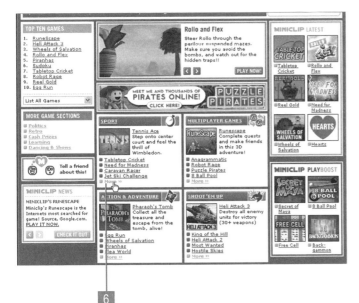

Tabletop Cricket

It's all to play for in the final of the Ashes. Can you outplay the defiant opposition?

BMX Freestyle

Pull some radical tricks in this adrenaline fueled game!

Jet Ski

Intense wave riding action in this thrilling 3D jet ski game.

Need for Madness

Perform extreme stunts to finish first in this crazy need for madness game!!

Stay the Distance

Study the field, pick a horse and see if you can stay the distance and win the race.

Miniclip Rally

Zed, Monkey and Ninja challenge each other to race on their home tracks!

Rule The Beach

Take on the opposition in this 3D volleyball game.

Hockey Showdown

Get your skates on and lead your team to victory.

Pressure Shot

Can Europe hold up under the pressure in the 2004 Ryder Cup?

Superbike GP

High speed, 3D superbike racing.

Table Tennis

Amazingly realistic table tennis game!

Trial Bike Pro

Try the Pro version for the real advanced players.

Exploring the online games site www.miniclip.com (cont.)

Ready to play

6 Let's get down to the serious business of having some fun! Obviously you can choose any game you like, and to find out the full lowdown in a genre, click on More.

7 You'll see a huge list of games, with the underlined title all you need to click on to load up the game. We click on Table Tennis.

8

Did you know ?

You can sign up for the latest new game info via email, by entering your email address and clicking Go in the box provided in the top-right of the Miniclip site.

Exploring the online games site www.miniclip.com (cont.)

Shockwave download

8 As we've mentioned, many online games require the use of a plug-in to function carefully – that's the case here. We're told we need Shockwave, a free plug-in used by millions across the world. Fill in simple name and email details, and click Next to work your way through the couple of steps needed to install the plug-in correctly. It really shouldn't take very long.

9 That done, the game should load, and here it is – simple but fun table tennis. Game objectives and controls are in the little window below the main game window.

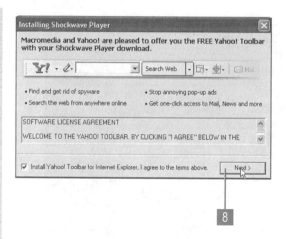

8

9

Timesaver tip

Keen gaming fans will want to go to www.miniclip.com/toolbar/ and download the Miniclip Toolbar, which sells itself as the 'only toolbar for FREE gaming'. Exclusive content, game updates, early game releases and customisable features can all be yours when you download this nifty little utility. Find out how to download it in our step-by-step tutorial.

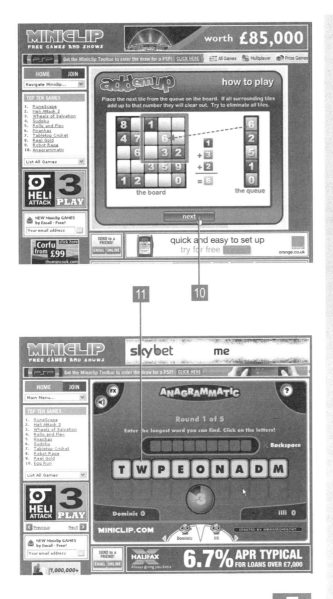

Different games

10 Many games, such as this title AddemUp, have a tutorial at the beginning for you to follow, so you can get the hang of what exactly it is that you're meant to be doing. It's as wise to use these, as there's nothing more annoying than trying to play a game without the foggiest idea of what's going on. If there's a few screens of instructions, like here, just click Next to cycle through.

11 Perhaps the most fun is when you choose a game that pits you against another human being. This Anagrammatic game, for example, sees us trying to make the longest word possible from a series of letters, in a Countdown kind of way, against a fellow user ('lukasz'). It really gets the competitive juices flowing!

8

Timesaver tip

One thing gamers love to do is chat, whether it's to moan about continually getting stuck in a certain part of a challenge, to boast about a high score, or just to have a general banter about anything and everything. Miniclip fans dying for some conversation should go to http://forums.miniclip.com/ for some top game chat. Before you can post your own opinions, you'll need to register.

Exploring the online games site www.miniclip.com (cont.)

Challenge me!

12 When you finish many of the games, such as Anagrammatic, you can go back to a kind of electronic waiting room, where you see who else is online, how many games you've played and won, and what your rating is. You can choose to challenge other users if you're really up for a series of games – doing this really ups the ante and starts getting you addicted! Click Play under a player's icon to play that particular person. Let battle commence!

12

For your information

The help section of the site, at www.miniclip.com/faqs.htm, is as extensive as you'd wish, with advice on what to do if a game isn't working, what to do if you get stuck, how to purchase games, and what to do in multi-player games. If you reckon you're going to be a regular user of the site, you may want to click Printer-friendly on this page, so you can print out the help pages to refer to later.

Timesaver tip

The Games Store, at www.miniclip.com/store.htm, lets you buy a massive selection of games, at pretty reasonable prices. It's a good idea to click Play The Demo first before buying, so that you can see if the game really is for you.

Toolbar fun

13 The Miniclip toolbar is well worth downloading, for exclusive content and news. A real godsend if you're a keen gamer. At www.miniclip.com/toolbar, click on Click Here under Get it FREE now!.

14 It's a three-step process to complete the installation, and it really shouldn't take very long. You'll then never be far away from the centre of the online gaming action.

8

Did you know ?

Miniclip.com even offers free games for you to download for your own website, which could prove to be a real boon and selling point to other users. Go along to www.miniclip.com/Downloads.htm to find out just what you need to do to help people access some really fun and addictive games.

Your life online: multimedia 269

Digging out the very best online games

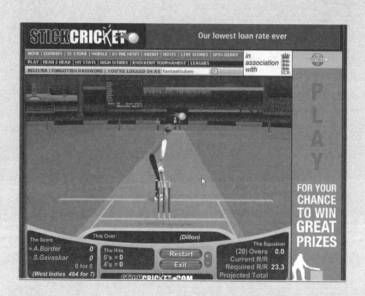

As we've said, the amount of games out there on the internet is staggering, so there's no way we can cover even a hundredth of them in this small boxout. What you'll probably find on your travels is that some sites are just host to one popular game, whilst other sites, such as Miniclip, are host to dozens.

If you'll excuse us recommending our own personal games for a second, we're big fans of both Stick Cricket (www.stickcricket.com) – one of the most addictive sporting games online, as recommended by *The Guardian* – and Zoo Keeper, a classic puzzler (recently released on the successful Nintendo handheld the DS) that you can find at www.bobpitch.com/zookeeper/zk.html. These are just personal preferences, however, and you're bound to find your own personal favourites. The more cerebral of you out there will find plenty of number-based brain crunching at Sudoku.com, the site for the puzzler that seems to have taken over so many newspapers and magazine over the last year.

Game fans wanting more of a selection can try RealArcade (www.realarcade.com) and Shockwave.com (www.shockwave.com), both of which have some graphically pleasing, addictive and challenging games for you to get your teeth into. Look out for cash games as well, where you can compete for the chance to win real money.

So a brief selection there – the real fun lies in your own explorations, and maybe even finding that rare gem of a game that no one else has picked up on. Have fun!

BobPitch.com

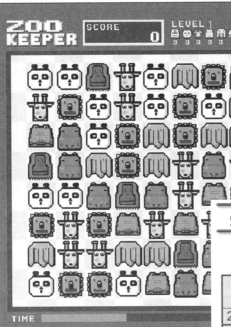

sudoku
one of the
Puzzles by Pappocom

" Fill in the grid so that every row, every column, and every 3x3 box contains the digits 1 through 9. "

6		1		4		5	
	8	3		5	6		
2							1
8		4		7			6
	6				3		
7		9		1			4
5							2
	7	2		6	9		
4		5		8		7	

Roll your mouse on and off the grid.
You may have to wait for the page to load fully.

That's all there is to it.

There's no math involved.
The grid has numbers, but
nothing has to add up to anything else.
You solve the puzzle with reasoning
and logic.

It's fun. It's challenging. It's addictive!

Solving time is typically
from 10 to 30 minutes,
depending on your skill and experience.

From here, you can check out the **tips** on how
to solve Sudoku puzzles, browse the **forums**
for more tips, or check the **solutions** to the
Sudokus you see in print.

WINDOWS
PROGRAM
FREE
TRIAL

Download a 28-day
free trial of **Sudoku**,
or **buy** it for $14.95

Building your first website

Introduction

There's no doubt about it – building your first website is one of the most rewarding things you can do online. Whether you want to build a serious, commercial site that can help you make a healthy profit, or just a couple of pages talking about your family and your life, getting your own web presence is regarded as one of the most popular things you can do online.

First off, we need to make a few things clear. You don't need to be an expert-level programmer, for starters – there's some superb software out there to help you build web pages in a matter of minutes. You can also use some online services to get your site up and ready, and we'll be looking at one such site, Moonfruit (www.moonfruit.com) in this chapter, as well as some of its rivals in the web design market. Secondly, remember that you can make a website about pretty much anything, with the only real limit being your imagination. If you like, you can start off by just building a simple home page all about yourself and your hobbies – something which you can do quite quickly, but which can gradually build up your confidence in the arena of web design.

What you do need, however, when you start your web design odyssey is a decent plan of action. If you're not clear and focused in your aims, then the chances are that your site is going to end up as an unholy mish-mash of different ideas, themes and graphics, which will only serve to confuse anybody who happens to click onto your site. Make sure you know what you're going to be focusing your website on – it sounds like an obvious thing to say, but you'd be surprised at the sheer number of people out there who just go into web design blind and hope that it will all turn out well in the end. We have to say – chances are that it won't. We'll look at planning in more detail in the first part of this chapter, before going on to the

What you'll do

Plan your first website

Build your first website with Moonfruit

Upload your site to the internet with CuteFTP

Find alternatives to Moonfruit

Get more website design tips

specifics of using the Moonfruit site and getting something concrete online to show your friends and family. Finally, we'll be looking at how to use a third-party piece of FTP software – CuteFTP – to upload your site.

For your information

The popularity of web design has spilled over into the high street newsagents. Go into any branch of WHSmiths and you'll see a healthy collection of magazines dedicated to building a website, ranging from beginner's guides to advanced tomes. These magazines are well worth a look, as many of them are published monthly and can thus keep up with all the latest trends and movements.

Jargon buster

Website – a place on the web comprising of text, pictures, sound and video which you can read or interact with.

Timesaver tip

You might want to create some kind of checklist when you're planning a website, so you can tick off that you've covered each preliminary area as you go through it. Elements that would appear on this list include your site's fundamental structure, what the basic layout of the pages is going to be, how people are going to navigate around your site, what color schemes you're going to use, how you're going to provide content, what the site's physical dimensions are going to be, how people are going to be able to contact you, whether or not you're going to add a Search facility, whether there are any similar sites you want to link to… there's a lot to think about!

Yes, building your first website can be a mite daunting. Get a workable plan written down on paper, however, with a decent structure and concrete ideas, and you'll soon realise that you can make life a good deal easier for yourself.

Over the next few pages, we're going to look at some excellent online resources which will help with your planning and content building for your site. Obviously, the content you put on your site depends on what you've decided it's going to be about, but things such as free games, free recipes and a free 'Word of the day' on your site are just some of the ideas which we'll highlight as ways of getting your potential site visitors interested. Simply looking at different websites can be a real eye-opener as well – helping you to see what works and what fails in the world of web design.

We really can't underestimate the importance of good planning when it comes to building a website – get this aspect right, and the battle is half won.

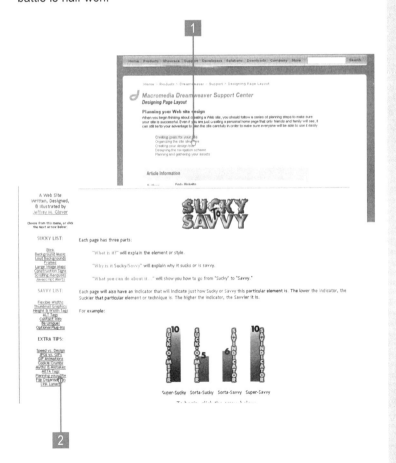

Get some help

1 If you're going to get some help and tips, why not get them from the experts, and people who have been there, done that? At www.macromedia.com/support/ dreamweaver/layout/site_planni ng/, the guys who produce superb site-building package Macromedia Dreamweaver have some great hints and tips on creating goals for your site, organising your structure, creating your design look and more.

2 It may have a bit of a cringeworthy name, but Sucky to Savvy at http://jeffglover.com/ss.php offers some excellent planning tips, and highlights common mistakes and design no-no's.

9

Jargon buster

Web page – the basic web document. It may just be a single screenful or you may have to scroll down to read it all.

Planning your first website (cont.)

Content matters

3 Right, let's start to think about adding some funky content to our site, to really entice visitors and give them some reason to come back to your site. If you want news feeds for your website, offering the latest headline from various news sites, try the link at www.easybyte.com/products/. Offering this kind of service to site visitors can hardly fail to impress.

4 If yours is the kind of site where free games would be appropriate and welcomed, try the offerings at www.groovynet.com/javagames.

5 HTMLGames at www.htmlgames.com is also very popular for this kind of thing, offering a variation of the classic game Othello. Click here to get the code.

6 The free information at http://fantomaster.com/faarticles 0.html will be of special interest to webmasters and people interested generally in building websites. You can copy and paste the articles into your own website for free.

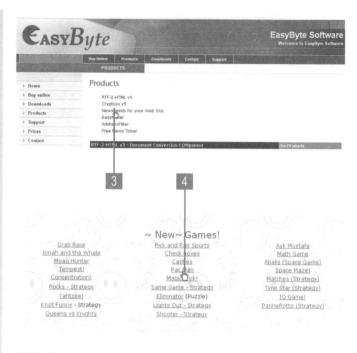

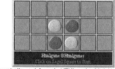

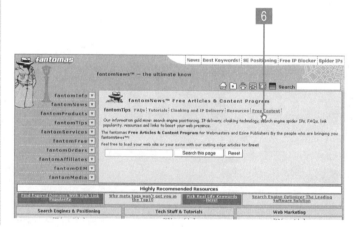

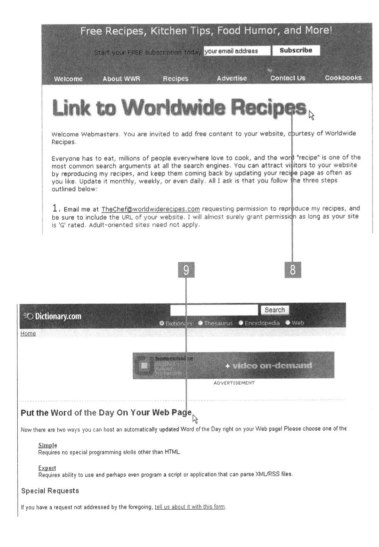

More content

7 Try www.addme.com/dispenser.htm for a tool which lets you inform readers about recent articles about search engines and website promotion, published in the AddMe! Newsletter. Keeping your visitors entertained with new content is vital if you want them to pay repeat visits to your site.

8 How about some free recipes for your site visitors? The popularity of cookery in general could mean that this will prove to be a popular addition to your site. Try www.wwrecipes.com/link.htm to see what you need to do to offer this service to people – it's all explained pretty clearly.

9 Wordsmiths will also be in heaven if you offer a 'word of the day' service – try http://dictionary.reference.com/help/linking/wordoftheday.html for the lowdown on what to do.

9

Planning your first website (cont.)

Super sites

10 Just to re-enforce the fact that you can get some great ideas from existing websites out there, here are a few sites that might float your boat and give you some creative ideas. First off, have a look at the stylish NASA site, at www.nasa.gov.

11 Budweiser's site at www.budweiser.com is sleek, fun and multimedia-rich – helping the promotion of the brand no end. Take a look and see what you think.

12 The Rolex site at www.rolex.com employs some beautifully stylized design to again strengthen the perception of the brand itself. Get your website right and it can be a massive boost for the product that you're trying to sell. These are just three examples out of hundreds of thousands of course – have fun exploring and seeing if you can implement any similar ideas, graphics or themes on your own site! Don't go stealing, though...

For your information

Obviously there are thousands of good websites out there which you can browse through to get a feel of how things work in the world of web design. A few further diverse examples which we recommend include The Tate Online (www.tate.org.uk), Harvey Nichols (www.harveynichols.com) and the General Motors site (www.gm.com). Ask yourself: what do these sites do right? Do they have any weaknesses? Are there any ideas they utilise which you could put your own spin on for your website? Curiosity online is a big plus point when it comes to getting your website clear in your head.

As we've already mentioned, there's some cracking software out there to help you build a website – we could fill the whole of this book detailing them and explaining the best ways to use them. Many software packages promise that they can help you build a website in minutes, but it's wise to take these proclamations with a healthy dose of salt. Even if you could get a website online in 5 minutes, is it likely to be any good? If you're even vaguely serious about web design, a few hours spent getting things right is the very least you should be prepared to spend on your pride and joy. Saying that, it's certainly nice when you can get something up and running quickly, and to that end, we're going to look at how Moonfruit (www.moonfruit.com) approaches the issue. This easy-to-use online service can get your web presence up and running with the minimum of hassle – you can download a free trial from the site as well. Moonfruit utilises the impressive SiteMaker website building tool, and we'll show you just how to get to grips with it below.

Building your first site with Moonfruit

Let's go

1. To take advantage of Moonfruit's free trial, go to www.moonfruit.com and click on the Free Trial link on the right-hand side. You get a 14-day free trial, which should be ample for you to give the service a thorough going over, and get something decent online.

2. Once you've signed up for the free trial, it's time to get going. Step one asks you – what kind of site are you going to create? Choices include gaming, family and friends or business. Make your selection and click Next.

3. Choose a suitable design style next. Take time to think whether plain, grunge or metallic, or any of the other picks, would suit your content. Decide and then click Next again.

Step one - Site type

Step two - Design

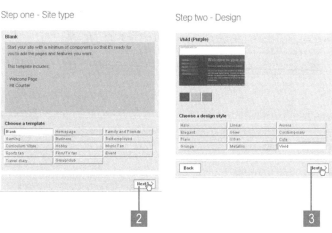

Timesaver tip

Use the Search from the home page to seek out similar examples of Moonfruit sites in genres that you're interested in. You can then see what works and what doesn't.

9

Building your first site with Moonfruit (cont.)

Continuing the setup

4 Some fundamentals to decide next, including a memorable (hopefully) URL, site name, category and descriptions to help search engines. Take your time with these basics, and then click on Next once more.

5 A new window will open for your site, prime for your customising to begin. Read the text carefully and remember there's a Help button to give you any useful pointers if anything flummoxes you.

6 If you click Edit this page, you can start work. Editing content is simply a matter of clicking on the small grey crosses which should show up on the left of each area. Note the helpful advice dotted around the dialog windows that appear. To edit your title text, select it and then type what you wish to write. Constant clicking of the Save button is good for safety's sake.

Step three - Site information

Timesaver tip

Click on Tour from the home page to be given a whistle stop guided tour of what you can expect with the Moonfruit service.

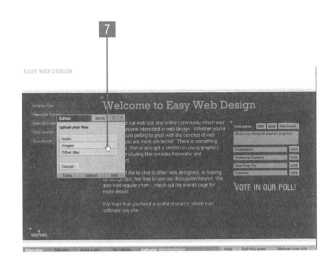

Image friendly

7 Adding images is a breeze –
you can decide to use what
Moonfruit gives you, or upload
your own images to your site.
This is an excellent way to really
put your own stamp of authority
on proceedings. In the editing
window interface, click on
Upload and then choose the
relevant option, which is Images
in this instance.

8 Then browse your hard drive for
the folder where your images
are – it makes sense to have a
folder prepared beforehand with
the files which you're going to
be likely to use. Images must be
in JPEG, GIF or SWF format.
Click Upload now to get your
image from your hard drive
uploaded to the server.

9 Hopefully your upload has been
successful – if it has, you'll see
this window. Choose Upload
another if you have another
image to upload. This process is
fast, user-friendly and powerful
– just what the doctor ordered.

Did you know ?

If you really like the Moonfruit free trial, why not subscribe to
a paid-for version? These offer advanced features including
much more storage space and the number of pages you can
build (the free version is limited to 15 pages), and are well
worth exploring. Prices start at £2.99 a month, which isn't
bad at all. Click on Pricing info from the home page to get
the full lowdown of the prices.

Building your first site with Moonfruit (cont.)

Get interactive

10 You can now start to branch out a bit – what about giving your site some elements of interactivity, to make people really feel involved? Click Add from the editing window, then Library file or your file.

11 You should now see a decent selection of the things you can add to your site. Choose an option and hit Use file – we've gone for Poll (short).

12 The great thing about Moonfruit is that you can move things around to your heart's content, simply by clicking on the crosses and dragging them over to your desired position. If things end up in the wrong place, it's no one's fault but your own!

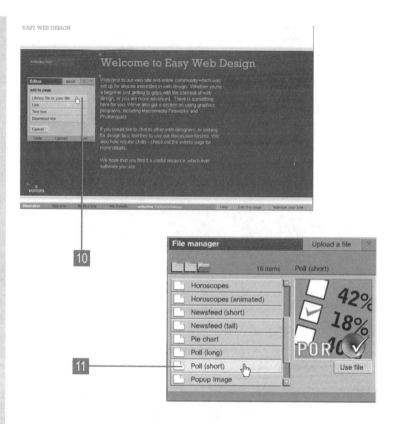

Timesaver tip

Moonfruit has a Siteleader Forum where you can pick up great tips from experienced users of the software. You can also find out how to promote your site more effectively, and add to the wishlist of product enhancements. Click Forum from the home page to find out more.

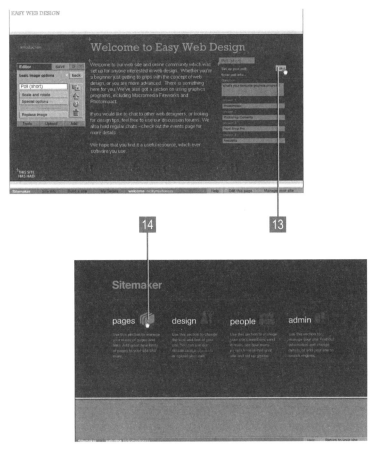

Poll fun

13 We're creating a poll, so come up with our suitable questions, and possible answers, and then click OK.

14 Successful work on Moonfruit demands that you get to grips with SiteMaker's SiteManager, which lets you manage your pages, design, people and admin elements. First off, click Manage My Site from the bottom-right. Then choose which part of your site you want to control – we go for Pages.

15 How about adding a discussion board to your site, so people can talk about any issues related to the site, or just life in general? From the screen that appears, choose Forum from under Choose a page type to add. Then select a name for the new menu item (Message Board seems appropriate) and click OK.

9

Add a menu item to site...

Please enter a name for your new menu item, and click on OK.

Menu name: Message Board

Cancel   OK

Did you know ?

SiteMaker has been responsible for over 750,000 websites being built – pretty impressive. Some of these look rather good, as well – click Gallery at the bottom of the site's home page to see some great examples. These should act as a good inspiration to you to build the best site you can with the software.

Building your first site with Moonfruit (cont.)

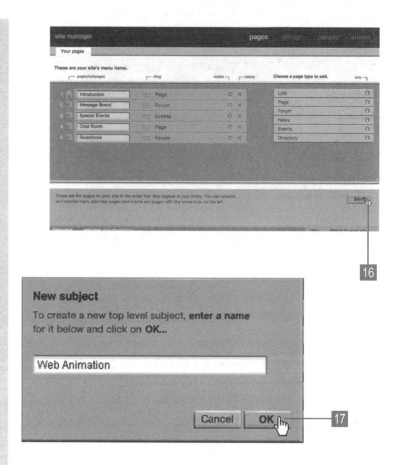

Choices, choices

16 After you click Save, you'll see a list of your site's menu items. Edit them by clicking on their titles. Think carefully about adding these added features to your site – they could mean the difference between dozens of visitors or hundreds.

17 We click on Messageboard to set all the necessary preferences for our forum. Try and set some interesting or relevant topics for people to chat about. Click OK when you decide on a topic.

18 We then enter our chat room page – follow the instructions to set the room's functionality, in a similar way as we did with the online poll.

ⓘ For your information

Click on Support on the home page and then FAQs to get a list of the frequently asked questions on the site, and concise, helpful answers, divided into topic areas.

Music matters

19 You can even add some music to your site, although it might be wise to use this option sparingly, to avoid annoying people! Go to Manage my Site again, then click on Design then Audio. You can now start to select a site-wide playlist for your site. Click on Add a track.

20 Moonfruit has tracks you can use, or you can upload your own selections – make sure that they're all legal and you're not infringing any copyright by doing so. Once the permissions have been gone through, you can edit the track list – just click on a track to hear what it sounds like and decide whether you want to use it or not. Again, just click Use file if you like a particular file.

9

Did you know ?

You can try www.quickonthenet.com for another online site builder, which can help you get a decent effort built in next to no time. Further options include DoYourOwnSite (www.doyourownsite.co.uk), aimed primarily at the eCommerce market and SiteRightNow (www.siterightnow.com).

Building your first site with Moonfruit (cont.)

The end

21 Now just keep on editing, adding, deleting, moving everything around... how long you go on depends on what kind of site you're designing and how complicated it is. When things are as easy as, for example, just clicking on Add a track to add some music, you can afford to experiment.

22 Our final site goes online after further editing, and has everything it should have. It was only our first effort, so we're going to improve on it and start using some of the techniques we've learned with different online and third-party options – a web designer's work is never done!

Jargon buster

FTP – stands for File Transfer Protocol, and FTP clients basically act as go-betweens between your own personal PC and your web server.

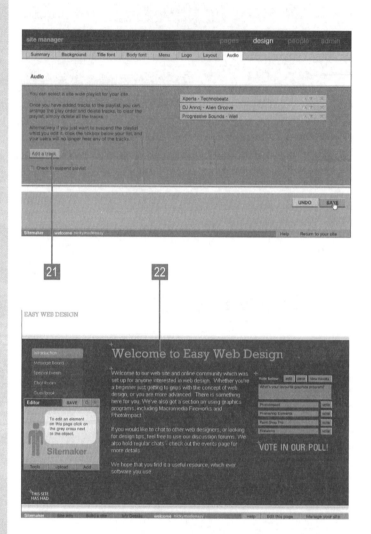

For your information

To take a tour of all of CuteFTP Home's features, go to www.cuteftp.com/cuteftp/tour.asp. From here, you can get to grips with all of the important activities and tasks Cute carries out for you.

However you've decided to go about building your website, you're going to need to make sure it's online. Obviously, if you've built your site online with Moonfruit or another online site creator, as we've done, this part of the process is unnecessary – but if you've used a piece of third-party software, the process known as 'uploading' comes into play. Everyone needs to see the fruits of their labours, after all – especially if they've created something to be proud of. Uploading your files to the web sounds complicated, but is actually thankfully pretty simple.

It's made easier by the software that's available to help you out in the task – there is a wealth of what are known as 'FTP clients' out there to help you do what you need to do. Some packages that you may use for building your website, such as Dreamweaver, come with built-in FTP clients, or you may choose to use a third-party service, such as WS FTP or CuteFTP. We're going to focus on the latter of these two options to see how it works.

Uploading your site with CuteFTP

Starting off

1 Find out all about CuteFTP Home at www.cuteftp.com/cuteftp. At the bottom of the page, click on Click here for a free 30-day trial. Selecting this option lets you decide whether you want to purchase the full version in the future. Once its finished installing, click Continue to start using the trial version.

2 The main Cute interface will load up. To start entering all the necessary details of how you want to connect, click on the Site Manager icon in the top-left hand corner of the main window.

3 Make sure you're in the General tab of the dialog window that opens. It's now time to enter the necessary details about your site – including host address, username and password. If you want to, you can add some 'comments' as well.

9

Uploading your site with CuteFTP (cont.)

Different tabs

4 Now click on the Type tab. Under here, you need to have a look at various options to do with the server type and data connection type. When you get more confident with uploading your files, you can start playing around with these options, but for the moment you may just want to stick with the default offerings.

5 The Options tab, meanwhile, lets you configure specific firewall settings – use the Proxy and Socks buttons to do so. Don't forget the buttons at the bottom of the screen which allow you to exit, delete or rename, or just get some more help on what's going on.

6 Feel free to also explore the Actions tab as well, which has further options to do with specific rules and folders. When you're happy, click Connect. You'll be asked to enter your web hosting password once a connection has been made. Click OK.

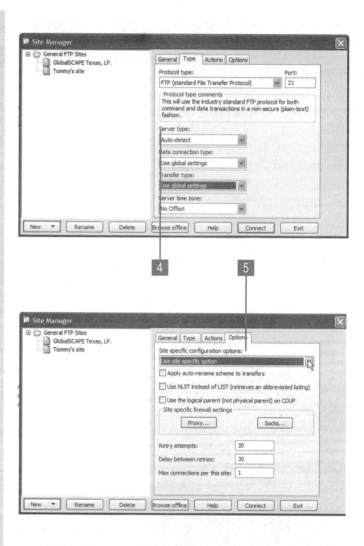

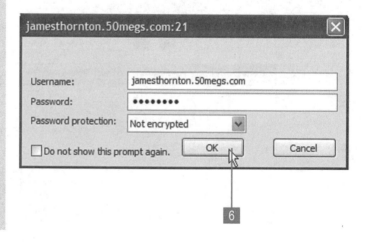

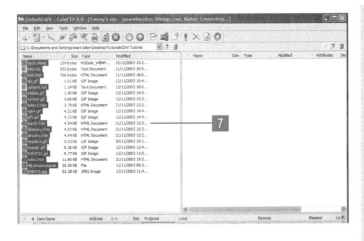

Cute in action

7 If the connection has been successful, it's time to get down to the all-important business of transferring your files from your hard drive onto the web space. Browse and find all your files in the left-hand window. Select them all and prepare to drag them into the window on the right-hand side.

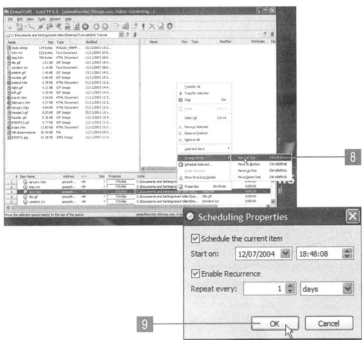

8 A lower window will show you the list of your files and a progress report. You can even set the order of how the files are uploaded, showing the flexibility and user-friendliness of the program. Right-click on a file to get a menu of options, scroll down to Change Order and then click Move to Top or any of the other three choices.

9 Scheduling uploads lets you pace your tasks to suit how you work – very convenient. Underneath Change Order from the previous step's pull-down menu is Schedule Selected. Choose this option to be able to set the date parameters for your upload. Very convenient!

9

Timesaver tip

Occasionally, your connection may crash or go down, for whatever reason. If this happens, don't panic – to start the transfer again, click on the Reconnect button on the top toolbar. This icon has a big green arrow, if you're not sure what to look for. Reconnecting should get you back up and running quickly.

Uploading your site with CuteFTP (cont.)

Final steps

10 The same menu with Change Order and Schedule Selected also has a Load and Save option. Click it and select Save queue if you want to leave your PC before the transfer has finished. You'll then be able start off from the same point when you next boot up. Choose a memorable filename and then click Save.

11 If you're experiencing problems connecting, try the Reconnect button we mentioned in our Timesaver Tip. Otherwise, click the far right-hand Global Options icon in the top toolbar, and then the Connection tab. You can now recalibrate various settings, and see which one helps your transfers complete successfully.

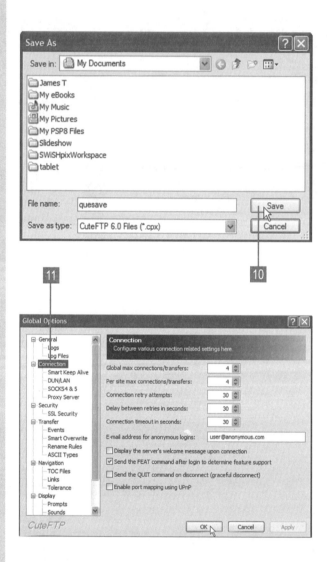

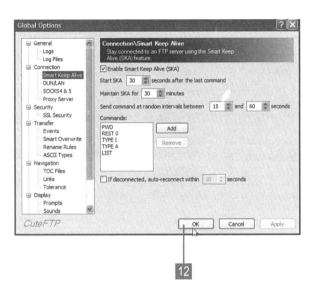

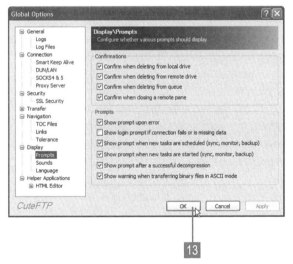

Uploading your site with CuteFTP (cont.)

Final steps

12 Under Connection you'll see an option called Smart Keep Alive. This option allows you to command CuteFTP to maintain a connection and stay connected to an FTP server. Set your options and click OK.

13 Under Global Options, Display, you'll see Prompts. Going into here allows you to turn off some of the multitude of prompts that Cute gives you as it goes about its day-to-day business – useful once you've started growing in confidence and knowing your way around. Uncheck a box to deselect it and click OK.

9

Finding alternatives to Moonfruit

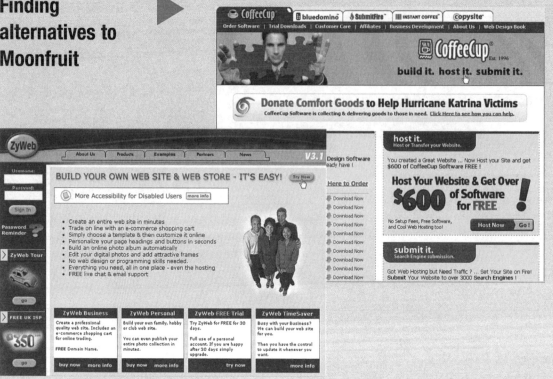

So we've seen how to build a website with an online service – what's the story when it comes to third-party software? The huge range of programs out there may leave you somewhat stumped.

A good place to start is to ask yourself: what kind of program are you after? Do you want a program that does all the hard work for you, but which may not offer you the kind of customisation and flexibility that you're after? Or do you want a program which lets you get into the nitty-gritty of hand-coding, which is fine if you're very computer-literate, but very scary if you're only just starting out on the internet? How much are you prepared to spend – does a free trial of a popular program satisfy your needs, or do you want to splash out a couple of hundred pounds on a full-version of a powerful piece of software? Many of your answers will depend on whether you're building your website for fun, or whether you want to start making some serious money out of the hobby.

Anyway, web design programs you really should give at least some attention to include CoffeeCup HTML Editor (www.coffeecup.com) ZyWeb Site Builder (www.zyweb.com), NetObjects Fusion 8 (www.netobjects.com), Macromedia Dreamweaver (www.macromedia.com), Serif WebPlus 9 (www.serif.com), HotDog Professional (www.sausage.com), CuteSITE Builder (www.cuteftp.com/cutesitebuilder) and XaraWebstyle (www.xara.com/products/webstyle).

We can't stress enough that this is just the tip of the iceberg when it comes to web design, but taking a look at the programs mentioned will certainly set you off on the right track.

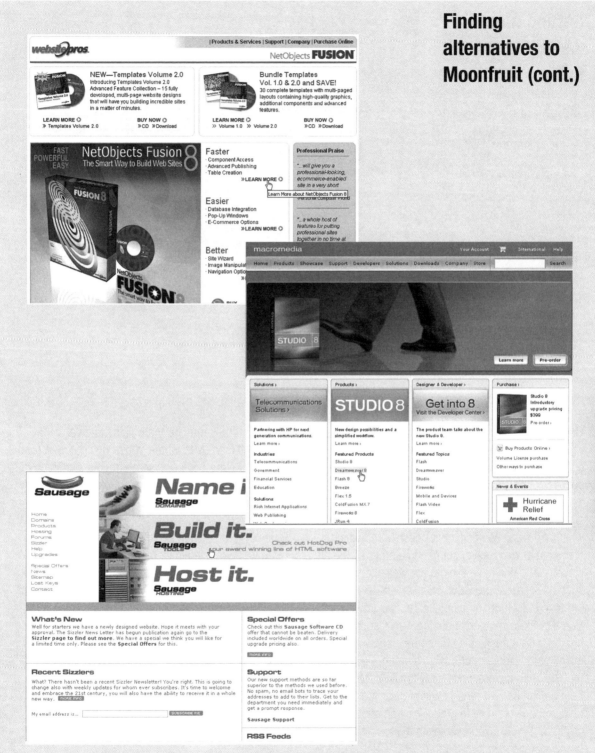

Getting more website design tips

One of the best ways to improve your website design is just to take time out and go on the internet – it seems obvious to say it, but seeing how the successful big boys design their sites can be a real help. That's not to say that you should copy their ideas, of course, but you can gain vital clues as to what works on sites and what doesn't; and which elements of web design seem common to all the big players. And don't just stick to the well-known sites such as Amazon, the BBC, eBay or whatever – take the time to look at some smaller, home-grown sites. Some of these may have glaring errors such as broken links, garish colour schemes, spelling mistakes or simple poor design elements – but some may be stylish, sleek and highly focused. Noticing both design howlers and pearls of design genius can help you on your way to producing something to be proud of. Discuss your work with friends and family, or maybe even work colleagues who you don't know

that well – they may be more likely to give you a honest opinion as to where you're going wrong (and right) than your chums. If some of your mates have designed their own sites, take a look at their handiwork as well – but don't go nicking their ideas!

Online, the amusingly titled Web Pages That Suck (www.webpagesthatsuck.com/) can show you some classic no-no's of site creation; you could also take a look at Shocking Sites (www.shockingsites.co.uk) or KillerSites.com for some useful tips and resources (www.killersites.com).

Go into web design with an open mind, ready to learn, adapt and take constructive criticism – and remember that ultimately you should be enjoying yourself and having fun, so don't get too bogged down in the seriousness of it all!

Technical support

Introduction

It's a fact of internet life that, sooner of later, you're going to run into problems which seem to have no answers. Internet Explorer may decide to give up the ghost, your PC may decide to start crashing for no apparent reason, your Inbox may start to get uncontrollable levels of spam, or your website may simply refuse to look correct in different people's browsers... the potential for problems is, there's no doubt about it, huge.

This is a rather negative view of proceedings, however. The issue shouldn't be about panicking when difficulties arise, because you may as well fret about the sun rising in the morning. No, what you need to do is keep a clear head, and realise that there are plenty of places to go online to get the help and advice you need, or at least a firm push in the right direction.

You could also try the computer press, of course, but the disadvantage here is the relative paucity of computer help magazines left out there in the market – the last couple of years have seen many titles forced to bow to market pressures and close. What's more, with most (though not all) computer magazines being printed monthly, you may have to wait an age for your question to be answered – a period of time which may see you solving the problem anyway.

No, the simple solution is to go online and seek out the answer. Obviously, if your computer has totally shut down and refused to start up, this could be a problem, but access to computers these days is much improved – chances are that you'll either have a PC-owning friend nearby or, in the worst-case scenario, a cheap internet café that will let you log on for half an hour or so and explain your predicament to a team of experts.

What you'll do

Get help online from Tech Support Guy

Find more online help sites

We're going to look at a few online help sites in this chapter, with our main focus being on the excellent 'Tech Support Guy' website, at www.helponthenet.com. This lively forum is one of our favourites, for its no-nonsense tone and comprehensiveness of subject matter, and is well worth at least a look if you've got a problem that has left you scratching your head.

We'll do our own mini troubleshooting guide, later on in the book, but for the moment, we'll put Tech Support Guy through its paces and see what it comes up with.

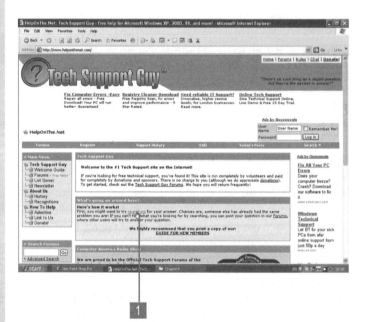

As the home page to Tech Support Guy says, if you're looking for free technical support online, you've found it! This online area of help forums is run completely by volunteers and paid for by sponsors, although the site won't say no to an appreciative donation! Below, we'll show you how to register and start to get the most out of the huge swathes of knowledge that the site is home to.

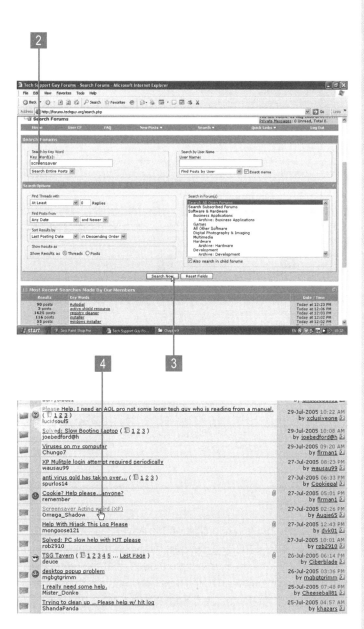

Getting help online from Tech Support Guy

Initial steps

1 Here's what the home page at www.helponthenet.com looks like. The main menu is down the left-hand side, and in the centre of the screen are a few welcome pointers. The site recommends that you try searching for an answer first – someone else in the past may have had exactly the same problem as you. If this is the case, you won't need to go through the process of asking a question at all. So we click on the underlined Searching link.

2 You'll be presented with a list of searching options next. What's the keyword involved in your problem? We're having problems with our PC screen savers, so we type in 'screensaver' under Keyword.

3 You can then choose to set the time period of posts that you want to analyse, as well as which forums you want to investigate. When you're happy, click on Search Now.

4 Your results will come back. Some of the threads returned may not be relevant, but we click on one that is – the discussion entitled Screensaver acting weird.

10

Getting help online from Tech Support Guy (cont.)

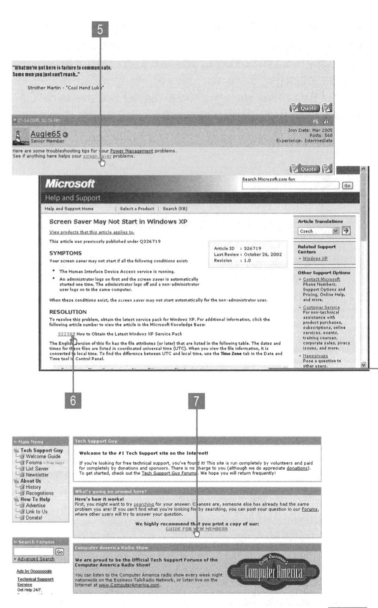

Answer please!

5 This takes us to a discussion from July 2005. This reply from a user typifies the help you can find on the site. The words 'screen saver' are underlined, which tells you that if you click on them, they'll act as a web link, and take you off to another web page which has more info. So we do just that.

6 The link, indeed, takes us to the Microsoft Help and Support Center, and its article on what to do if screen savers don't start in Windows XP. The Resolution looks like what we could be after, so we click on the article it points us to. You'll find this a lot on the site – a question takes you off on a trip round a few links on the internet, hopefully ending up at the correct answer.

7 Success! Microsoft's help solved our woes. We're still a beginner on the site, though, so let's do a bit of research and registration. Back at the home page, the site recommends that you print its help guide for new members, so we click on GUIDE FOR NEW MEMBERS.

Timesaver tip

Don't forget that you can click on the Advanced Search link from the home page to access as many search options as you're likely to need. Remember, though, that the more you narrow down your search, the less likely you are to get the exact answer that you need. Sometimes a more general search can be just the ticket!

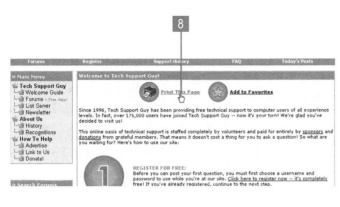

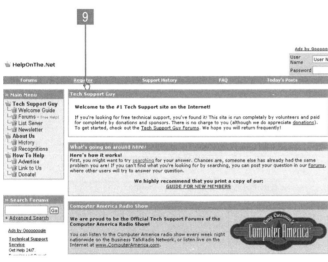

Beginner's help

8 Click Print this Page to print off the step-by-step novice's guide that the site gives you.

9 As the site recommends, it's time to register. Registration is important as it'll allow you to post your problems on any of the forums later. From the home page, click on Register.

10 Read the rules of the forum – it's important to abide by these. Click Register.

For your information

The different forums you can find at http://forums.techguy.org/ are many and varied. Topics covered include programs such as Word, PowerPoint and Excel, digital photography, multimedia problems, all the common Windows Operating Systems, online games and much, much more. There's even space in the forums for tips and tricks and general chit-chat, just to make you feel really at home.

10

Getting help online from Tech Support Guy (cont.)

Fill in the details

11 Fill in as much of the additional information, such as your experience level and whether or not you want to receive emails from the system administrator from time to time, and then click Complete Registration.

12 To successfully validate your registration, you'll need to go to your email account that you entered when you signed up. The site will have sent you an email welcoming you to the forums. Halfway down the email you'll see a long website URL; you need to click on this link to activate your registration.

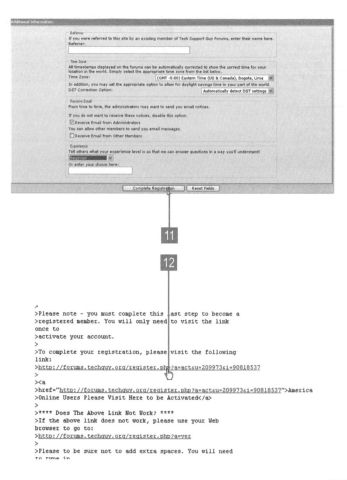

See also

We mentioned this in Chapter 3 of the book, but when you're taking part in popular chat rooms or forums such as the Tech Support Guy forums, the rules of Netiquette become extremely important.

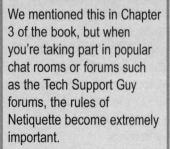

Timesaver tip

So you've got an internet problem – that's no excuse for bad language, a hectoring tone, over-the-top comments or a nasty tone when you write what's up. Stay calm and balanced and you'll far more likely to get the answer you need. And don't criticise someone's answer, either – it may not be what you're after, but is that because you didn't provide them with enough information? And even if you did, if they've gone to the time and trouble of writing back to you, with no personal gain involved, then the least they deserve is a thanks, or a 'Yes, but...' and a further explanation of what's up if you haven't got the desired answer. Basically, treat everyone online how you'd like to be treated, and you should be fine.

Go to the forums

13 Now that you've successfully registered, you can really get motoring. If you've got a problem online that's bugging you, and which doesn't seem to be answered in the forums, you can post your own question. Near the top of the screen, click on Go to Forums.

14 Knowing your problem, work out which forum you should post the query in. Be careful and precise here, as you don't want to annoy fellow users by posting a teaser that is not appropriate to its forum. We choose a Window XP-related forum.

See also

If you do have a website of your own, perhaps after building one in Chapter 9 of this book, you can link to the Tech Support Guy site for free, giving you a degree of extra kudos. The code you need is at www.helponthenet.com/linking .html – you don't even need to ask the site's permission to set up the link.

10

Getting help online from Tech Support Guy (cont.)

Post your question

15 You'll see all the threads in the forum – just double-check that there's not something already there which answers your question, or gives you ideas about how best to solve what's going on. Click New thread if you still think that your problem is unique and hasn't been tackled anywhere.

16 It's now time to write your question. Bear in mind our tips about Netiquette, here and in Chapter 3 of the book, and write slowly, clearly and concisely, giving the potential respondent as much information as possible. The more info you give them, the likelier it is that you'll get the answer you're after. When you're done, click Submit New Thread – fingers crossed that some kind soul can come to your salvation!

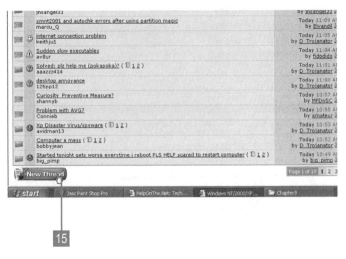

15

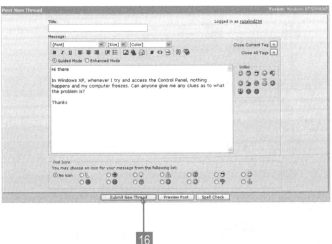

16

For your information

If the site regularly digs you out of some nasty PC holes, why not show your appreciation by making a small donation? All proceeds will be used by the site to pay for computer hardware, the internet connection and other such fees. Get all the info you need about making a contribution at www.helponthenet.com/donate.html.

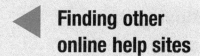
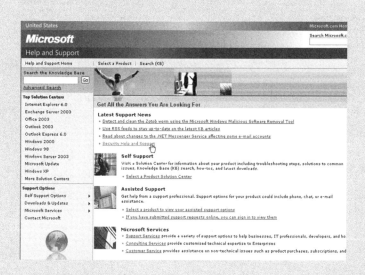

Thankfully, there are plenty of help sites on the net, so you may want to make use of as many of them as possible – or you may just want to stick to one favoured destination such as www.helponthenet.com, if you find that it regularly answers your problems. The more you contribute to a forum, the more you'll get known and welcomed by other users. You may even, as your expertise grows, start to realise that you can answer some of the questions yourself! Help should be a two-way thing, after all.

Other destinations to possibly give a whirl include www.pcpitstop.com, which can help you out with all sorts of solutions if your PC is acting a tad sluggish, and the help area from the Microsoft giants, at http://support.microsoft.com. The amount of answers here on all sorts of PC-related issues is staggering.

Your ISP should also come up trumps with technical support, although you may find that they're rather more keen to point you in the direction of premium-rate phonelines than free websites – funny, that. AOL has some decent help at www.help.aol.com, Tiscali's service is at www.tiscali.co.uk/help, whilst Wanadoo's area can be found at www.wanadoo.co.uk/help. That's just the tip of the iceberg for ISP help, obviously, so make sure you consult your provider's help area before getting fraught.

So there we are – a wealth of help and advice exists online. Once you've sorted out your problems, you can concentrate on the wealth of superlative content that can be found online – as we've seen in the course of this book, the internet truly does have the power to change your life, making virtually every aspect of your working and leisure time more convenient, informative and fun. Enjoy yourself!

10

Finding other online help sites (cont.)

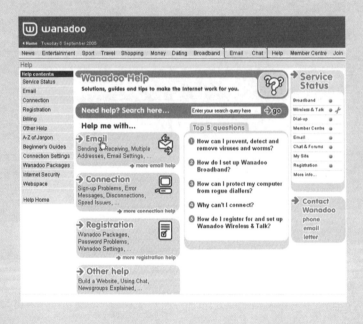

Jargon buster

Attachment – a file attached to your email message which complements the body text. Attachments are often photos, music files or Word documents.

Avatar – an icon which represents who you are online, often used in chat rooms. Avatars are often funny and light-hearted.

Blog – a website where you can post your thoughts and opinions, in a kind of electronic diary. You can populate your blog with photos and links to get more people interested. Most blogs are very simple to use, and you don't need any complicated programming knowledge to set one up. 'Blogging' has taken off significantly over the last couple of years.

Broadband – this is a term for high-speed internet access delivered via your telephone line, cable or satellite. Surfing with broadband revolutionises your internet experience and lets you access exciting features such as audio and video smoothly and quickly.

Browse – move from one site to another on the web, enjoying the scenery and following up leads. Also called surfing.

Browser – a program that allows you to access the world wide web. Popular browsers include Internet Explorer, Netscape and Opera.

Chat room – a special place on the web where you can go and talk to like-minded users about virtually every topic under the sun.

Download – to transfer files from one place to another – often from a website to your desktop.

Download websites such as www.download.com help you download useful files, programs and utilities to aid your internet life.

eCommerce – a general term for conducting business or transactions online. Commercial eCommerce products help you set up shop online, selling your wares and potentially making money, if you're selling something people want!

Email – is short for 'electronic mail'. In its most basic form, an email is simply a text message sent between two computers over the internet.

FAQ – the FAQs section of a website are the 'Frequently Asked Questions'. Reading these can often help you out if you're stuck on a site, or don't understand what something does.

Favorites – also known as bookmarks, your Favorites are saved web links in your browser, which when clicked on take you directly to that site. Having well-organised Favorites speeds up your internet access, and means that you can avoid the tedious process of typing in long or complicated web addresses.

Flames – these are abusive messages, often found in groups or emails, in response to anything regarded as a stupid comment.

Folder – useful devices for holding your PC files, documents and programs in some sort of order.

FTP (File Transfer Protocol) – the method usually used for transferring files across the internet.

Google – the world's most popular search engine.

The UK version is at www.google.co.uk. Worth an inclusion here as the phrase 'to Google' something, meaning to run a search for it online, has entered the national vocabulary.

Hard drive – a vital part of your PC, housing all of the programs and information on your computer.

Home page – the first page your browser loads when you open it up.

HTML (HyperText Markup Language) – is the universal language of the web, in which all pages are written.

Instant Message – these are messages sent across the internet for immediate access by the recipient. They're a super-quick alternative to email and still very popular.

Internet – literally, a network of networks, a grid of computers carrying information around the world. The internet allows services such as the world wide web and email to exist.

Internet telephony – technology which allows you, essentially, to make phone calls over the Net. Internet telephony software is often free, helping you save stacks of money on your regular phone calls.

ISP (Internet Service Provider) – your ISP is the company that connects you to the internet. Major ISPs include Wanadoo, PlusNet and NTL.

JavaScript - a programming language which helps web designers create more advanced sites.

Links – these basically take you around the web. By clicking on a link you'll be taken to a different website or page.

Modem – a hardware device which you connect to your PC and a phone line. It turns computer data into sound, so that it can be sent down a phone line and understood by your computer.

MP3 – a worldwide standard for digital audio compression, helping the transmission of music across the internet.

Net – short for internet. And internet is short for interlinked networks, which is what it is.

Netiquette – a way of behaving online, especially in regards to email, chat rooms, newsgroups and other methods of communicating with users. If you shout, swear, abuse people and generally act inappropriately online, you are showing bad Netiquette.

Operating System – the program that makes your computer work. The latest OS for PCs is Windows XP, whilst Apple Macs have OS X to play with.

Page – or web page, a document displayed on the web. It may be plain or formatted text; and may hold pictures, sounds and videos.

Password - many websites ask you for a password, known only to you, to access their services. Passwords are often a combination of words and numbers; when you're setting yours, try to have a few different passwords that are not easily guessable – for added peace of mind.

Phishing – an internet scam where fake emails are sent to you, often purporting to be from eBay, PayPal, Barclays etc, trying to con you into revealing your financial information or passwords.

Pop-up – a pop-up advert is a small window that appears on top of your current web page, often advertising an internet service. Sometimes pop-ups give you useful information or pointers, but often they're annoying and disrupt your normal internet life. Many pop-up blocking programs now exist to try and tackle this problem.

Search engine – a powerful resource such as Google (www.google.co.uk) which helps you find websites and internet content quickly.

Shouting – writing of messages or newsgroup articles entirely in capitals. Not a good idea as they are harder to read.

Signature – normally used in relation to email, your signature is a small text file that can be added to the end of all your outgoing emails automatically. Your signature normally includes your name and contact details, or a company disclaimer if it's a business or work email address.

Spam – unwanted junk email which clutters up your Inbox. Spam has become a huge problem over the last few years, but a series of companies and software programs are working hard to try and alleviate the problem.

Surfing – following links to move from one web page to another, at the same or a different site.

Upload – when you've built a website, you need to upload it to the web for people to see. Uploading is simply the technical term for copying all your text and images to the web.

URL (Uniform Resource Locator) – is simply a technical way of referring to a web address.

Virus – a malicious computer program which spreads across computer systems, doing damage such as destroying files and crashing computers.

Webmail – instead of having to use a dedicated email program such as Outlook Express or Eudora, webmail allows you to read and send mail from a website, via your browser. Popular webmail providers include Hotmail (www.hotmail.com) and Yahoo! (uk.yahoo.com). The advantage of webmail is that it means that wherever in the world you are, as long as there's a working computer and internet connection, you can access your email.

Web page – the basic web document. It may just be a single screenful or you may have to scroll down to read it all.

Website – a place on the web comprising of text, pictures, sound and video which you can read or interact with.

World Wide Web – the most visible and one of the simplest and most popular ways of using the internet. It consists of billions of web pages, which can be viewed through browsers.

Troubleshooting guide

Connecting

Customisation: making it work for me

Help/technical

Multimedia

Recommended alternatives

Searching

Index

H

Health encyclopaedia 240
Health information online 245
Health websites 245
History 24
    clearing 25
    closing panel 27
    options 25
Holiday planning at Expedia 230
Home page 38, 53
Hotmail 80
HTML Games website 276

I

Identities, in Outlook Express 75
Images
    for webpages 281
    search sites 57
    searching 54
IncrediMail 79
Instant Messaging 90
    alternative programs 95
Internet, setting up access 1
Internet banking 143
Internet Connection Wizard 70
Internet Explorer 15
    History 24
    Search 20
Internet phone calls 154
Internet radio 249
ISP (Internet Service Provider) 1
    choosing 3
    contracts 6
    price deals 12
ISP Review 12
ITunes 259

J

Job hunting online 137
Jobmatch 141
Jobs via email 139
Junk mail 120

K

KillerSites.com 294

L

Language Tools at Google 51
LAUNCHcast Radio 91
Links toolbar 28
Live365.com 249

M

Macromedia Dreamweaver 275
Mail account.
    setting up 69
MailWasher, spam removal 120
ManyFishInTheSea 100
MapQuest 223
Match 100
McAfee 112
    FreeScan 116
    Internet Security Suite 119
Men's Health website 245
Microfilter 8, 9
Microsoft support website 303
Miniclip toolbar 269
Miniclip.com 263
Monster, job site 142
Moonfruit 279
Mozilla Firefox 49
MP3 websites 256
MSN Maps & Directions 223
MSN Search 20

Viruses 111, 112

W

Waitrose online 169
Wanadoo 6
Web page
    printing 32
    saving 36
Web Pages That Suck website 294
Webmail 78
Website
    adding images 281
    building 279
    building services 292
    creating 273
    design ideas 278
    design tips 294
    planning 275

X

XaraWebstyle 292

Y

Yahoo!
anti-spam resource centre 123
    chat rooms 86
    Games 91
    Messenger 90

Z

ZyWeb Site Builder 292